AIR FRYER COOKBOOK FOR BEGINNERS

2000 Days of Amazingly Quick and Delicious Recipes to Fry, Grill, Roast, and Bake Pro Meals in No Time. Foolproof Tips for First-Time Success

STEPHAN TYLER

© Copyright 2022 – Stephan Tyler - All rights reserved.

The content contained within this book may not be reproduced, duplicated or transmitted without direct written permission from the author or the publisher.

Under no circumstances will any blame or legal responsibility be held against the publisher, or author, for any damages, reparation, or monetary loss due to the information contained within this book. Either directly or indirectly.

Legal Notice:

This book is copyright protected. This book is only for personal use. You cannot amend, distribute, sell, use, quote or paraphrase any part, or the content within this book, without the consent of the author or publisher.

Disclaimer Notice:

Please note the information contained within this document is for educational and entertainment purposes only. All effort has been executed to present accurate, up to date, and reliable, complete information. No warranties of any kind are declared or implied. Readers acknowledge that the author is not engaging in the rendering of legal, financial, medical or professional advice. The content within this book has been derived from various sources. Please consult a licensed professional before attempting any techniques outlined in this book.

By reading this document, the reader agrees that under no circumstances is the author responsible for any losses, direct or indirect, which are incurred as a result of the use of information contained within this document, including, but not limited to, — errors, omissions, or inaccuracies.

LET'S START

Table of Contents

INTRODUCTION 1
CHAPTER 1. AIR FRYER BASICS AND BENEFITS 3
- How to Start Cooking in An Air Fryer? 4
- How to Clean and Maintain Your Air Fryer 5
- Benefits of Using an Air Fryer 6

CHAPTER 2. BREAKFAST AND BRUNCH 1
1. Breakfast Turkey Sausage 1
2. Breakfast Casserole 1
3. Egg Chorizo Casserole 1
4. Zucchini Spinach Egg Casserole 1
5. Ham Cheese Casserole 2
6. Ham Cheese Egg Muffins 2
7. Crustless Cheese Egg Quiche 2
8. Broccoli Casserole 2
9. Cauliflower Muffins 2
10. Zucchini Bread 2
11. Egg Bites 3
12. Healthy Breakfast Donuts 3
13. Feta Pepper Egg Muffins 3
14. Sun-dried Tomatoes Egg Cups 3
15. Vanilla Raspberry Muffins 3
16. Simple Cheese Sticks 4
17. Hearty Pickle Chips 4
18. Early Morning Mushroom and Egg Bowl 4
19. Cheesy Omelet 4
20. Classic Bacon Asparagus Meal 4
21. Healthy Ham-A-Cup 4
22. The Simple Egg 5
23. Quick and Spicy Hot Dogs 5
24. Glazed Carrot Chips and Cheese 5
25. Chinese-Style Baby Carrots 5
26. Kale Chips 5
27. Morning Cocktail Meatball 5
28. Blueberry Breakfast Cobbler 6
29. Strawberry Breakfast Tarts 6
30. Everything Bagels 6
31. Maple-Glazed Doughnuts 6
32. Fried Chicken and Waffles 7
33. Puffed Egg Tarts 7
34. Early Morning Steak and Eggs 7
35. Lemon Vanilla Cupcakes with Yogurt Frost 8
36. Saucy Vegetable Chicken 8
37. Creamy Mushroom & Spinach Omelet 8
38. Caprese Sandwich with Sourdough Bread 8
39. Almond & Cinnamon Berry Oat Bars 8
40. Cinnamon Mango Bread 9
41. Honey Banana & Hazelnut Cupcakes 9
42. Cherry in Vanilla Almond Scones 9
43. Sweet Caramel French Toast 9
44. Smoky Cheese & Mustard Rarebit 9
45. Corn & Chorizo Frittata 10
46. Carrot & Broccoli Cheddar Quiche 10
47. Breaded Cauliflowers in Alfredo Sauce 10
48. Crunchy Asparagus with Cheese 10
49. Vanilla Brownies with White Chocolate & Walnuts 10
50. Bacon Bombs 11
51. Breakfast Pockets 11
52. Avocado Flautas 11
53. Sausage Cheese Wraps 11
54. Chicken Omelet 11
55. Sausage Burritos 12
56. Sausage Patties 12
57. Cinnamon Cream Doughnuts 12
58. Sausage Frittata 12
59. Potato Jalapeno Hash 12
60. Bread Rolls 13
61. Cheese Parsley Omelet 13
62. Egg Ham Pockets 13
63. Spanish Frittata 13
64. Cauliflower Hash 13

CHAPTER 3. LUNCH 15
65. Honey Mustard Pork Tenderloin 15
66. Rosemary Lamb Chops 15
67. Juicy Steak Bites 15
68. Greek Lamb Chops 15
69. Beef Roast 15
70. Herb Butter Rib-Eye Steak 16
71. Beef Jerky 16
72. Beef Patties 16
73. Beef Sirloin Roast 16
74. Bacon-Wrapped Filet Mignon 16
75. Beef Burgers 16
76. Season and Salt-Cured Beef 17
77. Sweet & Spicy Meatballs 17
78. Spiced Pork Shoulder 17
79. Fish Sticks 17
80. Grilled Cheese and Greens Sandwiches 18
81. Veggie Tuna Melts 18
82. California Melts 18
83. Vegetable Pita Sandwiches 18
84. Stuffed Portobello Mushrooms 19
85. Crustless Veggie Quiche 19
86. Beans and Greens Pizza 19
87. Grilled Chicken Mini Pizzas 19
88. Chicken Croquettes 20
89. Chicken and Fruit Bruschetta 20

CHAPTER 4. DINNER 21
90. Bow Tie Pasta Chips 21
91. Crispy Curry Potato Cubes with Coriander Salsa 21
92. Roasted Potatoes with Paprika Powder 21
93. Portobello Mushroom Pizzas with Hummus 21
94. Cordon Bleu and Letscho Vegetables 22
95. Cauliflower with An Herb Crust 22
96. Chestnut Recipe (Low Carb) 22

97. Puff Pastry Pockets with Salmon 22
98. Sliced Turkey 23
99. Baked Sausages 23
100. Fried Rice with Sesame-Sriracha Sauce 23
101. Roast Chicken 23

CHAPTER 5. SNACKS AND APPETIZERS 25

102. French Fries 25
103. Crispy Tofu Buffalo Bites 25
104. Curried Sweet Potato Fries with Creamy Cumin Ketchup 25
105. Fried Hot Dogs 26
106. Sweet Potato Chips 26
107. Parmesan Truffle Fries 26
108. Chicken Nuggets 26
109. Mini Popovers 26
110. Air Fryer Risotto Balls 27
111. Chicken Empanadas 27
112. Mozzarella Balls 27
113. Swedish Meatballs 27
114. Stuffed Mushrooms 28
115. Mexican Street Style Corn on the Cob 28
116. Ranch Potatoes 28
117. Spicy Cheese Dip 28
118. Zucchini Patties 28
119. Cinnamon Maple Chickpeas 29
120. Spicy Chickpeas 29
121. Crispy Cauliflower Florets 29
122. Air Fried Walnuts 29
123. Baked Cheese Dip 29
124. Onion Dip 29
125. Ricotta Dip 30
126. Garlic Cheese Dip 30
127. Spinach Dip 30
128. Spicy Almonds 30
129. Spicy Brussels Sprouts 30
130. Herb Mushrooms 30
131. Fish Nuggets 31
132. Cumin and Squash Chili 31
133. Feisty Banana Fritters 31
134. Curly Fries 31
135. Cauliflower Popcorns 31
136. Crispy Pickle Slices 31
137. Beef Taquitos 32
138. Cheese Sandwich 32
139. Roasted Pecans 32
140. Pizza Toast 32
141. Baked Pears with Blue Cheese and Honey 32
142. Baked Tomatoes with Parmesan and Mozzarella 33
143. Loaded Potato Bites 33
144. Cheddar Tortilla Chips 33
145. Mustard Cheddar Twists 33
146. Hash Brown Bruschetta 33
147. Breaded Beef Cubes 34
148. Waffle Fries Poutine 34
149. Endive in Curried Yogurt 34
150. Tortilla Chips 34
151. Panko Artichoke Hearts 34
152. Steak Fries 34
153. Breaded Green Olives 35
154. Apple Rolls 35
155. Pita Chips 35
156. Mozzarella Eggroll Sticks 35
157. Crab and Spinach Cups 35
158. Cajun Dill Pickle Chips 36
159. Sriracha Wings 36
160. Rosemary Cashews 36
161. Beef Enchilada Dip 36
162. Cheesy Stuffed Sliders 36
163. Philly Egg Rolls 37
164. Mozzarella Cheese Sticks 37
165. Crispy Sausage Bites 37
166. Puffed Asparagus Spears 37
167. Wonton Poppers 38
168. Party Pull Apart 38

CHAPTER 6. SIDE DISHES 39

169. Ranch Seasoned Air Fryer Chickpeas 39
170. Spanakopita Bites 39
171. Cheesy Spinach Wontons 39
172. Onion Rings 39
173. Delicata Squash 40
174. Egg Rolls 40
175. Crispy Fried Okra 40
176. Baked Sweet Potato Cauliflower Patties 40
177. Falafel 40
178. Zucchini Parmesan Chips 41
179. Lemony Green Beans 41
180. Roasted Corn 41
181. Spinach Frittata 41
182. Pecan Crusted Eggplant 41
183. Buffalo Cauliflower 41
184. Roasted Waldorf Salad 42
185. Melting Baby Potatoes 42
186. Roasted Spicy Corn 42
187. Cauliflower Quesadillas 42
188. Sweet Potato Hash Browns 43
189. Roasted Five-Spice Broccoli 43
190. Mediterranean Style Veggies 43
191. Corn Fritters 43
192. Roasted Italian Bell Peppers 44
193. Tex-Mex Corn and Beans 44
194. Mushroom Veggie Kabobs 44
195. Potatoes Au Gratin 44
196. Perfect Potato Pancakes 45
197. String Bean Fries 45
198. Four-Cheese Phyllo Triangles 45
199. Summer Vegetable Gratin 45
200. Polenta Pie 46
201. Bean and Rice Dish 46
202. Cheesy Potato Mash Casserole 46

203. Simple Squash Casserole........................... 46
204. Ginger Pork Lasagna 47
205. Scrambled Basil and Potato..................... 47
206. Sweet Pea Wontons.................................. 47
207. Onion Bread Pudding 47
208. Spicy Acorn Squash with Feta 48
209. Herb-Roasted Root Vegetables 48
210. Crispy Roasted Potatoes with Caper Vinaigrette 48
211. Roasted Beet & Pistachio Salad 48
212. Roasted Sweet & Sour Brussels Sprouts 49
213. Chimichurri Cauliflower "Steaks" 49
214. Spice-Roasted Carrots............................... 49
215. Summer Veggie Roast 49
216. Corn on the Cob 49
217. Twice-Baked Herb-Stuffed Potatoes 50

CHAPTER 7. POULTRY................................. 51

218. Chicken Tenders... 51
219. Sweet & Tangy Chicken 51
220. Parmesan Chicken Breast 51
221. Garlic Herb Turkey Breast 51
222. Simple & Juicy Chicken Breasts............... 52
223. Cauliflower Chicken Casserole 52
224. Greek Chicken 52
225. Baked Chicken Breast 52
226. Baked Chicken Thighs 52
227. Tasty Chicken Wings.................................. 52
228. Italian Turkey Tenderloin 53
229. Pesto Parmesan Chicken 53
230. Lemon Chicken Breasts 53
231. Spicy Chicken Wings 53
232. Fajita Chicken 53
233. One-Dish Chicken & Rice 53
234. Lebanese Turkey Burgers with Feta & Tzatziki 54
235. Sweet and Sour Chicken 54
236. Lemon Chicken Thighs.............................. 54
237. Southern Fried Chicken 54
238. Buffalo Chicken Wings 55
239. Chicken Parmesan with Provolone Cheese 55
240. Zingy & Nutty Chicken Wings 55
241. Pesto-Cream Chicken with Cherry Tomatoes .. 55
242. Peanut Chicken 56
243. Basil-Garlic Breaded Chicken Bake 56
244. Crispy Butter Chicken 56
245. South Indian Pepper Chicken 57
246. Honey and Wine Chicken Breasts 57
247. Roasted Veggie Chicken Salad.................. 57
248. Asian Turkey Meatballs............................. 57
249. Stir-Fried Chicken with Pineapple 58
250. Sweet and Sour Drumsticks 58
251. Chicken Satay 58
252. Orange Curried Chicken Stir-Fry 58
253. Tex-Mex Turkey Burgers 59
254. Barbecued Chicken Thighs 59
255. Garlic-Roasted Chicken with Creamer Potatoes 59
256. Ham and Cheese Stuffed Chicken Burgers........59
257. Mustard Chicken Tenders 59
258. Almond Flour Coco-Milk Battered Chicken ... 60
259. Ricotta and Parsley Stuffed Turkey Breasts ... 60
260. Bacon Lovers' Stuffed Chicken.................60
261. Crusted Chicken Tenders 60
262. Harissa-Rubbed Cornish Game Hens 61
263. Parmesan Chicken Tenders 61
264. Grilled Chicken Fajitas 61
265. Thai Basil Chicken 61
266. French Garlic Chicken 62
267. Chicken Strips with Satay Sauce 62
268. Chicken Pesto Parmigiana 62
269. Ginger Chicken 63
270. Chicken Jalfrezi...63
271. Sweet Rub Chicken Drumsticks 63
272. Buttermilk Marinated Chicken 64
273. Thyme Turkey Breast 64
274. Roasted Duck 64
275. Blackened Chicken Bake...........................64
276. Crusted Chicken Drumsticks 64
277. Roasted Turkey Breast 65
278. Brine Soaked Turkey 65
279. Lemon Pepper Turkey 65
280. Ground Chicken Meatballs 65
281. Parmesan Chicken Meatballs..................65
282. Italian Meatballs 66
283. Oregano Chicken Breast 66
284. Maple Chicken Thighs 66
285. Orange Chicken Rice.................................66
286. Deviled Chicken 66

CHAPTER 8. BEEF..67

287. Air Fried Grilled Steak 67
288. Texas Beef Brisket 67
289. Savory Beefy Poppers 67
290. Juicy Cheeseburgers 67
291. Copycat Taco Bell Crunch Wraps 68
292. Swedish Meatloaf 68
293. Carne Asada 68
294. Spicy Thai Beef Stir-Fry 69
295. Beef Casserole 69
296. Fajita Meatball Lettuce Wraps 69
297. Chimichurri Skirt Steak 69
298. Reuben Fritters 70
299. Charred Onions and Steak Cube BBQ 70
300. Steak and Mushroom Gravy....................70
301. Country Fried Steak 70
302. Spicy Grilled Steak.....................................71
303. Toothsome Greek Vegetable Skillet 71
304. Light Herbed Meatballs 71
305. Sirloin Steak 71
306. Buttered Filet Mignon 71
307. Savory Spiced & Herbed Skirt Steak................71

308. Steak with Bell Peppers 72	360. Herbed Lamb Loin Chops................................ 85
309. Corned Beef 72	361. Mustard Lamb Chops...................................... 85
310. Roasted Pepper Beef Prosciutto 72	362. Herbed Leg of Lamb.. 86
311. Honey Mustard Cheesy Meatballs................ 72	363. Cheesy Lamb Burgers..................................... 86
312. Garlic-Mustard Rubbed Roast Beef.............. 73	364. Spicy Lamb Burgers.. 86
313. Ginger Soy Beef 73	
314. Ginger-Orange Beef Strips 73	**CHAPTER 11. FISH AND SEAFOOD**............................ 87
315. Grilled Beef with Grated Daikon Radish 73	365. Bacon-Wrapped Shrimp 87
316. Grilled Tri-Tip Over Beet Salad 74	366. Crispy Paprika Fish Fillets 87
	367. Air Fryer Salmon 87
CHAPTER 9. PORK.. 75	368. Quick Paella... 87
317. Pork Taquitos... 75	369. Coconut Shrimp 87
318. Panko Breaded Pork Chops............................ 75	370. Cilantro-Lime Fried Shrimp........................... 88
319. Apricot Glazed Pork Tenderloins 75	371. Lemony Tuna.. 88
320. Pork Tenders with Bell Peppers 75	372. Grilled Soy Salmon Fillets.............................. 88
321. Barbecue Flavored Pork Ribs 76	373. Old Bay Crab Cake 88
322. Balsamic Glazed Pork Chops 76	374. Scallops and Spring Veggies 89
323. Rustic Pork Ribs 76	375. Fried Calamari.. 89
324. Keto Parmesan Crusted Pork Chops........... 76	376. Soy and Ginger Shrimp.................................. 89
325. Crispy Fried Pork Chops the Southern Way 76	377. Crispy Cheesy Fish Fingers 89
326. Fried Pork Quesadilla 77	378. Panko-Crusted Tilapia 90
327. Cilantro-Mint Pork BBQ Thai Style 77	379. Firecracker Shrimp.. 90
328. Tuscan Pork Chops.. 77	380. Lemon Pepper Shrimp 90
329. Italian Parmesan Breaded Pork Chops 77	381. Crumbed Fish.. 90
330. Crispy Roast Garlic-Salt Pork 78	382. Cajun Salmon 90
331. Peanut Satay Pork 78	383. Lime & Chili Salmon 90
332. Boozy Pork Loin Chops 78	384. Fish Patties 91
333. Pork Sausage with Mashed Cauliflower 78	385. Crispy Shrimp... 91
334. Farmhouse Pork with Vegetables 78	386. Coconut Crusted Fish Strips 91
335. Spicy Pork Meatballs 79	387. Fish Tacos 91
336. 30-Minute Hoisin Pork Loin Steak 79	388. Popcorn Shrimp 91
337. Pork Kebabs with Serrano Pepper 79	389. Shrimp Bang-Bang 91
338. Bacon-Wrapped Hot Dogs 79	390. Mexican Fish 92
339. Cheesy Ground Pork Casserole 79	391. Crispy Garlic Shrimp 92
340. Spicy Pork with Herbs and Candy Onions 80	392. Crispy Halibut Strips 92
341. Pork Steak with Mustard and Herbs 80	393. Pesto Haddock 92
342. Spicy and Creamy Pork Gratin 80	394. Breaded Flounder 92
343. Pork Tenderloin with Herbs 80	395. 3-Ingredients Catfish...................................... 93
344. Family Pork Loin Roast 80	396. Cajun Coated Catfish 93
345. Traditional Walliser Schnitzel....................... 81	397. Southern Style Catfish 93
346. Bolognese Sauce with a Twist 81	398. Sesame Seeds Coated Haddock 93
	399. Breaded Hake 93
CHAPTER 10. LAMB 83	400. Ranch Tilapia 94
347. Caraway, Sichuan 'n Cumin Lamb Kebabs 83	401. Tuna & Potato Cakes 94
348. Garlic Lemon-Wine on Lamb Steak 83	402. Spicy Shrimp... 94
349. Garlic-Rosemary Lamb BBQ............................ 83	403. Lemon Garlic Shrimp 94
350. Maras Pepper Lamb Kebab Recipe from Turkey ..83	404. Cheesy Shrimp 94
351. Saffron Spiced Rack of Lamb.......................... 84	405. Rice Flour Coated Shrimp.............................. 95
352. Simple Lamb BBQ with Herbed Salt 84	406. Shrimp Kebabs.. 95
353. Greek Lamb Meatballs 84	407. Fried Masala Fish 95
354. Glazed Lamb Chops 84	408. Scallops with Herb Sauce 95
355. Lamb Burgers... 84	409. Breaded Scallops 96
356. Oregano Lamb Chops 84	410. White Fish with Garlic 96
357. Lamb Steaks with Fresh Mint and Potatoes 85	411. Lobster Tails with Garlic Butter 96
358. Crunchy Cashew Lamb Rack 85	412. Lobster Stuffed Mushrooms 96
359. Lamb Meatballs 85	413. Beer Battered Cod 96

- 414. Calamari with Tomato Sauce 97
- 415. Salmon & Eggs 97
- 416. Tilapia with Egg 97
- 417. Seafood Super Veggie Fritters 97
- 418. Breaded Fish 97
- 419. Tuna with Roast Potatoes 97
- 420. Glazed Halibut Steak 98
- 421. Nacho-Crusted Shrimp 98
- 422. Sriracha and Honey Tossed Calamari 98
- 423. Kataifi-Wrapped Shrimp with Lemon-Garlic Butter 98
- 424. Grilled Barramundi with Lemon Butter 99
- 425. Cranberry Cod 99
- 426. Cod Fish Teriyaki with Oysters, Mushrooms & Veggies 99
- 427. Salmon with Dill Sauce 99
- 428. Black Cod with Grapes, Pecans, Fennel & Kale 100
- 429. Honey Glazed Salmon 100
- 430. Sweet & Sour Glazed Salmon 100
- 431. Salmon Parcel 100
- 432. Salmon with Broccoli 100
- 433. Salmon with Prawns & Pasta 100
- 434. Salmon Burgers 101
- 435. Chinese Cod 101
- 436. Cod Parcel 101
- 437. Cod Burgers 102
- 438. Spicy Catfish 102
- 439. Seasoned Catfish 102
- 440. Crispy Catfish 102
- 441. Cornmeal Coated Catfish 102
- 442. Glazed Haddock 103
- 443. Simple Haddock 103

CHAPTER 12. HEALTHY VEGETABLE RECIPES 105

- 444. Air Fryer Asparagus 105
- 445. Roasted Garlic Asparagus 105
- 446. Almond Flour Battered and Crisped Onion Rings 105
- 447. Crispy Nacho Avocado Fries 105
- 448. Chermoula-Roasted Beets 106
- 449. Fried Plantains 106
- 450. Parmesan Breaded Zucchini Chips 106
- 451. Bell Pepper-Corn Wrapped in Tortilla 106
- 452. Blooming Onion 107
- 453. Mexican Corn in A Cup 107
- 454. Honey Roasted Carrots 107
- 455. Crispy Sesame-Ginger Broccoli 108
- 456. Tomatoes Provençal 108
- 457. Roasted Cabbage 108
- 458. Crispy Brussels Sprouts 108
- 459. Caramelized Baby Carrots 108
- 460. Carrot with Zucchini 109
- 461. Broccoli with Olives 109
- 462. Basil Tomatoes 109
- 463. Stuffed Tomatoes 109
- 464. Parmesan Asparagus 109
- 465. Almond Asparagus 109
- 466. Spicy Butternut Squash 110
- 467. Sweet & Spicy Parsnips 110
- 468. Pesto Tomatoes 110
- 469. Rosemary-Roasted Red Potatoes 110
- 470. Roasted Radishes with Sea Salt 110
- 471. Garlic Zucchini and Red Peppers 110
- 472. Parmesan and Herb Sweet Potatoes 110
- 473. Roasted Brussels Sprouts with Orange and Garlic 111
- 474. Crispy Lemon Artichoke Hearts 111
- 475. Spiced Honey-Walnut Carrots 111
- 476. Roasted Grape Tomatoes and Asparagus 111
- 477. Stuffed Red Peppers with Herbed Ricotta and Tomatoes 111
- 478. Ratatouille 112
- 479. Parmesan-Thyme Butternut Squash 112
- 480. Crispy Garlic Sliced Eggplant 112
- 481. Dill-and-Garlic Beets 112
- 482. Citrus-Roasted Broccoli Florets 112
- 483. Tasty Hasselback Potatoes 113
- 484. Honey Sriracha Brussels Sprouts 113
- 485. Roasted Carrots 113
- 486. Roasted Parmesan Broccoli 113
- 487. Simple Baked Potatoes 113
- 488. Parmesan Green Bean 114
- 489. Roasted Asparagus 114
- 490. Healthy Air fryer Veggies 114
- 491. Baked Sweet Potatoes 114

CHAPTER 13. DEHYDRATED RECIPES 115

- 492. Squash Chips 115
- 493. Kiwi Chips 115
- 494. Cinnamon Apples Slices 115
- 495. Smoky Eggplant Bacon 115
- 496. Pineapple Chunks 115
- 497. Spicy Kale Chips 115
- 498. Asian Turkey Jerky 116
- 499. Chicken Jerky 116
- 500. Dehydrated Bell Peppers 116
- 501. Cinnamon Sweet Potato Chips 116
- 502. Shredded Carrots 116
- 503. Flavorful Almonds 116
- 504. Strawberry Slices 116
- 505. Banana Slices 117
- 506. Avocado Slices 117
- 507. Dried Raspberries 117
- 508. Green Apple Chips 117
- 509. Peach Wedges 117
- 510. Dried Mango Slices 117
- 511. Asian Tofu Jerky 117
- 512. Sun-Dried Tomatoes 117
- 513. Dried Green Bean 118
- 514. Cucumber Chips 118
- 515. Dried Beet Chips 118

- 516. Snap Pea Chips 118
- 517. Dried Okra 118
- 518. Lemon Slices 118
- 519. Dried Pear Chips 118
- 520. Dehydrated Almonds 118
- 521. Orange Slices 118

CHAPTER 14. SWEET AND DESSERTS 119

- 522. Fried Peaches 119
- 523. Apple Dumplings 119
- 524. Raspberry Cream Roll-Ups 119
- 525. Chocolate Cake 120
- 526. Chocolate Donuts 120
- 527. Fried Bananas with Chocolate Sauce 120
- 528. Apple Hand Pies 120
- 529. Chocolaty Banana Muffins 120
- 530. Blueberry Lemon Muffins 121
- 531. Sweet Cream Cheese Wontons 121
- 532. Cinnamon Rolls 121
- 533. Black and White Brownies 121
- 534. Baked Apple 121
- 535. Cinnamon Fried Bananas 121
- 536. Banana Cake 122
- 537. Cheesecake 122
- 538. Bread Pudding 122
- 539. Bread Dough and Amaretto Dessert 122
- 540. Pumpkin Pie 122
- 541. Wrapped Pears 123
- 542. Strawberry Donuts 123
- 543. Cocoa Cake 123
- 544. Apple Bread 123
- 545. Mini Lava Cakes 123
- 546. Carrot Cake 124
- 546. Ginger Cheesecake 124
- 548. Coffee Cheesecakes 124
- 549. Cocoa Cookies 124
- 550. Special Brownies 125
- 551. Sponge Cake 125
- 552. Walnut Raisin Pumpkin Bread 125
- 553. Summer Strawberry Crumble 125
- 554. Vegan Coconut Milk Cupcakes 126
- 555. Double Chocolate Walnut Cookies 126
- 556. Strawberry Toaster Pastries 126
- 557. Blueberry Muffins 126
- 558. Buttermilk Biscuits 127
- 559. Double Chocolate Brownies 127
- 560. Peach Cobbler 127
- 561. Snickerdoodles 127
- 562. Chia Cookies 128
- 563. Cranberry and Almond Cookies 128
- 564. Caramel Brownie Bites 128
- 565. Pumpkin Cookies 128
- 566. Pumpkin Cheesecake Bars 128
- 567. Pecan Cookies 129
- 568. Ricotta Cheesecake 129
- 569. Chocolate Chip Cookies 129
- 570. Chocolate Froth Cookies 129
- 571. Cinnamon Cookies 129
- 572. Sugar Cookies 129
- 573. Summer Citrus Sponge Cake 130
- 574. Vanilla Brownie Squares 130
- 575. Apple Pie 130
- 576. Dark Chocolate Lava Cakes 130
- 577. Chocolate Soufflé 130
- 578. Glazed Lemon Cupcakes 131
- 579. Sesame Banana Dessert 131
- 580. Triple Berry Lemon Crumble 131
- 581. Honey Hazelnut Apples 131
- 582. French Apple Cake 131
- 583. Raisin Apple Treat 132
- 584. Blackberries & Apricots Crumble 132
- 585. Coffee Cake 132

CHAPTER 15. EVERYDAY FAVORITES FOR YOUR FAMILY 133

- 586. Butternut Squash with Chopped Hazelnuts ... 133
- 587. Air Fried Shishito Peppers 133
- 588. Avocado Wedge Fries 133
- 589. Bacon Pinwheels 133
- 590. Candied Pecans 134
- 591. Cauliflower Parmesan Fritters 134
- 592. Cheesy Jalapeño Cornbread 134
- 593. Classic Latkes 134
- 594. Classic Poutine 135
- 595. Crispy Cinnamon Chickpeas 135
- 596. Crispy Green Tomatoes Slices 135
- 597. Air Fried Edamame 135
- 598. Frico 136
- 599. Garlicky Baked Cherry Tomatoes 136
- 600. Garlicky Knots with Parsley 136

CONCLUSION 137

Introduction

We are all fans of good food. It's not just our fuel; it's our mood manipulator. We all know how important it is to eat healthy when we are so hungry that we forget what healthy is. We often eat what we find most accessible. We know things do not always go as we expect. You will always find other attractions, like eating fast food, ready-to-eat meals, instant food, and processed food, and we find these very unhealthy!

Why settle for this lifestyle and let your body suffer from these not satisfying eating habits that you know will not benefit you at the very least? So, why not make good and healthy meals the easiest to have? Now this AIR FRYER COOKBOOK FOR BEGINNERS will save you in many ways! It not only air fries but also roasts, grills, bakes, and even dehydrates foods in a much healthier unexpected way!

An air fryer is just not an alternative to an oven; it is unique on its own in how it cooks. An air fryer is a kitchen appliance that circulates hot air to cook food in a way where it can get a satisfying crunch while remaining healthy and yummy. It does not create bumps in the food as a deep fryer does. It uses less oil, dehydrates water from the food, and cooks faster than a deep fryer.

We were not bragging about it, but many chefs have confirmed that an air fryer can make foods healthier and quicker. So, if you want to keep your family healthy, this cookbook is perfect for you. Use simple recipes to create delicious meals using the air fryer.

An air fryer is an excellent gift for housewives, bachelors, singles, and every person who loves cooking. Having an air fryer means you don't need to use the deep fryer so often. Utilizing this air fryer cookbook, you get many recipes you can use to make the best out of your air fryer. An air fryer lets you fix delicious meals for the family. If you want to replace your deep fryer or other kitchen gadgets with an air fryer, this cookbook will help you get started. It will even save you more space in your kitchen!

And here in this cookbook, there are many recipes that we prepare to help you start to try out this exciting kitchen gadget, and we promise these recipes will allow you to experiment a bit deeper with your taste. These recipes will have fantastic results that are fresh, succulent, brilliantly dark-colored, and delightful.

What more? It is also something to trust while on vacation. It always cooks the food thoroughly, so you can depend on this when relaxing in a motorhome with your favorite music. For all these reasons and many unspoken, we have complete confidence in the air fryer and the taste that the recipes will give you. It is truly the healthiest way to prepare food that everyone in your family will enjoy and keep coming back for more without realizing they are now eating better.

Now you know this fantastic air fryer is a must-try, so no more time-wasting! After this, you will learn its basics and benefits; you can pick a recipe to get started with healthier and better cooking in no time. Remember that healthy food doesn't mean you need to slave away in the kitchen or pay big bucks for hand-delivered meals. All you need is to try new, delicious recipes with your air fryer that is sure to become the new family's favorites. Your air fryer will soon be the most used item in your kitchen!

From this moment on, we believe you will prefer this air fryer cookbook instead of other cookbooks, as you know that you can make that same thing healthier in the least possible time.

This is it! Work your way through this cookbook. We promise that your hesitation about starting with your brand-new kitchen helper will put to rest in no time. Remember, every person starts out being a beginner; we all must learn what works best. Each time you make a new dish, you know more, and your experience grows. So, have fun with it and make the best of it! Live healthy, live strong.

Just a little break to ask you something that means a lot to me:

First of all, thank you for choosing my book *Air Fryer Cookbook for Beginners*. I know you could have picked between a significant number of cookbooks, but you chose this one, and for that, I am incredibly grateful.

I hope it will add value and quality to your everyday life.

If you will enjoy this book and find some benefit in reading this, I'd like to hear your thoughts and hope that you could take some time to post a review on Amazon. Your feedback and support will significantly improve my future projects and enhance this cookbook.

If you have purchased the paperback version through Amazon, go to your purchases section and Click "Write a Review" or scan the following QR code to write it quickly:

I want you to know that your review is essential.
I wish you all the best!

STEPHAN TYLER

Chapter 1. Air Fryer Basics and Benefits

Technology giving birth to different and unique inventions every day to satisfy the hunger for innovation in society. We can see it also in the everyday kitchen's modernization. Among all devices that have made life more comfortable with their usefulness and design, the Air Fryer is one of the best, a practical tool with many benefits.

An Air Fryer is a device that cooks food not by using oil but by heated air with no compromise on the dish's texture and flavor. Air Fryer is not only used for frying up food but can also be used for many other tasks such as grilling, baking, roasting, and many more. It ensures the food is cooked evenly and thoroughly. Its design is such that it fits in a compact area and works via electricity. It has many different parts:

The frying basket: It is a stainless-steel basket in which the food is placed for cooking. It can be replaced by any other utensils, such as a pizza pan.

The timer: The timer is set; accordingly, a red light indicates when the time has been finished.

The temperature controller: The temperature of the Air Fryer has a high range from 175° to 400°F. Adjust the temp knob to achieve the desired temperature.

The air inlet/outlet: It is used to release the hot air and steam that arises during the cooking process from the device's back. It is, therefore, important that the device is always kept in a spacious area.

How to Start Cooking in An Air Fryer?

Firstly, the Air Fryer must be in a spacious place to allow heat to escape and prevent damage to its parts. It should be put on top of a heat resistance surface.

Secondly, pull out the frying basket gently from the machine. It is recommended to preheat the device for 5 minutes before using it. Simply set the desired temperature for 5 mins, and then after the time is completed, pull out the basket.

Now place the food inside the container. Don't fill more than 2/3 of the container. The container can be greased with an oil spray to avoid sticking the food if required. If fatty foods are placed, add a little bit of water so that the container remains clean.

Now place the container gently inside and close the lid. The electric cord should be connected, and the time and temperature should be set. Both indicators should be on until the frying is completed.

The food can be stirred, flipped, or shaken as per requirement.

The food must be flipped at regular intervals for grilling until it gets a good color on both sides.

When finished, a sound will go off. Push the off button just once, then wait for 30 seconds for the device to turn off completely.

When done, serve the food in a serving dish and leave the basket out of the device for some time before putting it back in.

How to Clean and Maintain Your Air Fryer

Maintaining the Air Fryer

When buying the Air Fryer, quality needs to be addressed before anything else. Don't give in to purchase an Air Fryer based on reviews or prices. It should be bought from an established and authentic source.

Don't overfill the device; the fryer basket needs space. If it is overloaded, the food will not be properly cooked, and the taste and texture will be affected.

Don't place the Air Fryer just anywhere. It needs to be placed in an area that will allow some space. It should always be put on top of a heat resistance surface.

Please don't put the basket back in the fryer without cooling it down first. It should be cleaned and cool when reinserted.

Don't follow the instructions of temperature or time given on packages or recipes for ovens or microwaves. Air Fryer is a different device, which requires proper settings to be adjusted according to different cooking requirements.

Cleaning of the Air Fryer

The air fryer needs to be cleaned every month. If it is left without cleaning, it will start to smell. If some food pieces are stuck in the heating outlet, black smoke will begin to come out of the device when turned on.

When cleaning the device, it is important to keep in mind that no corrosive or strong chemicals should be used. Also, hard and abrasive brushes are to be avoided. They can cause damage to the stainless steel of the basket, which will be irreversible.

Before cleaning the equipment, the device should be turned off and left to completely cooled down. Then unplug the device and neatly place the cord to avoid hindrance.

Firstly, the basket needs to be cleaned thoroughly. The basket will accumulate grease over it due to use, and it will be difficult to remove. Use water and dishwashing liquid to clean the surface of the basket. If the stains are not easily removed, then leave the basket filled with water and dishwashing liquid for a certain amount of time. Then with a sponge, clean the basket.

After washing, the basket needs to be rubbed and dried with a kitchen towel. Once thoroughly dried, the basket should be reinserted.

Benefits of Using an Air Fryer

With the demand rising for fat-free and healthy food, air-fried food has also become a hot topic. With innovation striving to make every day more efficient, the air fryer has many benefits to improve daily lives. It has many advantages:

Multi-Purpose

It is not only a fryer but also a griller, a baker, or a pizza maker. Instead of purchasing tens of different devices, one can only buy an air fryer to fulfill one's kitchen's many requirements.

Healthier Food

With hot air instead of oil to cook the food, the food cooked has a significant reduction in oil and fat content. Fat is related to increasing the risk of many diseases, such as heart disease, hypertension, and obesity. It does all this without hindering the flavors of the food being cooked. Because the fryer evenly distributes heat, the air-fried food is as crispy as oil fried.

Reduces Time Consumption

An air fryer is set for a given time and cooks food at the provided temperature thoroughly. Usually, to get healthy cooked food, one must slave over a hot stove for some time, but time can be saved because of the air fryer.

Reduces Injury

There are many accidents involving the kitchen; either someone's finger is burned, or hot oil is splattered all over. The air fryer does not require oil or an open flame, so many injuries linked with it are not a worry.

Reheating

Leftover food can be easily reheated with the help of an air fryer. Usually, reheating food takes a lot of effort and time, but the air fryer does this very efficiently.

Easy to Use

Cooking is a complicated process requiring many skills, but the air fryer makes cooking very easy. You need only to put the ingredients inside the machine and push some buttons. Anyone, even someone with no prior experience with cooking, can make great meals

UNITS OF MEASUREMENT CONVERSION

- TSP = TEASPOON
- TBSP = TABLESPOON
- 1 TEASPOON = 5 gr
- 1 TABLESPOON = 15 gr
- 1 CUP = 250 gr
- ½ CUP = 125 gr
- ¼ CUP = 63 gr
- 1 LB = 500 gr
- 1 OZ = 30 gr

AIR FRYER TEMPERATURE CONVERSION

Fahrenheit (F) and Celsius (°C)

- 212 Fahrenheit (F) = 100 Celsius (°C)
- 250 F = 120°C
- 275 F = 140°C
- 300 F = 150°C
- 320 F = 160°C
- 325 F = 170°C
- 350 F = 180°C
- 375 F = 190°C
- 400 F = 200°C
- 410 F = 210°C
- 425 F = 220°C
- 480 F = 250°C

Chapter 2. Breakfast and Brunch

1. Breakfast Turkey Sausage
Preparation Time: 10 minutes
Cooking Time: 10 minutes
Servings: 8
Ingredients:
- 2 lbs. ground turkey
- 1 tsp. dried thyme
- 1 tsp. paprika
- 2 tsp. garlic powder
- 2 tsp. dry sage
- 2 tsp. fennel seeds
- 1 tsp. sea salt

Directions:
1. Add ground meat and remaining ingredients into the mixing bowl and mix until well combined. Take 2-3 tablespoon of meat mixture and flatten into patties.
2. Place the cooking tray in the air fryer basket. Place sausage patties in the air fryer basket. Air fry to 10 minutes at 370 F. Serve and enjoy.

2. Breakfast Casserole
Preparation Time: 10 minutes
Cooking Time: 45 minutes
Servings: 8
Ingredients:
- 12 eggs
- 1 tbsp. hot sauce
- 3/4 cup heavy whipping cream
- 2 cups cheddar cheese, shredded
- 12 oz. breakfast sausage
- Pepper
- Salt

Directions:
1. Heat large pan over medium-high heat. Add sausage in a pan and cook for 5-7 minutes or until meat is no longer pink. Add cooked sausage in a 9x13-inch baking dish.
2. In a large bowl, whisk eggs with hot sauce, cream, cheese, pepper, and salt. Pour egg mixture over sausage in baking dish.
3. Cover dish with foil. Place the baking dish in your air fryer basket. Bake to 40 minutes and temperature 350 F. Serve and enjoy.

3. Egg Chorizo Casserole
Preparation Time: 10 minutes
Cooking Time: 55 minutes
Servings: 6
Ingredients:
- 8 eggs
- 1 cup cheddar cheese, shredded
- 1 bell pepper, diced
- 4 oz. can green chilis, chopped
- 3/4 cup heavy cream
- 1/2 lb. ground chorizo sausage
- 1/4 tsp. pepper
- 1/2 tsp. salt

Directions:
1. Cook chorizo over medium-high heat in a pan for 8 minutes or until browned. In a bowl, whisk eggs with cream, pepper, and salt. Stir in cooked chorizo, cheese, bell pepper, and green chilis.
2. Pour egg mixture into the greased baking dish. Cover dish with foil. Place the baking dish in the air fryer basket. Bake for 40 minutes at a temperature of 350 F. Serve and enjoy.

4. Zucchini Spinach Egg Casserole
Preparation Time: 10 minutes
Cooking Time: 30 minutes
Servings: 8
Ingredients:
- 10 eggs
- 1/4 cup goat cheese, crumbled
- 4 cherry tomatoes, cut in half
- 1/3 cup cheddar cheese, grated
- 1/3 cup ham, chopped
- 1 small zucchini, sliced
- 1/2 cup spinach
- 2/3 cup heavy cream
- Pepper

- Salt

Directions:
1. In a bowl, whisk eggs with cream, pepper, and salt. Stir in cheddar cheese, ham, zucchini, and spinach. Pour egg mixture into the greased baking dish.
2. Top with goat cheese and cherry tomatoes. Cover dish with foil, then put it in the air fryer basket. Bake for 30 minutes at a temperature of 350 F. Serve and enjoy.

5. Ham Cheese Casserole
Preparation Time: 10 minutes
Cooking Time: 35 minutes
Servings: 12
Ingredients:
- 12 eggs
- 1/2 cup cheddar cheese, shredded
- 4 oz. cream cheese, cubed
- 2 cups ham, diced
- 1 cup heavy cream
- 1/4 tsp. pepper
- 1/4 tsp. salt

Directions:
1. Mix eggs with cream, pepper, and salt in a large bowl. Stir in cheddar cheese, cream cheese, and ham. Pour egg mixture into the greased 9*13-inch baking dish. Cover dish with foil.
2. Place the baking dish in the air fryer basket, then bake for 35 minutes at a temperature of 350 F. Serve and enjoy.

6. Ham Cheese Egg Muffins
Preparation Time: 10 minutes
Cooking Time: 20 minutes
Servings: 12
Ingredients:
- 12 eggs
- 1 3/4 cup cheddar cheese, shredded
- 2 cups ham, diced
- 1 tsp. garlic, minced
- 1/2 pepper
- 1/2 tsp. salt

Directions:
1. In a bowl, whisk eggs with garlic, pepper, and salt. Stir in cheddar cheese and ham. Pour egg mixture into the silicone muffin molds. Bake in your air fryer for 20 minutes at 375 F. Serve and enjoy.

7. Crustless Cheese Egg Quiche
Preparation Time: 10 minutes
Cooking Time: 45 minutes
Servings: 6
Ingredients:
- 12 eggs
- 12 tbsp. butter, melted
- 4 oz. cream cheese, softened
- 8 oz. cheddar cheese, grated
- Pepper
- Salt

Directions:
1. In a bowl, whisk eggs with butter, cream cheese, half cheddar cheese, pepper, and salt. Pour egg mixture into the greased 9.5-inch pie pan. Sprinkle remaining cheese on top. Cover dish with foil. Bake in your air fryer for 45 minutes at a temperature of 325 F. Serve and enjoy.

8. Broccoli Casserole
Preparation Time: 10 minutes
Cooking Time: 20 minutes
Servings: 4
Ingredients:
- 2 cups broccoli florets, chopped
- 1 cup cheddar cheese, grated
- 1/2 cup sour cream
- 1/2 cup heavy cream
- Pepper
- Salt

Directions:
1. In a bowl, whisk together heavy cream, sour cream, 1/2 cheddar cheese, pepper, and salt. Add broccoli florets into the baking dish.
2. Pour heavy cream mixture over broccoli. Top with remaining cheese. Cover baking dish with foil. Bake in your air fryer for 20 minutes at a temperature of 350 F. Serve and enjoy.

9. Cauliflower Muffins
Preparation Time: 10 minutes
Cooking Time: 25 minutes
Servings: 12
Ingredients:
- 5 eggs
- 1 cup cheddar cheese, shredded
- 1/2 tsp. garlic powder
- 1/2 cup onion, chopped
- 1/2 cup baby spinach
- 6 oz. ham, diced
- 3 cups cauliflower rice, squeeze out excess liquid
- Pepper
- Salt

Directions:
1. In a bowl, whisk eggs with cheese, garlic powder, pepper, and salt. Stir in onion, spinach, ham, and cauliflower rice. Pour egg mixture into the silicone muffin molds. Bake in your air fryer for 25 minutes at a temperature of 375 F. Serve and enjoy.

10. Zucchini Bread
Preparation Time: 10 minutes
Cooking Time: 60 minutes
Servings: 12
Ingredients:
- 2 eggs, lightly beaten
- 1 1/2 cups zucchini, grated
- 1/4 cup butter, melted
- 1 tsp. baking soda
- 1/2 cup sweetener

- 1/2 tsp. ground cinnamon
- 2 cups almond flour
- 1/2 tsp. salt

Directions:
1. Mix eggs plus butter in a small bowl. Mix almond flour, cinnamon, sweetener, baking soda, and salt in a mixing bowl.
2. Add zucchini and egg mixture and mix until well combined. Pour batter into the greased loaf pan. Place the loaf pan in the air fryer basket. Bake for 60 minutes at a temperature of 350 F. Slice and serve.

11. Egg Bites
Preparation Time: 10 minutes
Cooking Time: 10 minutes
Servings: 4
Ingredients:
- 4 eggs
- 1/4 cup cheddar cheese, shredded
- 4 bacon slices, cooked and crumbled
- 1/2 bell pepper, diced
- 1/2 onion, diced
- 1 tbsp. unsweetened almond milk
- Pepper
- Salt

Directions:
1. In a bowl, whisk eggs with cheese, milk, pepper, and salt. Stir in bacon, bell pepper, and onion. Pour egg mixture into the 4 silicone muffin molds. Put the muffin molds in the air fryer basket, then air fry for 10 minutes at a temperature of 300 F. Serve and enjoy.

12. Healthy Breakfast Donuts
Preparation Time: 10 minutes
Cooking Time: 20 minutes
Servings: 6
Ingredients:
- 4 eggs
- 1/2 tsp. instant coffee
- 1/3 cup unsweetened almond milk
- 1 tbsp. liquid stevia
- 3 tbsp. cocoa powder
- 1/4 cup butter, melted
- 1/3 cup coconut flour
- 1/2 tsp. baking soda
- 1/2 tsp. baking powder

Directions:
1. Put all the fixing into the large bowl and mix until well combined. Pour batter into the silicone donut molds. Place donut molds in the air fryer basket, then bake for 20 minutes at a temperature of 350 F. Serve and enjoy.

13. Feta Pepper Egg Muffins
Preparation Time: 10 minutes
Cooking Time: 20 minutes
Servings: 12
Ingredients:
- 4 eggs
- 1/2 cup egg whites
- 1 tsp. garlic powder
- 2 tbsp. feta cheese, crumbled
- 2 tbsp. green onion, chopped
- 4 fresh basil leaves, chopped
- 1/4 cup unsweetened coconut milk
- 1 red bell pepper, chopped
- Pepper
- Salt

Directions:
1. Mix eggs, egg whites, milk, garlic powder, pepper, and salt in a bowl. Stir in cheese, bell pepper, green onion, and basil. Pour egg batter into the silicone muffin molds. Bake in your air fryer for 20 minutes at 350 F. Serve and enjoy.

14. Sun-dried Tomatoes Egg Cups
Preparation Time: 10 minutes
Cooking Time: 20 minutes
Servings: 12
Ingredients:
- 6 eggs
- 1 1/2 tbsp. basil, chopped
- 2 tsp. olive oil
- 1/2 cup feta cheese, crumbled
- 4 cherry tomatoes, chopped
- 4 sun-dried tomatoes, chopped
- Pepper
- Salt

Directions:
1. In a bowl, whisk eggs with pepper and salt. Add remaining ingredients and stir well. Pour egg mixture into the silicone muffin molds. Bake in your air fryer for 20 minutes at a temperature of 400 F. Serve and enjoy.

15. Vanilla Raspberry Muffins
Preparation Time: 10 minutes
Cooking Time: 20 minutes
Servings: 12
Ingredients:
- 3 eggs
- 1/2 cup raspberries
- 1/2 tsp. vanilla
- 1/3 cup unsweetened almond milk
- 1/3 cup coconut oil, melted
- 1 1/2 tsp. baking powder
- 1/2 cup Swerve
- 2 1/2 cups almond flour

Directions:
1. Mix almond flour, baking powder, and sweetener in a large bowl. Stir in the coconut oil, vanilla, eggs, and almond milk. Add raspberries and fold well. Pour mixture into the silicone muffin molds. Bake in your air fryer to 20 minutes at a temperature of 350 F. Serve and enjoy.

16. Simple Cheese Sticks
Preparation time: 15 minutes
Cooking time: 8 minutes
Servings: 4
Ingredients:
- 6 cheese sticks, snake-sized
- ¼ cup parmesan cheese, grated
- 2 eggs
- 1 tablespoon Italian seasoning
- ¼ cup almond flour, whole wheat
- ¼ tablespoon rosemary, grounded
- 1 tablespoon garlic powder

Directions:
1. Take cheese sticks and set aside. Take a shallow bowl and beat eggs into the bowl. Mix cheese, flour, and seasonings in another bowl.
2. Roll the cheese sticks in the eggs and then in the batter. Now repeat the process till the sticks are well coated. Place it in the basket of the air fryer. Air fry for 6-7 minutes at 370 F. Serve and enjoy!

17. Hearty Pickle Chips
Preparation time: 15 minutes
Cooking time: 20 minutes
Servings: 4
Ingredients:
- 24 hamburger dill pickle chips
- 1/3 cup panko breadcrumbs, whole-wheat
- ¼ tsp. garlic powder
- ¼ cup egg white or fat-free liquid egg
- Dash cayenne pepper
- ¼ tsp. onion powder
- Ketchup; to dip
- Dash each salt and black pepper

Directions:
1. Warm your air fryer to 375 degrees F for 8 minutes. Spray oil in the fryer basket. Take a bowl and mix breadcrumbs with seasoning into it.
2. Blot pickle chips dry. Transfer them into a medium-small bowl, coat with egg whites to both sides. Remove the excess eggs and then coat with seasoned. Bake for 10 minutes, and another 10 minutes more to make it crispy. Serve and enjoy!

18. Early Morning Mushroom and Egg Bowl
Preparation time: 15 minutes
Cooking time: 13 minutes
Servings: 4
Ingredients:
- 8 chestnut mushrooms
- 8 tomatoes, halved
- 1 garlic clove, crushed
- 4 rashers smoked back bacon
- 7 ounces baby leaf spinach
- 4 whole eggs
- Chipotle as needed

Directions:
1. Warm your Air Fryer to 392 degrees F. Take the Air Fryer cooking basket and add mushrooms, tomatoes, and garlic. Spray with oil and season well. Add bacon, chipotle to the Air Fryer, and air fry for 10 minutes.
2. Take a microwave-proof bowl and add spinach, heat until wilt. Add wilt spinach into the microwave-proof bowl. Crack the eggs into the bowl and Air Fry for 2-3 minutes at 320 degrees F. Serve cooked eggs with bacon, enjoy!

19. Cheesy Omelet
Preparation time: 15 minutes
Cooking time: 13 minutes
Servings: 4
Ingredients:
- 2 eggs
- Pepper as needed
- Grated Cheddar as needed
- ½ cup onions, diced
- 2 teaspoons coconut aminos

Directions:
1. Preheat your Air Fryer up to 340 degrees F. Clean and chop the onion. Take a plate and cover with 2 teaspoon aminos. Transfer into the Air Fryer and bake for 8 minutes.
2. Beat eggs and add pepper with salt. Pour the egg mixture on onions and bake the mix for 3 minutes more. Add cheddar cheese and bake for 2 minutes more. Serve with fresh basil leaves. Enjoy!

20. Classic Bacon Asparagus Meal
Preparation time: 15 minutes
Cooking time: 20 minutes
Servings: 4
Ingredients:
- 1 bunch of asparagus
- 4 slices streaky bacon
- 1 teaspoon liquid stevia
- 1 and ½ tablespoons olive oil
- 1 teaspoon brown sugar
- Garlic pepper seasoning

Directions:
1. Warm your air fryer to 400 degrees F for 8 minutes. Trim the asparagus to your desired length. Take a bowl and add oil, garlic pepper, stevia to make a mixture
2. Coat the asparagus with the mix. Wrap one piece of bacon with an asparagus stalk. To secure the wrap, poke a toothpick. Place all the wraps in the basket in your Air Fryer. Air fry for 8 minutes. Serve and enjoy!

21. Healthy Ham-A-Cup
Preparation time: 15 minutes
Cooking time: 15 minutes
Servings: 6
Ingredients:
- 5 whole eggs
- 2 and ¼ ounces ham
- 1 cup milk
- 1/8 teaspoon pepper

- 1 and ½ cup Swiss cheese
- ¼ teaspoon salt
- ¼ cup green onion
- ½ teaspoon thyme

Directions:
1. Preheat your fryer to 350 degrees F. Crack your eggs in a bowl and beat it well. Add thyme onion, salt, Swiss cheese pepper, milk to the beaten eggs.
2. Prepare your baking forms for muffins and place ham slices in each baking form. Cover the ham with egg mixture. Transfer to Air Fryer and bake for 15 minutes. Serve and enjoy!

22. The Simple Egg
Preparation time: 15 minutes
Cooking time: 15 minutes
Servings: 6
Ingredients:
- 6 large eggs

Directions:
1. Preheat your air fryer 300 degrees F. Put the eggs in a single layer in your air fryer basket carefully. Bake for at least 8 minutes for a slightly runny yolk or 12 to 15 minutes for a firmer yolk.
2. Use tongs to remove the eggs from the air fryer carefully. Then take a bowl of icy water and immediately place them in it.
3. Let the eggs stand in the cold water for 5 minutes, then gently crack the shell underwater. After that, let the eggs stand for another minute or two, then peel and eat. Enjoy!

23. Quick and Spicy Hot Dogs
Preparation time: 15 minutes
Cooking time: 15 minutes
Servings: 6
Ingredients:
- 6 hot dogs
- 1 tablespoon mustard
- 6 tablespoons keto-friend spicy ketchup

Directions:
1. Preheat your air fryer to 380 degrees F. Transfer Hot Dogs to lightly greased Air Fryer cooking basket. Bake for 15 minutes, making sure to turn them halfway through. Serve with mustard and spicy ketchup, enjoy!

24. Glazed Carrot Chips and Cheese
Preparation time: 15 minutes
Cooking time: 15 minutes
Servings: 4
Ingredients:
- 3 carrots, sliced into sticks
- 1 tablespoon coconut oil
- 1/3 cup Romano cheese, freshly grated
- 2 teaspoons garlic powder
- Salt and pepper to taste

Directions:
1. Preheat your air fryer to 380 degrees F. Take a bowl, add all ingredients, and toss and coat them well. Transfer to Air Fryer cooking basket and air fry for 15 minutes. Once done, serve with your desired dipping sauce. Enjoy!

25. Chinese-Style Baby Carrots
Preparation time: 15 minutes
Cooking time: 15 minutes
Servings: 4
Ingredients:
- 1-pound baby carrots
- 2 tablespoons sesame oil
- ½ teaspoon Szechuan pepper
- 1 teaspoon five-spice powder
- 3-4 drops liquid stevia
- 1 large garlic clove, crushed
- 1-piece fresh ginger root, peeled and grated
- 2 tablespoons tamari sauce

Directions:
1. Warm your Air Fryer to 380 degrees F. Add all listed ingredients to the cooking basket. Air fry for 15 minutes, making sure to shake halfway through. Enjoy!

26. Kale Chips
Preparation time: 5 minutes
Cooking time: 5 minutes
Servings: 4
Ingredients:
- 2 and ½ tablespoons olive oil
- 1 and ½ teaspoon garlic powder
- 1 bunch kale, torn
- 2 tablespoons lime juice
- 1 and ½ teaspoons seasoned salt

Directions:
1. Preheat your Air Fryer to 195 degrees F. Add all listed ingredients to the cooking basket. Air fry for 4-5 minutes, making sure to shake halfway through. Enjoy!

27. Morning Cocktail Meatball
Preparation time: 15 minutes
Cooking time: 18 minutes
Servings: 4
Ingredients:
- ½ teaspoon salt
- 1 cup Romano cheese, grated
- 3 garlic cloves, minced
- 1 and ½ pounds pork, ground
- ½ cup scallions, chopped
- 2 eggs, whisked
- 1/3 teaspoon cumin powder
- 2/3 teaspoon ground black pepper
- 2 teaspoons basil

Directions:
1. Mix all ingredients in a bowl. Shape them into small sized balls. Preheat your Air Fryer to 345 degrees F. Transfer to Air Fryer cooking basket, air fry for 18 minutes. Serve and enjoy!

28. Blueberry Breakfast Cobbler

Preparation time: 15 minutes
Cooking time: 20 minutes
Servings: 4
Ingredients:
- 1/3 cup whole-wheat pastry flour
- ¾ teaspoon baking powder
- Dash sea salt
- ½ cup 2% milk
- 2 tablespoons pure maple syrup
- ½ teaspoon vanilla extract
- Cooking oil spray
- ½ cup fresh blueberries
- ¼ cup Granola or plain store-bought granola

Directions:
1. Mix the flour, baking powder, plus salt in a medium bowl. Add the milk, maple syrup, and vanilla and gently whisk just until thoroughly combined.
2. Preheat the air fryer to 350°F and setting the time to 3 minutes. Spray a 6-by-2-inch round baking pan with cooking oil and pour the batter into the pan. Top evenly with the blueberries and granola.
3. Bake at 350°F and set the time to 15 minutes. When the cooking is complete, the cobbler should be nicely browned, and a knife inserted into the middle should come out clean. Enjoy plain or topped with a little vanilla yogurt.

29. Strawberry Breakfast Tarts

Preparation time: 15 minutes
Cooking time: 10 minutes
Servings: 6
Ingredients:
- 2 refrigerated piecrusts
- ½ cup strawberry preserves
- 1 teaspoon cornstarch
- Cooking oil spray
- ½ cup low-fat vanilla yogurt
- 1-ounce cream cheese, at room temperature
- 3 tablespoons confectioners' sugar
- Rainbow sprinkles, for decorating

Directions:
1. Place the piecrusts on a flat surface. Cut each piecrust into 3 rectangles, for 6 total using a knife or pizza cutter. Discard any unused dough from the piecrust edges.
2. Mix the preserves and cornstarch in a small bowl, ensuring there are no lumps of cornstarch remaining. Scoop 1 tablespoon of the strawberry mixture onto the top half of each piece of piecrust.
3. Fold the bottom of each piece up to enclose the filling. Using the back of a fork, press along the edges of each tart to seal. Insert the crisper plate into the basket.
4. Warm at 375°F and set the time to 3 minutes. Spray the crisper plate with cooking oil. Working in batches, spray the breakfast tarts with cooking oil and place them into the basket in a single layer. Do not stack the tarts.
5. Bake at 375°F and set the time to 10 minutes. When the cooking is complete, the tarts should be light golden brown. Let the breakfast tarts cool thoroughly before removing them from the basket.
6. In a small bowl, stir together the yogurt, cream cheese, and confectioners' sugar. Spread the breakfast tarts with the frosting and top with sprinkles.

30. Everything Bagels

Preparation time: 10 minutes
Cooking time: 10 minutes
Servings: 2
Ingredients:
- ½ cup self-rising flour, plus more for dusting
- ½ cup plain Greek yogurt
- 1 egg
- 1 tablespoon water
- 4 teaspoons everything-bagel spice mix
- Cooking oil spray
- 1 tablespoon butter, melted

Directions:
1. Mix the flour and yogurt until a tacky dough form in a large bowl, using a wooden spoon. Put the dough to a lightly floured work surface and roll the dough into a ball.
2. Cut the dough into 2 pieces and roll each piece into a log. Form each log into a bagel shape, pinching the ends together.
3. In a small bowl, whisk the egg and water. Brush the egg wash on the bagels. Put 2 teaspoons of the spice mix on each bagel and gently press it into the dough.
4. Insert the crisper plate into the basket. Preheat the air fryer at 330°F and set the timer to 3 minutes.
5. Spray the crisper plate with cooking spray. Drizzle the bagels with the butter and place them into the basket. Bake at 330°F for 10 minutes. When the cooking is complete, the bagels should be lightly golden on the outside. Serve warm.

31. Maple-Glazed Doughnuts

Preparation time: 10 minutes
Cooking time: 14 minutes
Servings: 8
Ingredients:
- 1 can jumbo flaky refrigerator biscuits
- Cooking oil spray
- ½ cup light brown sugar
- ¼ cup butter
- 3 tablespoons milk
- 2 cups confectioners' sugar, + more for dusting (optional)
- 2 teaspoons pure maple syrup

Directions:
1. Insert the crisper plate into the basket. Preheat your air fryer at 350°F for 3 minutes. Remove the biscuits

from the tube and cut out each biscuit's center with a small, round cookie cutter.
2. Spray the crisper plate with cooking oil. Working in batches, place 4 doughnuts into the basket. Air fry at 350°F for 5 minutes.
3. Mix the brown sugar, butter, and milk in a small saucepan over medium heat until the butter is melted plus the sugar is dissolved, for 4 minutes. Remove, and whisk in the confectioners' sugar and maple syrup until smooth.
4. Dip the slightly cooled doughnuts into the maple glaze. Place them on a wire rack and dust with confectioners' sugar (if using). Let rest just until the glaze sets. Enjoy the doughnuts warm.

32. Fried Chicken and Waffles
Preparation time: 10 minutes
Cooking time: 30 minutes
Servings: 4
Ingredients:
- 8 whole chicken wings
- 1 teaspoon garlic powder
- Chicken seasoning, for preparing the chicken
- Freshly ground black pepper
- ½ cup all-purpose flour
- Cooking oil spray
- 8 frozen waffles
- Pure maple syrup, for serving (optional)

Directions:
1. Mix the chicken and garlic powder in a medium bowl and season with chicken seasoning and pepper. Toss to coat.
2. Put the chicken in a resealable plastic bag, then add the flour. Shake it to coat the chicken thoroughly.
3. Preheat the air fryer to 400°F and set the timer to 3 minutes. Oil the crisper plate using cooking oil. Put the chicken from the bag into the basket using tongs. Spray them with cooking oil.
4. Air fry at 400°F and set the timer to 20 minutes. After 5 minutes, remove the basket, shake the wings, and re-insert the basket to resume air frying. Shake the basket every 5 minutes.
5. Remove the cooked chicken; cover to keep warm. Rinse the basket and crisper plate with warm water. Insert it back into the unit.
6. Air fry at 360°F and set the time to 3 minutes. Oiled the crisper plate with cooking spray. Working in batches, place the frozen waffles into the basket. Do not stack them. Spray the waffles with cooking oil.
7. Air fry at 360°F and set the timer to 6 minutes. Serve the waffles with the chicken and a touch of maple syrup, if desired.

33. Puffed Egg Tarts
Preparation time: 15 minutes
Cooking time: 20 minutes
Servings: 2
Ingredients:
- 1/3 sheet frozen puff pastry, thawed
- Cooking oil spray
- ½ cup shredded Cheddar cheese
- 2 eggs
- ¼ teaspoon salt, divided
- 1 teaspoon minced fresh parsley (optional)

Directions:
1. Insert the crisper plate into the basket and the basket into the unit. Preheat your air fryer to 390°F and set the timer to 3 minutes.
2. Lay the puff pastry sheet on a piece of parchment paper and cut it in half. Spray the crisper plate with cooking oil. Transfer the 2 squares of pastry to the basket, keeping them on the parchment paper.
3. Bake at 390°F and set the timer to 20 minutes. After 10 minutes, use a metal spoon to press down each pastry square's center to make a well.
4. Divide the cheese equally between the baked pastries. Carefully crack an egg on top of the cheese, and sprinkle each with the salt. Resume cooking for 7 to 10 minutes.
5. When the cooking is complete, the eggs will be cooked through. Sprinkle each with parsley (if using) and serve.

34. Early Morning Steak and Eggs
Preparation time: 8 minutes
Cooking time: 14 minutes
Servings: 4
Ingredients:
- Cooking oil spray
- 4 (4-ounce) New York strip steaks
- 1 teaspoon granulated garlic, divided
- 1 teaspoon salt, divided
- 1 teaspoon freshly ground black pepper, divided
- 4 eggs
- ½ teaspoon paprika

Directions:
1. Insert the crisper plate into the basket and the basket into the air fryer. Preheat to 360°F and set the timer to 3 minutes.
2. Spray the crisper plate with cooking oil. Place 2 steaks into the basket; do not oil or season them at this time.
3. Air fry at 360°F and set the time to 9 minutes. After 5 minutes, open the unit and flip the steaks. Sprinkle each with ¼ teaspoon of granulated garlic, ¼ teaspoon of salt, and ¼ teaspoon of pepper.
4. Resume cooking until the steaks register at least 145°F on a food thermometer. When the cooking is complete, transfer the steaks to a plate and tent with aluminum foil to keep warm.
5. Spray 4 ramekins with olive oil. Crack 1 egg into each ramekin. Sprinkle the eggs with the paprika and the remaining ½ teaspoon each of salt and pepper. Working in batches, place 2 ramekins into the basket.
6. Bake at 330°F and set the timer to 5 minutes. When the cooking is complete, and the eggs are cooked to 160°F, remove the ramekins and repeat the step with the remaining 2 ramekins. Serve the eggs with the steaks.

35. Lemon Vanilla Cupcakes with Yogurt Frost

Preparation time: 15 minutes
Cooking time: 8 minutes
Servings: 5
Ingredients:
Lemon Frosting:
- 1 cup natural yogurt
- Sugar to taste
- 1 orange, juiced
- 1 tbsp. orange zest
- 1 cup cream cheese

Cake:
- 2 lemons, quartered
- ½ cup flour + extra for basing
- ¼ tsp. salt
- 2 tbsp. sugar
- 1 tsp. baking powder
- 1 tsp. vanilla extract
- 2 eggs
- ½ cup softened butter
- 2 tbsp. milk

Directions:
1. In a bowl, add the yogurt and cream cheese. Mix until smooth. Add the orange juice and zest; mix well. Gradually add the sweetener to the taste while stirring until smooth. Make sure the frost is not runny. Set aside.
2. For cupcakes: Place the lemon quarters in a food processor and process it until pureed. Add the baking powder, softened butter, milk, eggs, vanilla extract, sugar, and salt. Process again until smooth.
3. Preheat Air Fryer to 400 F. Flour the bottom of 10 cupcake cases and spoon the batter into the cases ¾ way up. Place them in the air fryer and bake for 7-8 minutes. Remove and let cool. Design with the frosting and serve.

36. Saucy Vegetable Chicken

Preparation time: 15 minutes
Cooking time: 10 minutes
Servings: 4
Ingredients:
- 4 chicken breasts, cut into cubes
- 2 carrots, sliced
- 2 mixed bell peppers, cut into strips
- 1 cup snow peas
- 15 oz. broccoli florets
- 1 scallion, sliced

Sauce:
- 3 tbsp. soy sauce
- 2 tbsp. oyster sauce
- 1 tbsp. brown sugar
- 1 tsp. sesame oil
- 1 tsp. cornstarch
- 1 tsp. sriracha
- 2 garlic cloves, minced
- 1 tbsp. grated ginger
- 1 tbsp. rice wine vinegar

Directions:
1. Warm Air Fryer to 370 F. Place the chicken, bell peppers, and carrot in a bowl. In another bowl, combine the sauce ingredients.
2. Coat the chicken mixture with the sauce. Put on a lined baking dish, then bake for 5 minutes. Add snow peas and broccoli and cook for an additional 8 to 10 minutes. Serve garnished with scallion.

37. Creamy Mushroom & Spinach Omelet

Preparation time: 15 minutes
Cooking time: 8 minutes
Servings: 2
Ingredients:
- 4 eggs, lightly beaten
- 2 tbsp. heavy cream
- 2 cups spinach, chopped
- 1 cup chopped mushrooms
- 3 oz. feta cheese, crumbled
- A handful of fresh parsley, chopped

Directions:
1. Oiled the air fryer basket with cooking spray. In a bowl, whisk eggs and until combined. Stir in spinach, mushrooms, feta cheese, parsley, salt, and pepper.
2. Pour into a baking dish and Bake in the fryer for 8 minutes at 350 F. Serve immediately with a touch of tangy tomato relish.

38. Caprese Sandwich with Sourdough Bread

Preparation time: 15 minutes
Cooking time: 14 minutes
Servings: 2
Ingredients:
- 4 slices sourdough bread
- 2 tbsp. mayonnaise
- 2 slices ham
- 2 lettuce leaves
- 1 tomato, sliced
- 2 slices Mozzarella cheese

Directions:
1. On a clean board, lay the sourdough slices and spread with mayonnaise. Top 2 of the slices with ham, lettuce, tomato, and Mozzarella cheese.
2. Season with salt and black pepper. Top with the remaining slices to form two sandwiches. Transfer to the air fryer. Bake for 14 minutes at 340 F, flipping once. Serve hot.

39. Almond & Cinnamon Berry Oat Bars

Preparation time: 15 minutes
Cooking time: 30 minutes
Servings: 6
Ingredients:
- 3 cups rolled oats
- ½ cup ground almonds
- ½ cup flour
- 1 tsp. baking powder

- 1 tsp. ground cinnamon
- 3 eggs, lightly beaten
- ½ cup canola oil
- 1/3 cup milk
- 2 cups mixed berries

Directions:
1. In a bowl, add oats, almonds, flour, baking powder, and cinnamon and stir well. In another bowl, whisk eggs, oil, and milk. Stir the wet ingredients gently into the oat mixture.
2. Fold in the berries. Pour the mixture into the pan and place it in the fryer. Bake for 30 minutes at 330 F. When ready, check if the bars are nice and soft.

40. Cinnamon Mango Bread
Preparation time: 15 minutes
Cooking time: 35 minutes
Servings: 8
Ingredients:
- ½ cup melted butter
- 1 egg, lightly beaten
- ½ cup brown sugar
- 1 tsp. vanilla extract
- 3 ripe mangos, mashed
- 1 ½ cups plain flour
- 1 tsp. baking powder
- ½ tsp. grated nutmeg
- ½ tsp. ground cinnamon

Directions:
1. Oiled a loaf tin using a cooking spray and line with baking paper. In a bowl, whisk melted butter, egg, sugar, vanilla, and mango. Sift in flour, baking powder, nutmeg, and cinnamon; stir without overmixing.
2. Put the batter into the tin, then place it in the air fryer. Bake for 35 minutes at 300 F. Make sure to check at the 20-25-minute mark. When ready, let cool before slicing it.

41. Honey Banana & Hazelnut Cupcakes
Preparation time: 15 minutes
Cooking time: 30 minutes
Servings: 6
Ingredients:
- ½ cup melted butter
- ½ cup honey
- 2 eggs, lightly beaten
- 3 ripe bananas, mashed
- 1 tsp. vanilla extract
- 1 ½ cups flour
- 1 tsp. baking powder
- ½ tsp. baking soda
- 1 tsp. ground cinnamon
- ½ cup chopped hazelnuts
- ½ cup dark chocolate chips

Directions:
1. Spray a 6-hole muffin tray with oil spray. In a bowl, whisk butter, honey, eggs, banana, and vanilla. Sift in flour, baking powder, baking soda, and mix well. Stir in hazelnuts and chocolate.
2. Pour the mixture into the muffin holes. Place in the air fryer. Bake for 30 minutes at 350 F, checking them at the around 20-minute mark.

42. Cherry in Vanilla Almond Scones
Preparation time: 15 minutes
Cooking time: 14 minutes
Servings: 4
Ingredients:
- 2 cups flour
- 1/3 cup sugar
- 2 tsp. baking powder
- ½ cup sliced almonds
- ¾ cup chopped cherries, dried
- ¼ cup cold butter, cut into cubes
- ½ cup milk
- 1 egg
- 1 tsp. vanilla extract

Directions:
1. Line air fryer basket with baking paper. Mix flour, sugar, baking powder, almonds, and dried cherries. Put the butter into the dry ingredients with hands to form a sandy, crumbly texture. Whisk together egg, milk, and vanilla extract. Pour into the dry ingredients and stir to combine.
2. Sprinkle a board with flour, lay the dough onto the board, and give it a few kneads. Form or shape the dough into a rectangle, then cut into squares. Arrange the squares in the air fryer's basket and air fry for 14 minutes at 390 F. Serve immediately.

43. Sweet Caramel French Toast
Preparation time: 15 minutes
Cooking time: 10 minutes
Servings: 3
Ingredients:
- 6 slices white bread
- 2 eggs
- ¼ cup heavy cream
- 1/3 cup sugar mixed with 1 tsp. cinnamon
- 6 tbsp. caramel
- 1 tsp. vanilla extract

Directions:
1. In a bowl, whisk eggs and cream. Dip each piece of bread into the egg and cream. Dip the bread into the sugar and cinnamon mixture until well-coated. On a clean board, lay the coated slices.
2. Spread three of the slices with about 2 tbsp. of caramel each around the center. Place the remaining three slices on top to form 3 sandwiches.
3. Spray the air fryer basket with oil. Arrange the sandwiches into the fryer and bake for 10 minutes at 340 F, turning once halfway through cooking. Serve.

44. Smoky Cheese & Mustard Rarebit
Preparation time: 15 minutes
Cooking time: 10 minutes
Servings: 2

Ingredients:
- 4 bread slices
- 1 tsp. smoked paprika
- 2 eggs
- 1 tsp. Dijon mustard
- 4 oz. cheddar cheese, grated
- Salt and black pepper to taste

Directions:
1. Preheat the Air fryer to 370 F. In a bowl, whisk the eggs and stir in mustard, cheddar cheese, paprika, salt, and pepper. Spread the mixture on the bread. Place them in the fryer basket and bake the slices for 10 minutes.

45. Corn & Chorizo Frittata
Preparation time: 15 minutes
Cooking time: 6 minutes
Servings: 2
Ingredients:
- 3 eggs
- 1 large potato, boiled and cubed
- ½ cup of frozen corn
- ½ cup feta cheese, crumbled
- 1 tbsp. chopped parsley
- ½ chorizo, sliced
- Olive oil to grease
- Salt and black pepper to taste

Directions:
1. Preheat Air Fryer to 330 F. Beat the eggs with some salt and pepper in a bowl. Stir in all of the remaining ingredients. Put the batter into a greased baking dish and place it in the fryer. Bake for 6 minutes. Serve.

46. Carrot & Broccoli Cheddar Quiche
Preparation time: 15 minutes
Cooking time: 30 minutes
Servings: 2
Ingredients:
- 4 eggs
- 1 cup whole milk
- 1 broccoli heads cut into florets
- 2 medium tomatoes, diced
- 4 medium carrots, diced
- ¼ cup Feta cheese, crumbled
- 1 cup grated cheddar cheese
- Salt and black pepper to taste
- 1 tsp. chopped parsley

Directions:
1. Put the broccoli and carrots in a food steamer and cook until soft, about 10 minutes. In a jug, crack in the eggs, add the parsley, salt, and pepper. Beat the eggs while adding the milk gradually until a pale mixture is attained.
2. Once the broccoli and carrots are ready, strain them through a sieve, and set aside. In a 3x3-inch quiche dish, add the carrots and broccoli. Put the tomatoes on top, then the feta and cheddar cheese following.
3. Leave a little bit of cheddar cheese. Pour the egg mixture over the layering and top with the remaining cheddar cheese. Place the dish in the air fryer and bake at 350 F for 20 minutes.

47. Breaded Cauliflowers in Alfredo Sauce
Preparation time: 15 minutes
Cooking time: 15 minutes
Servings: 4
Ingredients:
- 4 cups cauliflower florets
- 1 tbsp. butter, melted
- ¼ cup alfredo sauce
- 1 cup breadcrumbs
- 1 tsp. sea salt

Directions:
1. Whisk the alfredo sauce along with the butter. In a shallow bowl, combine the breadcrumbs with the sea salt.
2. Dip each cauliflower floret into the alfredo mixture first, and then coat in the crumbs. Drop the prepared florets into the Air fryer. Set the temperature to 350 F and air fry to 15 minutes. Shake the florets twice.

48. Crunchy Asparagus with Cheese
Preparation time: 15 minutes
Cooking time: 10 minutes
Servings: 6
Ingredients:
- 1 lb. asparagus spears
- ¼ cup flour
- 1 cup breadcrumbs
- ½ cup Parmesan cheese, grated
- 2 eggs, beaten
- Salt and black pepper to taste

Directions:
1. Preheat the Air fryer to 370 F. Combine the breadcrumbs and Parmesan cheese in a small bowl. Season with salt and pepper. Line a baking sheet with parchment paper.
2. Dip half of the spears into the flour first, then into the eggs, and finally coat with crumbs. Arrange them on the sheet and bake for about 8 to 10 minutes.
3. Repeat with the other half of the spears. Serve with melted butter, hollandaise sauce, and freshly squeezed lemon.

49. Vanilla Brownies with White Chocolate & Walnuts
Preparation time: 15 minutes
Cooking time: 20 minutes
Servings: 6
Ingredients:
- 6 oz. dark chocolate
- 6 oz. butter
- ¾ cup white sugar
- 3 eggs
- 2 tsp. vanilla extract
- ¾ cup flour
- ¼ cup of cocoa powder

- 1 cup chopped walnuts
- 1 cup white chocolate chips

Directions:
1. Line a pan inside the Air Fryer with baking paper. Dissolve chocolate and butter over low heat in a saucepan. Keep stirring until you obtain a smooth mixture. Let cool slightly and whisk in eggs and vanilla.
2. Sift flour and cocoa and stir to mix well. Sprinkle the walnuts over and add the white chocolate into the batter. Pour the batter into a pan that fits in the fryer and bake for 20 minutes at 340 F. Serve with ice cream.

50. Bacon Bombs

Preparation time: 10 minutes
Cooking time: 10 minutes
Servings: 4
Ingredients:
- 3 center-cut bacon slices
- 3 large eggs, lightly beaten
- 1 oz. 1/3-less-fat cream cheese, softened
- 1 tbsp. chopped fresh chives
- 4 oz. fresh whole wheat pizza dough
- Cooking spray

Directions:
1. Sear the bacon slices in a skillet until brown and crispy, then chop into fine crumbles. Add eggs to the same pan and cook for 1 minute, then stir in cream cheese, chives, and bacon. Mix well, then allow this egg filling to cool down.
2. Spread the pizza dough and slice into four -5inches circles. Divide the egg filling on top of each circle and seal its edge to make dumplings.
3. Place the bacon bombs in the Air Fryer basket and spray them with cooking oil. Air Fry at 350 degrees F temperature for 6 minutes. Serve warm.

51. Breakfast Pockets

Preparation time: 10 minutes
Cooking time: 11 minutes
Servings: 6
Ingredients:
- 1 box puff pastry sheet
- 5 eggs
- ½ cup loose sausage, cooked
- ½ cup bacon, cooked
- ½ cup cheddar cheese, shredded

Directions:
1. Stir and cook eggs in a skillet for 1 minute, then mix with sausages, cheddar cheese, and bacon. Spread the pastry sheet and cut it into four rectangles of equal size.
2. Divide the egg mixture over each rectangle. Fold the edges around the filling and seal them. Place the pockets in the Air Fryer basket. Air Fry at 370 degrees F for 10 minutes. Serve warm.

52. Avocado Flautas

Preparation time: 10 minutes
Cooking time: 16 minutes
Servings: 8
Ingredients:
- 1 tbsp. butter
- 8 eggs, beaten
- ½ tsp. salt
- ¼ tsp. pepper
- 1 ½ tsp. cumin
- 1 tsp. chili powder
- 8 fajita-size tortillas
- 4 oz. cream cheese, softened
- 8 slices cooked bacon

Avocado Crème:
- 2 small avocados
- ½ cup sour cream
- 1 lime, juiced
- ½ tsp. salt
- ¼ tsp. pepper

Directions:
1. In a skillet, melt butter and stir in eggs, salt, cumin, pepper, and chili powder, then stir cook for 4 minutes. Spread all the tortillas and top them with cream cheese and bacon.
2. Then divide the egg scramble on top and finally add cheese. Roll the tortillas to seal the filling inside. Place 4 rolls in the Air Fryer basket.
3. Air Fry at 400 degrees F for 12 minutes. Cook the remaining tortilla rolls in the same manner. Meanwhile, blend avocado crème ingredients in a blender, then serve with warm flautas.

53. Sausage Cheese Wraps

Preparation time: 10 minutes
Cooking time: 3 minutes
Servings: 8
Ingredients:
- 8 sausages
- 2 pieces American cheese, shredded
- 8-count refrigerated crescent roll dough

Directions:
1. Roll out each crescent roll and top it with cheese and 1 sausage. Fold both the top plus bottom edges of the crescent sheet to cover the sausage and roll it around the sausage.
2. Place 4 rolls in the Air Fryer basket and spray them with cooking oil. Air Fry at 380 degrees F for 3 minutes. Cook the remaining rolls in the same manner. Serve fresh.

54. Chicken Omelet

Preparation time: 10 minutes
Cooking time: 18 minutes
Servings: 4
Ingredients:
- 4 eggs
- ½ cup chicken breast, cooked and diced

- 2 tbsp. shredded cheese, divided
- ½ tsp. salt, divided
- ¼ tsp. pepper, divided
- ¼ tsp. granulated garlic, divided
- ¼ tsp. onion powder, divided

Directions:
1. Spray 2 ramekins with cooking oil and keep them aside. Crack two large eggs into each ramekin, then add cheese and seasoning. Whisk well, then add ¼ cup chicken.
2. Place the ramekins in a baking tray. Set the baking tray inside the Air Fryer, bake at 330 degrees F for 18 minutes. Serve warm.

55. Sausage Burritos
Preparation time: 10 minutes
Cooking time: 10 minutes
Servings: 6
Ingredients:
- 6 medium flour tortillas
- 6 scrambled eggs
- ½ lb. ground sausage, browned
- ½ bell pepper, minced
- 1/3 cup bacon bits
- ½ cup shredded cheese
- Oil, for spraying

Directions:
1. Mix eggs with cheese, bell pepper, bacon, and sausage in a bowl. Spread each tortilla on the working surface and top it with ½ cup egg filling.
2. Roll the tortilla like a burrito, then place 3 burritos in the Air Fryer basket. Spray them with cooking oil, Air Fry at 330 degrees F for 5 minutes. Cook the remaining burritos in the same manner. Serve fresh.

56. Sausage Patties
Preparation time: 10 minutes
Cooking time: 20 minutes
Servings: 4
Ingredients:
- 1 1/2 lbs. ground sausage
- 1 tsp. chili flakes
- 1 tsp. dried thyme
- 1 tsp. onion powder
- ½ tsp. each paprika and cayenne
- Sea salt and black pepper, to taste
- 2 tsp. brown sugar
- 3 tsp. minced garlic
- 2 tsp. Tabasco
- Herbs for garnish

Directions:
1. Toss sausage ground with all the spices, herbs, sugar, garlic, and tabasco sauce in a bowl. Make 1.5-inch-thick and 3-inch round patties out of this mixture.
2. Place the sausage patties in the Air Fryer basket. Air Fry at 370 degrees F for 20 minutes. Flip the patties when cooked halfway through, then continue cooking.

57. Cinnamon Cream Doughnuts
Preparation time: 10 minutes
Cooking time: 8 minutes
Servings: 4
Ingredients:
- 1/2 cup Sugar
- 2 1/2 tbsp. butter
- 2 large egg yolks
- 2 1/4 cups all-purpose flour
- 1 1/2 tsp. baking powder
- 1 tsp. salt
- 1/2 cup sour cream

To garnish:
- 1/3 cup white Sugar
- 1 tsp. cinnamon
- 2 tbsp. butter, melted

Directions:
1. Beat egg with sugar and butter in a mixer until creamy, then whisk in flour, salt, baking powder, and sour cream. Mix well until smooth, then refrigerate the dough for 1 hour.
2. Spread this dough into ½ inch thick circle, then cut 9 large circles out of it. Make the hole at the center of each circle. Place the doughnuts in the Air Fryer basket.
3. Air Fry at 350 degrees F temperature for 8 minutes. Air fries the doughnuts in two batches to avoid overcrowding. Mix sugar, cinnamon, and butter and glaze the doughnuts with this mixture. Serve.

58. Sausage Frittata
Preparation time: 15 minutes
Cooking time: 20 minutes
Servings: 4
Ingredients:
- 1/4-pound sausage, cooked and crumbled
- 4 eggs, beaten
- 1/2 cup shredded Cheddar cheese blend
- 2 tbsp. red bell pepper, diced
- 1 green onion, chopped
- 1 pinch cayenne pepper
- cooking spray

Directions:
1. Beat eggs with cheese, sausage, cayenne, onion, and bell pepper in a bowl. Spread the egg mixture in a 6x2 inch baking tray, greased with cooking spray.
2. Set the baking tray inside the Air Fryer, then bake at 360 degrees F for 20 minutes. Slice and serve.

59. Potato Jalapeno Hash
Preparation time: 15 minutes
Cooking time: 24 minutes
Servings: 6
Ingredients:
- 1 1/2 lbs. potatoes, peeled and diced
- 1 tbsp. olive oil
- 1 red bell pepper, seeded and diced
- 1 small onion, chopped

- 1 jalapeno, seeded and diced
- 1/2 tsp. olive oil
- 1/2 tsp. taco seasoning mix
- 1/2 tsp. ground cumin
- salt and black pepper to taste

Directions:
1. Soak the potato in cold water for 20 minutes, then drain them. Toss the potatoes with 1 tbsp. olive oil. Spread them in the Air Fryer basket. Air Fry at 370 degrees F for 18 minutes.
2. Meanwhile, toss onion, pepper, olive oil, taco seasoning, and all other ingredients in a salad bowl. Add this vegetable mixture to the Air Fryer basket. Continue air frying at 356 degrees F for 6 minutes. Serve warm.

60. Bread Rolls
Preparation time: 10 minutes
Cooking time: 28 minutes
Servings: 8
Ingredients:
- 8 Bread Slices
- 2 Potatoes boiled and mashed
- 1 tsp. Ginger grated
- 1 tbsp. Coriander powder
- 1 tsp. Cumin powder
- 1/2 tsp. Chili powder
- 1/2 tsp. Garam Masala
- 1/2 tsp. Dry Mango powder
- 1&1/2 tsp. Salt
- 1 Large Bowl of Water
- Cooking Oil

Directions:
1. Mix mashed potatoes with ginger and all the spices. Divide this mixture into 16 balls and keep them aside. Slice the bread slices into half to get 16 rectangles.
2. Dip each in water for 1 second, then place one potato ball at the center and wrap the slice around it. Place half of these wrapped balls in the Air Fryer basket and spray them with cooking oil.
3. Air Fry at 390 degrees F for 18 minutes. Flip the balls after 10 minutes of cooking, then continue air frying. Cook the remaining balls in the same manner. Serve fresh.

61. Cheese Parsley Omelet
Preparation time: 15 minutes
Cooking time: 6 minutes
Servings: 2
Ingredients:
- 2 eggs
- 1/4 cup milk
- Pinch of salt
- ¼ cup chopped parsley
- 1 tsp. breakfast seasoning
- 1/4 cup shredded cheese
- Black pepper to taste

Directions:
1. Whisk eggs with milk, salt, seasoning, and black pepper in a bowl. Spread this mixture in a baking pan. Top the egg with cheese.
2. Set the baking pan inside the Air Fryer. Bake at 300 degrees F for 6 minutes. Garnish with parsley. Serve.

62. Egg Ham Pockets
Preparation time: 15 minutes
Cooking time: 5 minutes
Servings: 2
Ingredients:
- 2 ramekins
- 2 eggs
- 2 slices of ham
- Butter
- Salt, to taste
- Black pepper, to taste
- Cheese, for topping

Directions:
1. Layer two ramekins with butter and place one ham slice in each ramekin. Crack an egg into each ramekin and top it with salt and black pepper. Bake in your air fryer at 400 degrees F for 5 minutes. Garnish with cheese and serve.

63. Spanish Frittata
Preparation time: 15 minutes
Cooking time: 8 minutes
Servings: 6
Ingredients:
- 6 large eggs
- 1 chorizo sausage, sliced
- 1 cup summer squash, boiled and cubed
- Olive oil
- 2 tbsp. chopped parsley
- 1 wheel of feta
- Salt/pepper, to taste

Directions:
1. Add squash and sausage to the Air Fryer basket and spray them with cooking oil. Roast at 300 degrees F for 3 minutes.
2. Transfer the squash and sausage to a bowl. Whisk in eggs, parsley, salt, and black pepper. Spread this mixture in a baking pan.
3. Set the baking pan inside the Air Fryer, then bake at 350 degrees F for 5 minutes. Slice and serve.

64. Cauliflower Hash
Preparation time: 15 minutes
Cooking time: 10 minutes
Servings: 4
Ingredients:
- 2 cups cauliflower, finely grated
- 2 tbsp. potato starch
- Salt, to taste
- Pepper powder, to taste
- 2 tsp. chili flakes
- 1 tsp. garlic

- 1 tsp. onion powder
- 2 tsp. vegetable oil

Directions:
1. Soak cauliflower in water for 5 minutes, then drain well. Sauté cauliflower shreds with 1 tsp. oil in a skillet for 4 minutes.
2. Transfer the shreds to a bowl and add potato starch, salt, black pepper, chili flakes, garlic, and onion powder. Mix well, then make four flat patties out of this mixture.
3. Place cauliflower hash in the Air Fryer basket and spray them with cooking oil. Air Fry at 300 degrees F for 10 minutes. Flip each hash when cooked halfway through, then resume cooking. Serve fresh.

Chapter 3. Lunch

65. Honey Mustard Pork Tenderloin
Preparation Time: 10 minutes
Cooking Time: 26 minutes
Servings: 4
Ingredients:
- 1 lb. pork tenderloin
- 1 tsp. sriracha sauce
- 1 tbsp. garlic, minced
- 2 tbsp. soy sauce
- 1 ½ tbsp. honey
- ¾ tbsp. Dijon mustard
- 1 tbsp. mustard

Directions:
1. Add sriracha sauce, garlic, soy sauce, honey, Dijon mustard, and mustard into the large zip-lock bag and mix well. Add pork tenderloin into the bag. Put in the refrigerator overnight.
2. Warm air fryer to 380 F. Spray air fryer tray with cooking spray, then place marinated pork tenderloin on a tray and air fry for 26 minutes. Turn pork tenderloin after every 5 minutes. Slice and serve.

66. Rosemary Lamb Chops
Preparation Time: 10 minutes
Cooking Time: 6 minutes
Servings: 4
Ingredients:
- 4 lamb chops
- 2 tbsp. dried rosemary
- ¼ cup fresh lemon juice
- Pepper
- Salt

Directions:
1. Mix lemon juice, rosemary, pepper, and salt in a small bowl. Brush mixture over lamb chops. Place lamb chops on air fryer tray and air fry at 400 F for 3 minutes. Turn lamb chops to the other side and cook for 3 minutes more. Serve and enjoy.

67. Juicy Steak Bites
Preparation Time: 10 minutes
Cooking Time: 9 minutes
Servings: 4
Ingredients:
- 1 lb. sirloin steak, cut into bite-size pieces
- 1 tbsp. steak seasoning
- 1 tbsp. olive oil
- Pepper
- Salt

Directions:
1. Warm air fryer to 390 F. Add steak pieces into the large mixing bowl. Add steak seasoning, oil, pepper, and salt over steak pieces and toss until well coated.
2. Transfer steak pieces on air fryer pan and air fry for 5 minutes. Turn steak pieces to the other side and cook for 4 minutes more. Serve and enjoy.

68. Greek Lamb Chops
Preparation Time: 10 minutes
Cooking Time: 10 minutes
Servings: 4
Ingredients:
- 2 lbs. lamb chops
- 2 tsp. garlic, minced
- 1 ½ tsp. dried oregano
- ¼ cup fresh lemon juice
- ¼ cup olive oil
- ½ tsp. pepper
- 1 tsp. salt

Directions:
1. Add lamb chops in a mixing bowl. Add remaining ingredients over the lamb chops and coat well. Arrange lamb chops on the air fryer tray and air fry at 400 F for 5 minutes. Turn lamb chops and air fry for 5 minutes more. Serve and enjoy.

69. Beef Roast
Preparation Time: 10 minutes
Cooking Time: 45 minutes
Servings: 6
Ingredients:
- 2 ½ lbs. beef roast
- 2 tbsp. Italian seasoning

Directions:
1. Arrange roast on the rotisserie spite. Rub roast with Italian seasoning, then insert into the air fryer. Roast at 350 F for 45 minutes. Slice and serve.

70. Herb Butter Rib-Eye Steak
Preparation Time: 10 minutes
Cooking Time: 14 minutes
Servings: 4
Ingredients:
- 2 lbs. rib eye steak, bone-in
- 1 tsp. fresh rosemary, chopped
- 1 tsp. fresh thyme, chopped
- 1 tsp. fresh chives, chopped
- 2 tsp. fresh parsley, chopped
- 1 tsp. garlic, minced
- ¼ cup butter softened
- Pepper
- Salt

Directions:
1. Mix butter plus herbs in a small bowl. Rub herb butter on rib-eye steak and place it in the refrigerator for 30 minutes. Place marinated steak on air fryer pan and air fry at 400 F for 12-14 minutes. Serve and enjoy.

71. Beef Jerky
Preparation Time: 10 minutes
Cooking Time: 4 hours
Servings: 4
Ingredients:
- 2 lbs. London broil, sliced thinly
- 1 tsp. onion powder
- 3 tbsp. brown sugar
- 3 tbsp. soy sauce
- 1 tsp. olive oil
- 3/4 tsp. garlic powder

Directions:
1. Add all ingredients except meat to the large zip-lock bag. Mix until well combined. Add meat to the bag. Seal bag and massage gently to cover the meat with marinade.
2. Let marinate the meat for 1 hour. Arrange marinated meat slices on an air fryer tray and dehydrate at 160 F for 4 hours. Serve.

72. Beef Patties
Preparation Time: 10 minutes
Cooking Time: 13 minutes
Servings: 4
Ingredients:
- 1 lb. ground beef
- ½ tsp. garlic powder
- ¼ tsp. onion powder
- Pepper
- Salt

Directions:
1. Warm air fryer to 400 F. Add ground meat, garlic powder, onion powder, pepper, and salt into the mixing bowl and mix until well combined.
2. Make even shape patties from meat mixture and arrange an air fryer pan. Place pan in the air fryer. Air fry patties for 10 minutes Turn patties after 5 minutes. Serve and enjoy.

73. Beef Sirloin Roast
Preparation Time: 10 minutes
Cooking Time: 50 minutes
Servings: 8
Ingredients:
- 2½ pounds sirloin roast
- Salt and ground black pepper, as required

Directions:
1. Rub the roast with salt and black pepper generously. Insert the rotisserie rod through the roast.
2. Insert the rotisserie forks, one on each rod's side, to secure the rod to the chicken. Arrange the drip pan at the bottom of the Air Fryer.
3. Adjust the temperature to 350 degrees F. Roast for 50 minutes. Place the roast onto a platter for 10 minutes before slicing. With a sharp knife, cut the roast into desired sized slices and serve.

74. Bacon-Wrapped Filet Mignon
Preparation Time: 10 minutes
Cooking Time: 15 minutes
Servings: 2
Ingredients:
- 2 bacon slices
- 2 (4-ounce) filet mignon
- Salt and ground black pepper, as required
- Olive oil cooking spray

Directions:
1. Wrap 1 bacon slice around each filet mignon and secure with toothpicks. Season the fillets with the salt and black pepper lightly.
2. Arrange the filet mignon onto a cooking rack and spray with cooking spray. Arrange the drip pan at the bottom of the Air Fryer.
3. Adjust the temperature to 375 degrees F. Air fry for 15 minutes. When cooking time is complete, remove the rack from the air fryer and serve hot.

75. Beef Burgers
Preparation Time: 15 minutes
Cooking Time: 18 minutes
Servings: 4
Ingredients:
For Burgers:
- 1-pound ground beef
- ½ cup panko breadcrumbs
- ¼ cup onion, chopped finely
- 3 tablespoons Dijon mustard
- 3 teaspoons low-sodium soy sauce
- 2 teaspoons fresh rosemary, chopped finely
- Salt, to taste

For Topping:
- 2 tablespoons Dijon mustard
- 1 tablespoon brown sugar
- 1 teaspoon soy sauce
- 4 Gruyere cheese slices

Directions:

1. Mix all the fixing in a large bowl, then make 4 equal-sized patties from the mixture. Arrange the patties onto a cooking tray. Adjust the air fryer to 370 degrees F. Air fry for 15 minutes.
2. Meanwhile, in a small bowl, add the mustard, brown sugar, and soy sauce and mix well for the sauce. When cooking time is complete, remove and coat the burgers with the sauce. Top each burger with 1 cheese slice. Return to the air fryer to broil for 3 minutes. Serve hot.

76. Season and Salt-Cured Beef
Preparation Time: 15 minutes
Cooking Time: 3 hours
Servings: 4
Ingredients:
- 1½ pounds beef round, trimmed
- ½ cup Worcestershire sauce
- ½ cup low-sodium soy sauce
- 2 teaspoons honey
- 1 teaspoon liquid smoke
- 2 teaspoons onion powder
- ½ teaspoon red pepper flakes
- Ground black pepper, as required

Directions:
1. In a zip-top bag, place the beef and freeze for 1-2 hours to firm up. Put the meat onto your cutting board, then cut against the grain into 1/8-¼-inch strips.
2. Mix the remaining fixing in a large bowl. Add the steak slices and coat with the mixture generously.
3. Refrigerate to marinate for about 4-6 hours. Remove the beef slices from the bowl, and with paper towels, pat dries them.
4. Divide the steak strips onto the cooking trays and arrange them in an even layer. Set your air fryer to 160 degrees F. Dehydrate the steak strips for 3 hours. After 1½ hours, switch the position of cooking trays.
5. Meanwhile, in a small pan, add the remaining ingredients over medium heat and cook for about 10 minutes, stirring occasionally. When cooking time is complete, remove the trays, then serve.

77. Sweet & Spicy Meatballs
Preparation Time: 20 minutes
Cooking Time: 30 minutes
Servings:
Ingredients:
For Meatballs:
- 2 pounds lean ground beef
- 2/3 cup quick-cooking oats
- ½ cup Ritz crackers, crushed
- 1 (5-ounce) can evaporate milk
- 2 large eggs, beaten lightly
- 1 teaspoon honey
- 1 tablespoon dried onion, minced
- 1 teaspoon garlic powder
- 1 teaspoon ground cumin
- Salt and ground black pepper, as required

For Sauce:
- 1/3 cup orange marmalade
- 1/3 cup honey
- 1/3 cup brown sugar
- 2 tablespoons cornstarch
- 2 tablespoons soy sauce
- 1-2 tablespoons hot sauce
- 1 tablespoon Worcestershire sauce

Directions:
1. For meatballs, mix all the ingredients in a large bowl. Make 1½-inch balls from the mixture. Arrange half of the meatballs onto a cooking tray in a single layer. Set your air fryer to 380 degrees F. Air fry for 15 minutes. Remove, then repeat with the remaining meatballs.
2. For the sauce, in a small pan, add all the ingredients over medium heat and cook until thickened, stirring continuously. Serve the meatballs with the topping of sauce.

78. Spiced Pork Shoulder
Preparation Time: 15 minutes
Cooking Time: 55 minutes
Servings: 6
Ingredients:
- 1 teaspoon ground cumin
- 1 teaspoon cayenne pepper
- 1 teaspoon garlic powder
- Salt and ground black pepper, as required
- 2 pounds skin-on pork shoulder

Directions:
1. Mix the spices, salt, and black pepper in a small bowl. Arrange the pork shoulder onto a cutting board, skin-side down.
2. Season the inner side of pork shoulder with salt and black pepper. With kitchen twines, tie the pork shoulder into a long round cylinder shape.
3. Season the outer side of pork shoulder with spice mixture. Insert the rotisserie rod through the pork shoulder. Insert the rotisserie forks, one on each side of the rod, to secure the pork shoulder.
4. Set your air fryer to 350 degrees F, then roast for 55 minutes. Remove the pork from the air fryer and place onto a platter for about 10 minutes before slicing. Cut the pork shoulder into desired sized slices using a sharp knife and serve.

79. Fish Sticks
Preparation Time: 5 minutes
Cooking Time: 15 minutes
Servings: 4
Ingredients:
- 1-pound cod, wild-caught
- ½ teaspoon ground black pepper
- 3/4 teaspoon Cajun seasoning
- 1 teaspoon salt
- 1 1/2 cups pork rind
- 1/4 cup mayonnaise, reduced Fat
- 2 tablespoons water

- 2 tablespoons Dijon mustard

Directions:
1. Switch on the air fryer, insert fryer basket, grease it with olive oil, set the fryer at 400 degrees F, and preheat for 5 minutes
2. Meanwhile, place mayonnaise in a bowl and then whisk in water and mustard until blended. Place pork rinds in a shallow dish, add Cajun seasoning, black pepper, salt, and stir until mixed.
3. Cut the cod into 1 by 2 inches pieces, then dip into mayonnaise mixture and then coat with pork rind mixture.
4. Open the fryer; add fish sticks in it, spray with oil, close with its lid, and air fry for 10 minutes until nicely golden and crispy, flipping the sticks halfway through the frying. Transfer fish sticks onto a serving plate and serve.

80. Grilled Cheese and Greens Sandwiches

Preparation time: 15 minutes
Cooking time: 8 minutes
Servings: 4
Ingredients:
- 1½ cups chopped mixed greens
- 2 garlic cloves, thinly sliced
- 2 teaspoons olive oil
- 2 slices low-sodium low-fat Swiss cheese
- 4 slices low-sodium whole-wheat bread
- Olive oil spray, for coating the sandwiches

Directions:
1. In a 6-by-2-inch pan, mix the greens, garlic, and olive oil. Grill in the air fryer for 4 to 5 minutes, stirring once, until the vegetables are tender. Drain, if necessary.
2. Make 2 sandwiches, dividing half of the greens and 1 slice of Swiss cheese between 2 slices of bread. Lightly spray the outsides of the sandwiches with olive oil spray.
3. Grill the sandwiches in the air fryer for 6 to 8 minutes, turning with tongs halfway through, until the bread is toasted and the cheese melts. Cut each sandwich in half to serve.

81. Veggie Tuna Melts

Preparation time: 15 minutes
Cooking time: 11 minutes
Servings: 4
Ingredients:
- 2 low-sodium whole-wheat English muffins, split
- 1 (6-ounce) can chunk light low-sodium tuna, drained
- 1 cup shredded carrot
- 1/3 cup chopped mushrooms
- 2 scallions, white and green parts, sliced
- 1/3 cup nonfat Greek yogurt
- 2 tablespoons low-sodium stone-ground mustard
- 2 slices low-sodium low-fat Swiss cheese, halved

Directions:
1. Place the English muffin halves in the air fryer basket. Grill for 3 to 4 minutes, or until crisp. Remove from the basket and set aside.
2. In a medium bowl, thoroughly mix the tuna, carrot, mushrooms, scallions, yogurt, and mustard. Top each half of the muffins with one-fourth of the tuna mixture and a half slice of Swiss cheese.
3. Grill in the air fryer for 4 to 7 minutes, or until the tuna mixture is hot and the cheese melts and starts to brown. Serve immediately.

82. California Melts

Preparation time: 10 minutes
Cooking time: 4 minutes
Servings: 4
Ingredients:
- 2 low-sodium whole-wheat English muffins, split
- 2 tablespoons nonfat Greek yogurt
- 8 fresh baby spinach leaves
- 1 ripe tomato, cut into 4 slices
- ½ ripe avocado, peeled, pitted, and sliced lengthwise
- 8 fresh basil leaves
- 4 tablespoons crumbled fat-free low-sodium feta cheese, divided

Directions:
1. Put the English muffin halves into the air fryer. Air fry for 2 minutes, or until light golden brown. Transfer to a work surface. Spread each muffin half with 1½ teaspoons of yogurt.
2. Top each muffin half with 2 spinach leaves, 1 tomato slice, one-fourth of the avocado, and 2 basil leaves. Sprinkle each with 1 tablespoon of feta cheese.
3. Air fries the sandwiches in the air fryer for 3 to 4 minutes, or until the cheese softens and the sandwich is hot. Serve immediately.

83. Vegetable Pita Sandwiches

Preparation time: 15 minutes
Cooking time: 12 minutes
Servings: 4
Ingredients:
- 1 baby eggplant, peeled and chopped
- 1 red bell pepper, sliced
- ½ cup diced red onion
- ½ cup shredded carrot
- 1 teaspoon olive oil
- 1/3 cup low-fat Greek yogurt
- ½ teaspoon dried tarragon
- 2 low-sodium whole-wheat pita bread, halved crosswise

Directions:
1. In a 6-by-2-inch pan, stir together the eggplant, red bell pepper, red onion, carrot, and olive oil. Put the vegetable mixture into the air fryer basket and roast for 7 to 9 -minutes, stirring once, until the vegetables are tender. Drain if necessary.
2. In a small bowl, thoroughly mix the yogurt and tarragon until well combined. Stir the yogurt mixture

into the vegetables. Stuff one-fourth of this mixture into each pita pocket.
3. Place the sandwiches in the air fryer and air fry for 2 to 3 minutes, or until the bread is toasted. Serve immediately.

84. Stuffed Portobello Mushrooms
Preparation time: 15 minutes
Cooking time: 12 minutes
Servings: 4
Ingredients:
- 4 Portobello mushrooms, wiped clean with a damp cloth, stemmed, and gills removed
- 1 teaspoon olive oil
- 2 cups chopped fresh baby spinach
- 1 red bell pepper, chopped
- 1/3 cup chopped red onion
- 1/3 cup nonfat Greek yogurt
- 2 tablespoons nonfat cream cheese, at room temperature
- 2 tablespoons grated Parmesan cheese

Directions:
1. Rub the mushrooms with the olive oil. Place them in the air fryer basket, hollow-side up, and air-fry for 3 minutes. Carefully remove the mushroom caps because they will contain liquid. Drain the liquid out of the caps.
2. In a medium bowl, thoroughly mix the spinach, red bell pepper, red onion, yogurt, cream cheese, and Parmesan cheese. Stuff one-fourth of this mixture into each drained mushroom cap.
3. Return the caps to the air fryer basket. Air-fry for 6 to 9 minutes, or until the filling is hot and the mushroom caps are tender. Serve.

85. Crustless Veggie Quiche
Preparation time: 8 minutes
Cooking time: 22 minutes
Servings: 3
Ingredients:
- 4 egg whites
- 1 egg
- 1 cup frozen chopped spinach
- 1 red bell pepper, chopped
- ½ cup chopped mushrooms
- 1/3 cup minced red onion
- 1 tablespoon low-sodium mustard
- 1 slice low-sodium low-fat Swiss cheese, torn into small pieces
- Nonstick cooking spray with flour

Directions:
1. Mix the egg whites and egg in a medium bowl. Stir in the spinach, red bell pepper, mushrooms, onion, and mustard.
2. Mix in the Swiss cheese. Spray a 6-by-2-inch pan with nonstick cooking spray. Pour the egg mixture into the prepared pan.
3. Bake in your air fryer for 18 to 22 minutes, or until the egg mixture is puffed, light golden brown, and set. Cool for 5 minutes before serving.

86. Beans and Greens Pizza
Preparation time: 11 minutes
Cooking time: 19 minutes
Servings: 4
Ingredients:
- ¾ cup whole-wheat pastry flour
- ½ teaspoon low-sodium baking powder
- 1 tablespoon olive oil, divided
- 1 cup chopped kale
- 2 cups chopped fresh baby spinach
- 1 cup canned no-salt-added cannellini beans, rinsed, and drained
- ½ teaspoon dried thyme
- 1 piece low-sodium string cheese, torn into pieces

Dirctions:
1. Mix the pastry flour and baking powder in a small bowl. Add ¼ cup of water and 2 teaspoons of olive oil. Mix until a dough form.
2. On a floured surface, press or roll the dough into a 7-inch round. Set aside while you cook the greens.
3. In a 6-by-2-inch pan, mix the kale, spinach, and remaining teaspoon of the olive oil. Air-fry for 3 to 5 minutes, until the greens are wilted. Drain well.
4. Put the pizza dough into the air fryer basket. Top with the greens, cannellini beans, thyme, and string cheese. Air-fry for 11 to 14 minutes, or until the crust is golden brown and the cheese is melted. Cut into quarters to serve.

87. Grilled Chicken Mini Pizzas
Preparation time: 15 minutes
Cooking time: 6 minutes
Servings: 4
Ingredients:
- 2 low-sodium whole-wheat pita bread, split
- ½ cup no-salt-added tomato sauce
- 1 garlic clove, minced
- ½ teaspoon dried oregano
- 1 cooked shredded chicken breast
- 1 cup chopped button mushrooms
- ½ cup chopped red bell pepper
- ½ cup shredded part-skim low-sodium Mozzarella cheese

Directions:
1. Place the pita bread, insides up, on a work surface. Mix the tomato sauce, garlic, and oregano in a small bowl. Put and spread 2 tablespoons of the sauce on each pita half.
2. Top each with ¼ cup of shredded chicken, ¼ cup of mushrooms, and 2 tablespoons of red bell pepper. Sprinkle with the Mozzarella cheese.
3. Bake the pizzas in your air fryer for 3 to 6 minutes, or until the cheese melts and starts to brown and the pita bread is crisp. Serve immediately.

88. Chicken Croquettes

Preparation time: 15 minutes
Cooking time: 10 minutes
Servings: 8
Ingredients:
- 2 (5-ounce) cooked chicken breasts, finely chopped
- 1/3 cup low-fat Greek yogurt
- 3 tablespoons minced red onion
- 2 celery stalks, minced
- 1 garlic clove, minced
- ½ teaspoon dried basil
- 2 egg whites, divided
- 2 slices low-sodium whole-wheat bread, crumbled

Directions:
1. In a medium bowl, thoroughly mix the chicken, yogurt, red onion, celery, garlic, basil, and 1 egg white. Form the mixture into 8 ovals and gently press into shape.
2. In a shallow bowl, beat the remaining egg white until foamy. Put the bread crumbs on a plate. Dip the chicken croquettes into the egg white and then into the bread crumbs to coat.
3. Air-fry the croquettes, in batches, for 7 to 10 minutes, or until the croquettes reach an internal temperature of 160°F on a meat thermometer, and their color is golden brown. Serve immediately.

89. Chicken and Fruit Bruschetta

Preparation time: 15 minutes
Cooking time: 10 minutes
Servings: 4
Ingredients:
- 1 tablespoon unsalted butter, at room temperature
- 3 slices low-sodium whole-wheat bread
- ½ cup chopped peeled peaches
- ½ cup chopped fresh strawberries
- ½ cup fresh blueberries
- ¼ cup canned low-sodium chicken breast, drained
- 1 tablespoon freshly squeezed lemon juice
- 1 tablespoon honey

Directions:
1. Put the butter on the bread, then place it in the air fryer basket. Bake for 3 to 5 minutes, or until light golden brown.
2. Meanwhile, in a small bowl, gently mix the peaches, strawberries, blueberries, chicken, and lemon juice.
3. Remove the bread from the basket. Top each slice with one-third of the chicken mixture. Drizzle with the honey.
4. Return to the basket, batches, and bake for 2 to 5 -minutes, until the fruit starts to caramelize. Cut each into quarters and serve.

Chapter 4. Dinner

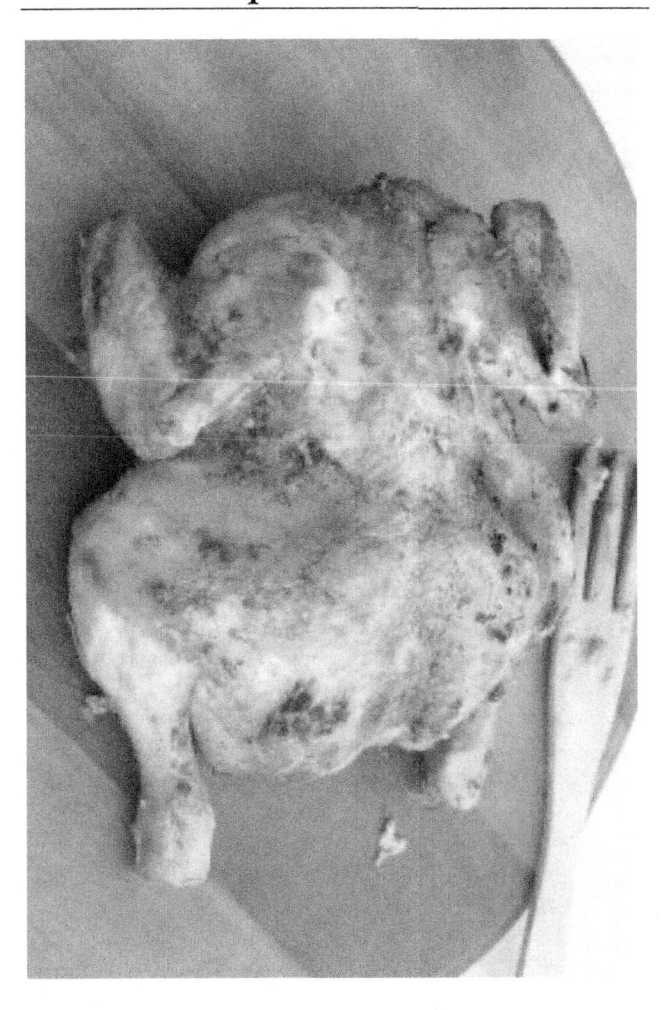

90. Bow Tie Pasta Chips
Preparation time: 15 minutes
Cooking time: 10 minutes
Servings: 4
Ingredients:
- 2 cups dry whole-wheat bow tie pasta
- 1 tablespoon olive oil
- 1 tablespoon nutritional yeast
- 1 1/2 teaspoon Italian Seasoning Blend
- 1/2 teaspoon salt

Directions:
1. Cook your pasta for 1/2 the time, as stated on the package. Mix the drained pasta with the olive oil, nutritional yeast, Italian seasoning, plus salt.
2. Put about half of the batter in your air fryer basket if yours is small; larger ones may be able to cook in one batch.
3. Set the air fryer to 390°F and air fry for 5 minutes. Shake the basket and air fry for 3 to 5 minutes more or until crunchy.

91. Crispy Curry Potato Cubes with Coriander Salsa
Preparation time: 15 minutes
Cooking time: 15 minutes
Servings: 4
Ingredients:
- 750 g waxy potatoes
- 1 tbsp. mild curry powder
- 1 tbsp. vegetable oil
- 1 small, ripe mango, sliced (fresh or canned)
- 15 g fresh coriander, finely chopped
- 1/2 lime juice and grated zest
- Freshly ground black pepper

Directions:
1. Preheat the Air fryer to 180 ° C. Peel the potatoes and cut them into 2 cm thick cubes. Soak them in water for 30 minutes. Then drain and dry with kitchen paper
2. Mix the curry powder with the oil in a bowl and turn the potato cubes in this mixture. Place the potato cubes in the cooking basket and slide the basket into the Air fryer. Set the timer to bake for 15-18 minutes until golden brown.
3. In the meantime, puree the mango in a blender with the coriander, the lemon peel, and the lime juice and season with salt and pepper. Serve the potato cubes with the salsa.

92. Roasted Potatoes with Paprika Powder
Preparation time: 15 minutes
Cooking time: 20 minutes
Servings: 4
Ingredients:
- 800 g waxy potatoes
- 2 tablespoons of olive oil
- 1 tbsp. hot paprika powder
- Freshly ground black pepper

Directions:
1. Preheat the Air fryer to 180 F. Peel the potatoes and cut them into 3 cm cubes. Soak them in water for at least 30 minutes. Then drain thoroughly and dry with kitchen paper.
2. Mix 1 tablespoon of olive oil with the paprika powder in a medium bowl and season it with pepper. Turn the potato cubes in the spicy oil.
3. Place the potato sticks in the cooking basket and push the basket into the Air fryer. Set the timer to bake for 20 minutes. Sprinkle with paprika powder. Serve.

93. Portobello Mushroom Pizzas with Hummus
Preparation time: 15 minutes
Cooking time: 9 minutes
Servings: 4
Ingredients:
- 4 large portobello mushrooms
- Balsamic vinegar
- Salt and black pepper
- 4 tablespoons oil-free pasta sauce
- 1 clove garlic, minced
- 3 oz. zucchini, shredded, chopped
- 2 tbsp. sweet red pepper, diced
- 4 olives kalamata olives, sliced

- 1 tsp. dried basil
- 1/2 cups hummus
- Fresh basil leaves or other herbs, minced

Directions:
1. Slice off the stems, then remove the gills with a spoon. Pat dries the insides and brush all sides with balsamic vinegar.
2. Sprinkle the inside with salt plus pepper. Put 1 tablespoon of pasta sauce inside each mushroom and flavor it with garlic.
3. Warm Air Fryer to 330F. Put the mushrooms as will fit in a single layer or use a rack to hold two layers. Air Fry for 3 minutes.
4. Remove and top each one with equal portions of zucchini, peppers, plus olives, then flavor it with dried basil, salt, plus pepper.
5. Put to the Air Fryer for 3 minutes. Check mushrooms, then rearrange if using a rack. Return to the Air Fryer for another 3 minutes or until mushrooms are tender.
6. Place on a plate, drizzle with hummus, and sprinkle with basil or other herbs. You can put the portobellos back into the air fryer briefly to warm the hummus if you want, then serve.

94. Cordon Bleu and Letscho Vegetables
Preparation time: 15 minutes
Cooking time: 30 minutes
Servings: 4
Ingredients:
- 4 chicken breasts
- 200 g Gruyère
- 4 slices ham
- 800 g red pointed peppers
- 500 g small green pointed peppers
- Corn cob
- 100 ml of vegetable stock
- 4 eggs
- 100 g Flour
- 100 g Panko flour
- 2 tbsp. olive oil

Directions:
1. First, cut a bag into the chicken breasts. Cut the cheese into bars and wrap it with ham. Put the wrapped pieces of cheese in your pockets. The filled chicken breasts can now be breaded by turning them first in flour, then in whole egg, and then in panko flour.
2. For the Letscho peppers, put onions and olive oil in a saucepan, pour in vegetable broth, and let simmer. Peel the corn and cook in salted water. Mix the soft boiled Letscho vigorously. Braise red and green peppers at 180 F for 15 minutes, cut the cooked corn from the stalk, and braise briefly.
3. Lightly oil the breaded chicken breasts with an oil sprayer or a brush and then bake at 180 F for 15 minutes in an air fryer. If these are a little thicker, the meat will take a little longer. Cut the cordon bleu into pieces and serve with the braised peppers, the letscho, and the corn.

95. Cauliflower with An Herb Crust
Preparation time: 15 minutes
Cooking time: 40 minutes
Servings: 4
Ingredients:
- 2 pieces cauliflower
- 500g butter
- 70g Panko flour
- 10g parsley
- 34g almonds
- Salt

Directions:
1. Remove the stalk from the cauliflower and place it in the Air fryer baking dish. Melt the butter in a saucepan and roast the almonds in a pan. Add to the cauliflower and salt.
2. Now bake in your air fryer the cauliflower at 160 F for 15 minutes, turn it over and bake for another 15 minutes. Turn the cauliflower again and let it steep at 140 F for 7 minutes.
3. Now lift the cauliflower out of the baking pan and mix the remaining butter with chopped parsley and panko flour. Bake this mixture again for 5 minutes at 170 F in the Air fryer baking pan. Brush the cauliflower with the herb crust and garnish with freshly chopped parsley.

96. Chestnut Recipe (Low Carb)
Preparation time: 15 minutes
Cooking time: 35-40 minutes
Servings: 4
Ingredients:
- 500-700 g chestnuts

Directions:
1. Let chestnuts stand in cold water for one hour. Take the chestnuts out of the water and cut them crosswise on a sieve with a small knife.
2. Spread chestnuts on the grill cup and bake at 170 degrees for 30 minutes, shaking occasionally. To avoid drying out, add about 80-100 ml of water to the hot air fryer's bottom. Serve.

97. Puff Pastry Pockets with Salmon
Preparation time: 15 minutes
Cooking time: 20 minutes
Servings: 6
Ingredients:
- 200 g smoked salmon
- 1 pack of puff pastry
- 1 bunch of dill
- 100 g crème Fraiche
- 2 eggs
- Half a lemon juice
- Salt. pepper
- 4 egg yolks

Directions:

1. Finely chop the salmon and chop the dill. Mix with remaining ingredients except for puff pastry. Whisk eggs.
2. Spread out the puff pastry. Cut into triangles. Brush with beaten egg. Spread it again, then brush with the egg from the outside. Place the puff pastry pockets on the grill plate and bake in your air fryer at 160 F for 20 minutes.

98. Sliced Turkey
Preparation time: 15 minutes
Cooking time: 25 minutes
Servings: 4
Ingredients:
- 500 g turkey breast fillet
- 2 carrots
- 1 bell pepper
- 1 zucchini (small)
- 2 cloves of garlic
- 4 tbsp. white wine
- 1 onion
- 4 tbsp. creme fraiche
- 2 tbsp. wine vinegar
- 1 bunch of parsley
- 500 g rice
- Salt, pepper, paprika powder

Directions:
1. Cook the rice according to the package insert. Cut zucchini and carrots into thin slices, core the peppers, wash, and cut into cubes.
2. Put a little oil in the hot air fryer. Add the carrots and air fry for 5 minutes. Add remaining vegetables and air fry again for 10 minutes.
3. Peel the garlic and onion and cut into fine cubes. Cut the turkey fillet into strips and add the onion and garlic to the hot air fryer.
4. Mix the wine and vinegar well and pour over the turkey meat. Let it air fryer for 10 minutes. Add salt, pepper, paprika powder, and refine with crème Fraiche. Chop parsley and pour over the sliced meat. Remove this from the hot air fryer and serve with rice.

99. Baked Sausages
Preparation time: 15 minutes
Cooking time: 12 minutes
Servings: 4
Ingredients:
- 8 sausages of your choice
- 1 pack of puff pastry
- Mustard
- Curry powder
- Ketchup

Directions:
1. Let the sausages steep in hot water. Cut the puff pastry into strips. Pat dries the sausages out of the water. Place on the puff pastry and roll it up.
2. Bake the sausages in your air fryer for 12 minutes until the dough turns golden yellow. Mix the ketchup and curry powder. Serve sausages with mustard and ketchup mix.

100. Fried Rice with Sesame-Sriracha Sauce
Preparation time: 15 minutes
Cooking time: 20-30 minutes
Servings: 4
Ingredients:
- 2 cups cooked white rice
- 1 tbsp. vegetable oil
- 2 tsp. toasted sesame oil
- Kosher salt
- ground black pepper
- 1 tsp. sriracha
- 1 tsp. soy sauce
- 1/2 tsp. sesame seeds, toasted, plus more for topping
- 1 large egg, lightly beaten
- 1 cup frozen peas and carrots, thawed

Directions:
1. Mix the rice, vegetable oil, 1 teaspoon sesame oil plus 1 tablespoon water in a bowl. Flavor it with salt plus pepper, then put it in a 7-inch round air fryer insert, metal cake pans, or foil pan.
2. Put it in a 5.3-quart air fryer and air fry at 350 degrees F, stirring halfway through, for 12 minutes.
3. Meanwhile, stir the sriracha, soy sauce, sesame seeds, plus remaining 1 tsp. sesame oil in a small bowl.
4. Open the air fryer, then put the egg over the rice. Close and air fry until the egg is cooked through, about 4 minutes.
5. Open again, add the peas and carrots and stir into the rice to distribute and break up the egg. Close and air fry 2 minutes more to heat the peas and carrots. Spoon the fried rice into bowls, drizzle with some of the sauce and sprinkle with more sesame seeds.

101. Roast Chicken
Preparation time: 15 minutes
Cooking time: 60 minutes
Servings: 3
Ingredients:
- Nonstick cooking spray, for the basket
- 1 small chicken
- 1 tbsp. olive oil
- Kosher salt
- ground black pepper
- 3 sprigs fresh rosemary, thyme, sage
- 1 head garlic, sliced in half
- 1/2 lemon

Directions:
1. Warm 3.5-quart air fryer at 370 degrees F and oiled the basket using a nonstick cooking spray. Massage the outside of the chicken using the olive oil.
2. Flavor the chicken inside and outside with 1 tablespoon salt plus several grinds of pepper. Fill the cavity with the herbs, garlic, plus lemon.
3. Put your chicken in the air fryer basket breast-side up. Roast the chicken until it is golden and crispy for 50 to 60 minutes. Serve.

Chapter 5. Snacks and Appetizers

102. French Fries
Preparation Time: 5 minutes
Cooking Time: 13 minutes
Servings: 6
Ingredients
- 2 Potatoes, medium or large
- 3/4 tbsp. Olive Oil
- 1/2 tsp. Salt
- 1/4 tsp. Black Pepper
- 1/2 tsp. Garlic powder

Directions:
1. Arrange the seasoned potato slices and place them at the bottom of your air fryer basket. Potatoes will be crispier if they'll be separated.
2. Air fry at 360°F for 20 minutes. Toss the fries halfway through. If you want fries to be crisper, allow cooking for 2 more additional minutes. Serve hot.

103. Crispy Tofu Buffalo Bites
Preparation Time: 10 minutes
Cooking Time: 15 minutes
Servings: 6
Ingredients:
- 13oz. Extra-firm Tofu
- 1/2 cup Franks Hot sauce
- 1/2cup Chickpea flour
- 1/2 tsp. Garlic powder
- Salt to taste
- 1 1/2 cup Panko breadcrumbs (Gluten-free version)
- 1/4 cup Rice flour
- 1 tablespoons of water to make a thick batter
- Oil spray

Directions:
1. Press the tofu for 30 minutes. Drain tofu, wrap in paper towels, or clean tea towels and place heavy items on top to press. Combine in a bowl chickpea flour, garlic powder, and salt.
2. Add in a little water to make the batter thick. Cut the tofu into sticks or nugget sized pieces. Coat tofu with rice flour, then in the chickpea flour batter. Coat it with the panko breadcrumbs.
3. Put the tofu into your air fryer basket. Spray oil on the tofu. Air fry at 400°F for a total of 15 minutes. Turn them after seven minutes until browned and crispy. Repeat with remaining tofu.
4. Put the air fryer tofu in a large mixing bowl and toss with the buffalo sauce to coat. Serve immediately with celery and ranch sauce.

104. Curried Sweet Potato Fries with Creamy Cumin Ketchup
Preparation Time: 10 minutes
Cooking Time: 60 minutes
Servings: 2
Ingredients:
For the Sweet Potato Fries:
- 2 small, sweet potatoes
- 2-3 tablespoons olive oil
- 1/2 teaspoon curry powder
- 1/4 teaspoon coriander
- 1/4 teaspoon sea salt

For the Creamy Cumin Ketchup:
- 1/4 cup ketchup
- 2 tablespoons vegan mayo
- 1/2 teaspoon ground cumin
- 1/8 teaspoon ground ginger
- Pinch of cinnamon

Directions:
1. Cut the sweet potatoes into about 1/4 sticks. They should be as wide around as your pinky finger, but longer is also fine.
2. Arrange the sweet potato sticks on a cookie sheet, and spray 2 tablespoons of the olive oil over them. Also, sprinkle on the coriander, curry powder, and sea salt.

3. Toss them well to coat them properly in the oil, spices, and salt. Add the rest of the oil, if required. Transfer the sweet potato fries to the air fryer basket. Air fryer at 370°F for about 20 minutes, shaking them after 10 minutes.
4. For the creamy cumin ketchup, whisk all of the ingredients together in a small bowl. Serve with the sweet potato fries.

105. Fried Hot Dogs
Preparation Time: 3 minutes
Cooking Time: 7 minutes
Servings: 2
Ingredients:
- 2 hot dogs
- 2 hot dog buns
- 2 tablespoons grated cheese

Directions:
1. Preheat Air Fryer to 390°F. Put 2 hot dogs into your air fryer basket. Air fry for about 5 minutes. Remove the hot dog from the air fryer.
2. Place the hot dog on a bun, add cheese if desired. Place dressed hot dog into the Air Fryer, and air fry for an additional 2 minutes.

106. Sweet Potato Chips
Preparation Time: 10 minutes
Cooking Time: 50 minutes
Servings: 2
Ingredients:
- 2 medium-sized Sweet Potatoes thinly sliced
- ¼ cup of Olive Oil
- 1 teaspoon of ground Cinnamon optional
- Salt and pepper to taste

Directions:
1. Thinly slice the sweet potatoes. Use a mandolin or a food processor. Soak the sweet potato slices in the cold water for 30 minutes.
2. Drain and pat dry the slices thoroughly. Repeat it multiple times till completely dry. Toss the sweet potato slices with salt, olive oil, pepper, and cinnamon (if using), ensuring every slice is coated with the oil.
3. Put the slices into your Air Fryer Basket. Press the start button to air fry the sweet potatoes at 390°F for 20 minutes.
4. Shake every 7 to 8 minutes for even cooking. Suppose it is still not crisp, air fry for an additional 5 minutes. Serve it hot with ketchup.

107. Parmesan Truffle Fries
Preparation Time: 10 minutes
Cooking Time: 15 minutes
Servings: 2
Ingredients:
- 2 large gold potatoes, peeled
- 1 tablespoon parsley flakes
- 1/2 teaspoon garlic powder
- 1 teaspoon black pepper, crushed
- 1/2 teaspoon truffle salt
- Olive oil spray
- 2 tablespoons Parmesan cheese

Directions:
1. Use a mandoline with a French fry setting, slice the whole potato using the spring-form handle to slice into French fries.
2. Place sliced potatoes in a bowl and spray with olive spray for about 3 seconds. Add garlic powder, black pepper, and parsley flakes. Place all of them into the Air Fryer Basket.
3. Air fry for about 5 minutes at 390°F. Take out the basket and flip fries to evenly cook the fries. Air fries another 8 minutes and remove from the Air Fryer and add to a bowl. Sprinkle with truffle salt and Parmesan cheese.

108. Chicken Nuggets
Preparation Time: 4 minutes
Cooking Time: 16 minutes
Servings: 4
Ingredients:
- 2 large chicken breasts, skinless, boneless, bite-sized pieces
- 1/2 teaspoon kosher salt
- Black pepper
- 2 tsp. olive oil
- 6 tbsp. whole wheat Italian seasoned breadcrumbs
- 2 tbsp. panko
- 2 tbsp. grated parmesan cheese
- Olive oil spray

Directions:
1. Warm Air Fryer at 400°F for 8 minutes. Put olive oil in one bowl plus the panko, breadcrumbs, and parmesan cheese in another.
2. Season the chicken using salt and pepper, put it in the bowl with the olive oil, and mix it well so the olive oil evenly coats all of the chicken.
3. Put a few chunks of chicken one at a time into the breadcrumb mixture to coat. Place them into the Air Fryer Basket. Then lightly spray the top of it with olive oil spray. Air fryer for 8 minutes, turning halfway until it gets golden.

109. Mini Popovers
Preparation Time: 5 minutes
Cooking Time: 20 minutes
Servings: 4-7
Ingredients:
- 1 cup milk room temperature
- 2 eggs room temperature
- 1 tbsp. butter melted
- 1 cup all-purpose flour
- Salt and pepper Pinch of each

Directions:
1. Oiled a heatproof silicone egg bite mold with nonstick spray. Add all the fixing to a blender, then process at medium speed for 30 seconds.

2. Fill each mold with a scant 2 tablespoon of batter. Place them into the Air Fryer Basket. Air fry at 400°F for 20 minutes.
  3. Place the egg bite mold on the lower tray of the Air Fryer. After it gets cooked quickly, pierce each popover with a sharp knife, then again place them in the Air Fryer Basket and continue air frying for 1-2 minutes more. Serve immediately.

110. Air Fryer Risotto Balls

Preparation Time: 20 minutes
Cooking Time: 10 minutes
Servings: 4
Ingredients:
Risotto:
- 1 tsp. olive oil
- 1 cup onions diced very small
- 4 cups vegetable broth
- 1 cup arborio rice
- 1 cup Parmesan cheese

Breading:
- 1 1/2 cups Bread Crumbs
- 2 eggs beaten

Directions:
  1. Add some olive oil to a deep and large saucepan and heat it over medium heat. Post this, add the onions and sauté until soft. Add dry rice to the pan and sauté for around 1 minute.
  2. After this, add 2 cups of veggie broth. Let the broth cook down while continually stir to avoid any burning. Once the liquid has been cooked properly, add 2 more cups of veggie broth.
  3. Continue with this process until all the liquid is absorbed and your rice is soft. This process should take around 20 minutes. Stir in Parmesan.
  4. Put risotto into a casserole dish or sheet pan. Cool for around 1-2 hours in the fridge. Take a small bowl and place the bread crumbs. In another container, store the beaten eggs.
  5. Remove the chilled risotto (rice mixture) from the fridge. Roll into 1-inch rice balls. Dip them into eggs then into bread crumbs to coat the entire ball. Place rolled and coated balls back into the fridge for 45 minutes.
  6. Remove from the fridge and place it on the trays of the Air Fryer in small batches. Air Fry at 400°F for a cooking time of 10 minutes. Shake for 8 minutes. The balls are properly done around 6-7 minutes, but the browning doesn't happen until minute 8-10. Serve with marinara sauce.

111. Chicken Empanadas

Preparation Time: 10 minutes
Cooking Time: 10 minutes
Servings: 6
Ingredients
- 2 pounds shredded chicken
- Package of chicken taco seasoning
- 1/2 onion diced
- 1 cup shredded cheese of choice (cheddar)
- 2 frozen pie crusts, thawed
- A dusting of flour (to roll out the crust)
- Spray cooking oil of choice (coconut or avocado oil)
- Garnishes (sour cream, salsa, guacamole)

Directions:
  1. Set the prescribed temperature of your air fryer and push start to begin preheating.
  2. Shred the meat properly. Take a medium bowl and mix the meat along with onion, sauce, and cheese. Roll out to each pie crust over the dusting of flour.
  3. Using a ramekin or small bowl to make a circle imprint on the dough. Cut out the circle finely. Cut additional circles by re-rolling the dough.
  4. Add a small amount of filling on each circle and fold over to form a half-circle shape. Pinch or crimp the dough and shut using a fork.
  5. Put the food to the Air Fry tray and air fry for around 10 minutes turning the empanadas halfway through. Garnish with salsa and sour cream or guacamole.

112. Mozzarella Balls

Preparation Time: 80 minutes
Cooking Time: 10 minutes
Servings: 12
Ingredients
- 2 cups fresh grated Mozzarella
- 3 tbsp. cornstarch
- 1 egg
- 1 cup Italian seasoned breadcrumbs
- 1 tbsp. oregano
- 1 1/2 tsp. garlic powder
- 1 tsp. salt
- 1 1/2 tbsp. Parmesan

Directions:
  1. Warm Air Fryer to 400°F. Line a baking sheet with the parchment. Make a thorough mixture of cornstarch and parmesan to shredded cheese.
  2. Roll the cheese into the bite-size balls and put it in the freezer (45- 60 mins). Beat your egg in a small bowl. Mix salt, garlic powder, plus bread crumbs and mix well in another bowl.
  3. Immerse your cheese balls in the egg and coat them well. Roll the egg coated balls in bread crumbs and place them back on a baking sheet. Put this in the freezer for around 20 mins.
  4. Repeat the egg and bread steps and place it in the Air Fryer basket. Air fry on 400°F for around 10 minutes while making sure to rotate frequently. When the balls begin to melt, transfer them back to your baking sheet. Let rest for a couple of minutes. Serve.

113. Swedish Meatballs

Preparation Time: 15 minutes
Cooking Time: 25 minutes
Servings: 4-6
Ingredients:
- 2 slices white bread
- 1/2 cup milk
- 8 ounces ground beef

- 8 ounces ground pork
- 1/4 yellow onion, grated
- 3/4 teaspoon ground allspice
- 1 large egg
- Kosher salt and freshly ground black pepper
- Nonstick cooking spray, for the tray
- Lingonberry jam, for serving

Directions:
1. Soak the bread in milk in a medium bowl for around 5 minutes. Squeeze out excess milk and tear into bite-sized pieces.
2. Mix the bread with the ground beef, 1 teaspoon salt, pork, onion, allspice, egg, and a few pepper grinds. Form this into small balls about the size of a heaping tablespoon.
3. Oil the basket of the Air Fryer using a cooking spray and fill it with the meatballs. Set it to 360°F.
4. Air fry while shaking the tray halfway through, until they are browned, tender, and cooked through for about 10 minutes. Serve them with lingonberry jam.

114. Stuffed Mushrooms
Preparation Time: 15 minutes
Cooking Time: 30 minutes
Servings: 4-6
Ingredients
- 1/4 cup breadcrumbs
- 1/4 cup grated Pecorino-Romano
- 1 teaspoon chopped fresh mint
- 1 clove garlic, minced
- 4 tablespoons olive oil
- 1 tablespoon chopped fresh parsley
- 36 white button mushrooms, stemmed
- Kosher salt and freshly ground black pepper
- 2 tablespoons shredded Mozzarella

Directions:
1. In a medium bowl, combine the Mozzarella, parsley, mint, garlic, 2 tablespoons of olive oil, breadcrumbs, Pecorino-Romano, 1/2 teaspoon salt, and 1/4 teaspoon pepper, and toss to blend.
2. In a large bowl, toss the mushrooms with the remaining 2 tablespoons of olive oil and arrange a small baking sheet or plate with the cavities facing up.
3. Divide the breadcrumb mixture among the mushrooms while filling the cavities and pressing down gently to secure.
4. Put half the mushrooms in a single layer in the basket of the Air Fryer. Set to 360°F and close the lid. Air fry until the filling is bubbling and browned, about 10 minutes. Repeat with the remaining mushrooms. Serve.

115. Mexican Street Style Corn on the Cob
Preparation Time: 5 minutes
Cooking Time: 15 minutes
Servings: 4
Ingredients:
- 4 ears shucked corn
- ½ cup Mexican Crema or Sour Cream
- ¼ cup Cotija Cheese grated
- 2 tbsp. cilantro finely chopped
- 2 tsp. chili powder
- Juice of 1 lime
- Oil for spraying Vegetable, Canola, or Avocado

Directions:
1. Wash and dry the corn. Place the corn on the tray in the Air Fryer basket in a single layer and lightly spray it with oil.
2. Set the Air Fryer temperature to 400°F and air fry for 15 minutes. After exactly 8 minutes, open the lid, turn corn, and lightly spray again, and then continue air frying. Once the time is up, remove corn to a platter.
3. Spread Mexican crema on sides of the corn. Sprinkle with cotija cheese, chili powder, and cilantro. Squeeze with lime before serving.

116. Ranch Potatoes
Preparation time: 15 minutes
Cooking time: 20 minutes
Servings: 2
Ingredients:
- 1/2 lb. baby potatoes, wash and cut in half
- 1/4 tsp. paprika
- 1/4 tsp. onion powder
- 1/4 tsp. garlic powder
- 1/4 tsp. parsley
- 1/2 tbsp. olive oil
- 1/4 tsp. dill
- 1/4 tsp. chives
- Salt

Directions:
1. Spray air fryer basket with cooking spray. Add all fixing into the bowl and toss well. Spread potatoes on an air fryer basket. Set to air fry at 400F for 20 minutes. Serve and enjoy.

117. Spicy Cheese Dip
Preparation time: 15 minutes
Cooking time: 30 minutes
Servings: 10
Ingredients:
- 16 oz. cream cheese, softened
- 1 cup sour cream
- 1/2 cup hot salsa
- 3 cups cheddar cheese, shredded

Directions:
1. Oil an 8-inch baking dish and set aside. Mix all the fixing above in a bowl until just combined and pour into the baking dish. Set your air fryer to bake at 350 for 30 minutes. Serve and enjoy.

118. Zucchini Patties
Preparation time: 15 minutes
Cooking time: 25 minutes
Servings: 6
Ingredients:

- 1 egg, lightly beaten
- 1 cup zucchini, shredded and squeeze out all liquid
- 1/4 tsp. red pepper flakes
- 1/4 cup Parmesan cheese, grated
- 2 tbsp. onion, minced
- 1/2 tbsp. Dijon mustard
- 1/2 tbsp. mayonnaise
- 1/2 cup breadcrumbs
- Pepper
- Salt

Directions:
1. Place the air fryer Basket onto your Baking Pan and spray with cooking spray. Add all listed fixing into the bowl and mix until well combined.
2. Make small patties from the zucchini mixture and place it on an air fryer basket. Air fry at 400°F for 25 minutes. Serve and enjoy.

119. Cinnamon Maple Chickpeas
Preparation time: 15 minutes
Cooking time: 12 minutes
Servings: 4
Ingredients:
- 15 oz. chickpeas, rinsed, drained, and pat dry
- 1 tbsp. olive oil
- 1/2 tsp. ground cinnamon
- 1 tbsp. maple syrup
- Pepper
- Salt

Directions:
1. Place the air fryer Basket onto the Baking Pan, then spray with cooking spray. Spread chickpeas on air fryer basket. Set to air fry at 375F for 12 minutes.
2. In a large bowl, mix cinnamon, maple syrup, oil, pepper, and salt. Add chickpeas and toss well. Serve and enjoy.

120. Spicy Chickpeas
Preparation time: 15 minutes
Cooking time: 12 minutes
Servings: 4
Ingredients:
- 14 oz. can of chickpeas, rinsed, drained, and pat dry
- 1/2 tsp. chili powder
- 1 tbsp. olive oil
- Pepper
- Salt

Directions:
1. Place the air fryer Basket onto the Baking Pan and spray with cooking spray. Add chickpeas, chili powder, oil, pepper, and salt into the bowl and toss well. Spread chickpeas on air fryer basket. Set to air fry at 375°F for 12 minutes. Serve and enjoy.

121. Crispy Cauliflower Florets
Preparation time: 15 minutes
Cooking time: 20 minutes
Servings: 4
Ingredients:
- 5 cups cauliflower florets
- 4 tablespoons olive oil
- 1/2 tsp. cumin powder
- 6 garlic cloves, chopped
- 1/2 tsp. salt

Directions:
1. Put the air fryer basket onto the baking ban and spray using cooking spray. Add all the fixing into the large bowl and toss well. Put cauliflower florets into the air fryer basket. Air fry at 400°F for 20 minutes. Serve and enjoy.

122. Air Fried Walnuts
Preparation time: 15 minutes
Cooking time: 5 minutes
Servings: 6
Ingredients:
- 2 cups walnuts
- 1 tsp. olive oil
- 1/4 tsp. chili powder
- Pepper
- Salt

Directions:
1. Place the air fryer Basket onto the Baking Pan, then spray the air fryer basket with cooking spray. Add walnuts, chili powder, oil, pepper, and salt into the bowl and toss well. Add walnuts into the air fryer basket. Air fry at 350°F for 5 minutes. Serve and enjoy.

123. Baked Cheese Dip
Preparation time: 15 minutes
Cooking time: 30 minutes
Servings: 12
Ingredients:
- 4 oz. cream cheese, cubed
- 1 1/2 cups cheddar cheese, shredded
- 1/2 cup mayonnaise
- 1 small onion, diced
- 1 1/2 cups Mozzarella cheese, shredded

Directions:
1. Oiled an 8-inch baking dish and set aside. Mix all the fixing into the mixing bowl. Pour mixture into the prepared baking dish. Set to bake at 400 F for 30 minutes, place the baking dish in the air fryer. Serve and enjoy.

124. Onion Dip
Preparation time: 15 minutes
Cooking time: 40 minutes
Servings: 8
Ingredients:
- 1 1/2 onions, chopped
- 1 cup Mozzarella cheese, shredded
- 1 cup cheddar cheese, shredded
- 1 1/2 cup mayonnaise
- 1/2 tsp. garlic powder
- 1 1/2 cup Swiss cheese, shredded
- Pepper

- Salt

Directions:
1. Oiled an 8-inch baking dish and set aside. Add all fixing listed into the mixing bowl and mix until well combined. Pour these into the prepared baking dish. Set to bake in your air fryer at 350 for 40 minutes. Serve and enjoy.

125. Ricotta Dip

Preparation time: 15 minutes
Cooking time: 15 minutes
Servings: 6
Ingredients:
- 1/4 cup parmesan cheese, grated
- 1/2 cup Mozzarella cheese, shredded
- 1 tbsp. rosemary, chopped
- 1 cup ricotta cheese, shredded
- 1 tbsp. lemon juice
- 2 tbsp. olive oil
- 2 garlic cloves, minced
- Pepper
- Salt

Directions:
1. Grease baking dish and set aside. Add all listed fixing into the mixing bowl and mix until well combined. Put the mixture into the baking dish. Set to bake in your air fryer at 400 F for 15 minutes. Serve and enjoy.

126. Garlic Cheese Dip

Preparation time: 15 minutes
Cooking time: 20 minutes
Servings: 12
Ingredients:
- 3 garlic cloves, minced
- 1 cup Mozzarella cheese, shredded
- 8 oz. cream cheese, softened
- 5 oz. Asiago cheese, shredded
- 1 cup sour cream

Directions:
1. Grease baking dish and set aside. Add all the fixing into the mixing bowl and mix until well combined. Pour mixture into the prepared baking dish. Set to bake in your air fryer at 350 F for 20 minutes. Serve and enjoy.

127. Spinach Dip

Preparation time: 15 minutes
Cooking time: 20 minutes
Servings: 12
Ingredients:
- 3 oz. frozen spinach, defrosted & chopped
- 2 cups cheddar cheese, shredded
- 8 oz. cream cheese
- 1 cup sour cream
- 1 tsp. garlic salt

Directions:
1. Grease baking dish and set aside. Add all fixing into the mixing bowl and mix until well combined. Transfer mixture into the baking dish. Set your air fryer to bake at 350 F for 20 minutes. Serve and enjoy.

128. Spicy Almonds

Preparation time: 15 minutes
Cooking time: 20 minutes
Servings: 6
Ingredients:
- 1 1/2 cups raw almonds
- 1/2 tsp. garlic powder
- 1/2 tsp. cumin
- 1 1/2 tsp. chili powder
- 2 tsp. Worcestershire sauce
- 1/2 tsp. cayenne
- 1/4 tsp. onion powder
- 1/4 tsp. dried basil
- 2 tbsp. butter, melted
- 1/2 tsp. sea salt

Directions:
1. Line the Baking Pan with foil and set aside. In a mixing bowl, whisk together butter, Worcestershire sauce, chili powder, cumin, garlic powder, basil, onion powder, cayenne, and salt.
2. Add almonds and toss to coat. Spread almonds onto the prepared baking pan. Set your air fryer to bake at 350°F for 20 minutes. Serve and enjoy.

129. Spicy Brussels Sprouts

Preparation time: 15 minutes
Cooking time: 35 minutes
Servings: 6
Ingredients:
- 2 cups Brussels sprouts, halved
- 1/4 tsp. cayenne pepper
- 1/4 tsp. garlic powder
- 1/4 cup olive oil
- 1/4 tsp. salt

Directions:
1. Line the Baking Pan with foil and set aside. Add all ingredients into the large bowl and toss well. Transfer Brussels sprouts on a baking pan. Set your air fryer to Bake at 400°F for 35 minutes. Serve and enjoy.

130. Herb Mushrooms

Preparation time: 15 minutes
Cooking time: 14 minutes
Servings: 4
Ingredients:
- 1 lb. mushrooms
- 1 tbsp. basil, minced
- 1 garlic clove, minced
- 1/2 tbsp. vinegar
- 1/2 tsp. ground coriander
- 1 tsp. rosemary, chopped
- Pepper
- Salt

Directions:

1. Place the air fryer Basket onto the Baking Pan and spray the air fryer basket with cooking spray. Add all the listed fixing into the large bowl and toss well. Spread mushrooms onto the baking pan. Air fry at 350°F for 14 minutes. Serve and enjoy.

131. Fish Nuggets
Preparation Time: 10 minutes
Cooking Time: 10 minutes
Servings: 4
Ingredients:
- 1-pound fresh cod
- 2 tablespoons olive oil
- ½ cup almond flour
- 2 large finely beaten eggs
- 1-2 cups almond meal
- Salt as needed

Directions:
1. Preheat your Air Fryer to 388 F.
2. Take a food processor and add olive oil, almond meal, salt, and blend. Take three bowls and add almond flour, almond meal, beaten eggs individually.
3. Take costs and cut them into slices of 1-inch thickness and 2-inch length. Dredge slices into flour, eggs, and crumbs.
4. Transfer nuggets to cooking basket and air fry for 10 minutes until golden. Serve and enjoy!

132. Cumin and Squash Chili
Preparation Time: 10 minutes
Cooking Time: 22 minutes
Servings: 4
Ingredients:
- 1 medium butternut squash
- 2 teaspoons cumin seeds
- 1 large pinch of chili flakes
- 1 tablespoon olive oil
- 1 and ½ ounces pine nuts
- 1 small bunch fresh coriander, chopped

Directions:
1. Take the squash and slice it. Remove seeds and cut them into smaller chunks. Take a bowl and add chunked squash, spice, and oil. Mix well.
2. Preheat your air fryer to 360 degrees F and add the squash to the cooking basket. Roast for 20 minutes, making sure to shake the basket from time to time to avoid burning.
3. Take a pan, place it over medium heat, add pine nuts to the pan, and dry toast for 2 minutes. Sprinkle nuts on top of the squash and serve. Enjoy!

133. Feisty Banana Fritters
Preparation Time: 10 minutes
Cooking Time: 8 minutes
Servings: 4
Ingredients:
- 4 small bananas, halved
- 1 cup flour
- Sesame seeds
- Salt, to taste
- ¼ cup water

Directions:
1. Preheat your Air Fryer to 340 degrees. Take a bowl and add flour, salt, sesame seeds, water, and mix them well. Coat the bananas with the flour mixture and transfer them to the fryer basket. Air fry for 8 minutes. Enjoy!

134. Curly Fries
Preparation Time: 10 minutes
Cooking Time: 15 minutes
Servings: 4
Ingredients:
- 2 potatoes
- 1 tablespoon extra-virgin olive oil
- 1 teaspoon pepper
- 1 teaspoon salt
- 1 teaspoon paprika

Directions:
1. Warm your Air Fryer to 350 degrees F.
2. Wash potatoes thoroughly and pass them through a spiralizer to get curly shapes. Take a bowl and add potatoes to the bowl, toss, and coat well with pepper, salt, oil, and paprika.
3. Transfer the curly fries to the air fryer cooking basket and air fry for 15 minutes. Sprinkle more salt and paprika, serve and enjoy!

135. Cauliflower Popcorns
Preparation Time: 15 minutes
Cooking Time: 12 hours
Servings: 4
Ingredients:
- 2 pounds head cauliflower, cut into small florets
- 2 tablespoons hot sauce
- 1 tablespoon fresh lime juice
- 1 tablespoon oil
- 1 tablespoon smoked paprika
- 1 teaspoon ground cumin

Directions:
1. In a bowl, add all the ingredients and toss to coat well. Arrange the cauliflower florets onto 2 cooking trays.
2. Arrange the drip pan at the bottom of the air fryer cooking chamber. Adjust the temperature to 130 degrees F. Dehydrate for 12 hours; when cooking time is complete, remove the trays and serve hot.

136. Crispy Pickle Slices
Preparation Time: 15 minutes
Cooking Time: 18 minutes
Servings: 8
Ingredients:
- 16 dill pickle slices
- ¼ cup all-purpose flour
- Salt, as required
- 2 small eggs, beaten lightly
- 1 tablespoon dill pickle juice
- ¼ teaspoon garlic powder
- ¼ teaspoon cayenne pepper

- 1 cup panko breadcrumbs
- 1 tablespoon fresh dill, minced
- Cooking spray

Directions:
1. Place the pickle slices over paper towels for about 15 minutes or until all the liquid is absorbed.
2. Meanwhile, mix the flour plus salt in a shallow dish. In another shallow dish, add the eggs, pickle juice, garlic powder, and cayenne and beat until well combined.
3. In a third shallow dish, mix the panko and dill. Coat the pickle slices with flour mixture, then dip into the egg mixture and finally coat with the panko mixture.
4. Spray the pickle slices with cooking spray. Arrange the pickle slices onto a cooking tray. Arrange the drip pan at the bottom of the air fryer cooking chamber. Set to 400 degrees F. Air fry for 18 minutes, remove and serve warm.

137. Beef Taquitos

Preparation Time: 15 minutes
Cooking Time: 8 minutes
Servings: 6
Ingredients:
- 6 corn tortillas
- 2 cups cooked beef, shredded
- ½ cup onion, chopped
- 1 cup pepper jack cheese, shredded
- Olive oil cooking spray

Directions:
1. Arrange the tortillas onto a smooth surface. Place the shredded meat over one corner of each tortilla, followed by onion and cheese.
2. Roll each tortilla to secure the filling and secure with toothpicks. Spray each taquito with cooking spray evenly. Arrange the taquitos onto a cooking tray, then put in the air fryer.
3. Set the temperature to 400 degrees F. Air fry for 8 minutes, remove and serve warm.

138. Cheese Sandwich

Preparation Time: 10 minutes
Cooking Time: 10 minutes
Servings: 2
Ingredients:
- 3 tablespoons butter, softened
- 4 white bread slices
- 2 cheddar cheese slices

Directions:
1. Spread the butter over each bread slice generously. Place 2 bread slices onto a cooking tray, buttered side down
2. Top each buttered bread slice with 1 cheese slice. Cover with the remaining bread slices, buttered side up. Arrange the sandwiches onto a cooking tray in your air fryer.
3. Adjust the temperature to 375 degrees F, then air fry for 10 minutes. Cut each sandwich in half vertically and serve warm.

139. Roasted Pecans

Preparation Time: 5 minutes
Cooking Time: 6 minutes
Servings: 2
Ingredients:
- 2 cups pecan halves
- 1 tbsp. butter, melted
- Salt

Directions:
1. Preheat the air fryer to 200 F. Add pecans, butter, and salt in a mixing bowl and toss well. Transfer pecans on air fryer tray and air fry for 4-6 minutes. Toss after every 2 minutes. Serve and enjoy.

140. Pizza Toast

Preparation Time: 5 minutes
Cooking Time: 10 minutes
Servings: 2
Ingredients:
- 4 Texas toast slices
- 8 oz. Mozzarella cheese, shredded
- ½ jar pizza sauce
- 4 basil leaves

Directions:
1. Arrange toast slices on air fryer drip pan and air fry at 380 F for 2 minutes. Remove the pan from the air fryer. Add pizza sauce, Mozzarella cheese, and basil leaves to each toast slice. Return pan in the air fryer and air fry until cheese is melted. Serve and enjoy.

141. Baked Pears with Blue Cheese and Honey

Preparation Time: 10 minutes
Cooking Time: 10 minutes
Servings: 4
Ingredients:
- 1 tbsp.. melted butter for greasing
- 4 ripe pears, halved and cored
- 1 tbsp.. chopped fresh thyme + more for topping
- 1 tbsp.. honey
- 6 tsp. soft blue cheese
- Salt and black pepper to taste
- Chopped pecans to garnish

Directions:
1. Insert the dripping pan at the bottom of the air fryer. Preheat at 400 F for 2 to 3 minutes. Lightly grease a 6-inch baking dish with melted butter.
2. Use a spoon to create a shallow hole at the center of each pear half and top with the thyme and honey. Arrange the pears in the baking dish with the open side up.
3. Slide the cooking tray upside down onto the middle rack of the air fryer, sit the baking dish on top, and close the lid. Bake for 10 minutes. Cook until the pears soften and are golden brown.
4. Remove from the air fryer when ready and to serve, transfer the pears to the plate, and spoon the blue cheese at the center of the pears. Season with salt, black pepper, add the pecans, and drizzle with some honey. Enjoy!

142. Baked Tomatoes with Parmesan and Mozzarella

Preparation Time: 10 minutes
Cooking Time: 10 minutes
Servings: 4
Ingredients:
- 4 Roma tomatoes halved
- 1 cup grated Parmesan cheese
- 1 cup grated Mozzarella cheese
- ½ cup chopped fresh basil
- Olive oil for drizzling

Directions:
1. Insert the dripping pan at the bottom of the air fryer and preheat at 400 F for 2 to 3 minutes.
2. Arrange the tomato halves on the cooking tray with an open side facing up and fill with the cheese and basil. Slide the tray onto the middle rack of the air fryer and close the lid.
3. Bake for 10 minutes. Remove the tray from the air fryer, allow to sit for 2 minutes, and serve afterward.

143. Loaded Potato Bites

Preparation Time: 10 minutes
Cooking Time: 15 minutes
Servings: 4
Ingredients:
- 3 Russet potatoes, cleaned and cut into 1-inch rounds
- ¼ cup butter
- ¼ cup chopped scallions
- 1 cup grated cheddar cheese
- 3 tbsp. chopped and cooked bacon bits

Directions:
1. Warm air fryer at 400 F for 2 to 3 minutes. Arrange the potato pieces on the cooking tray, spread the butter on top, and top with the scallions and cheese.
2. Bake for 15 minutes until the cheese melts and is bubbly. Remove the air fryer's tray, allow to sit for 2 minutes, garnish with the bacon, and serve afterward.

144. Cheddar Tortilla Chips

Preparation Time: 45 minutes
Cooking Time: 10 minutes
Servings: 6
Ingredients:
- 1 cup flour
- Salt and black pepper to taste
- 1 tbsp.. golden flaxseed meal
- 2 cups shredded Cheddar cheese

Directions:
1. Melt cheddar cheese in the microwave for 1 minute. Once melted, add the flour, salt, flaxseed meal, and pepper. Mix well with a fork.
2. On a board, place the dough, and knead it with hands while warm until the ingredients are well combined. Divide the dough into 2 and with a rolling pin, roll them out flat into 2 rectangles.
3. Use a pastry cutter to cut out triangle-shaped pieces and line them in 1 layer on a baking dish. Grease the frying basket with cooking spray.
4. Arrange some triangle chips in 1 layer in the basket without touching or overlapping; spray them with cooking spray. Air fry for 10 minutes. Serve with a cheese dip.

145. Mustard Cheddar Twists

Preparation Time: 25 minutes
Cooking Time: 20 minutes
Servings: 8
Ingredients:
- 2 cups cauliflower florets, steamed
- 1 egg
- 3 ½ oz. oats
- 1 red onion, diced
- 1 tsp. mustard
- 5 oz. cheddar cheese
- Salt and black pepper to taste

Directions:
1. Preheat the air fryer to 350 F.
2. Pulse the oats using a food processor until they are the consistency of breadcrumbs. Place the steamed florets in a cheesecloth and squeeze out the excess liquid.
3. Place the cauliflower florets in a large bowl. Add the rest of the ingredients to the bowl. Mix well with hands to combine the ingredients thoroughly. Take a little bit of the batter and twist it into a straw.
4. Place on a lined baking tray and repeat with the rest of the mixture. Air fry for 10 minutes, turn over, and air fry for an additional 10 minutes.

146. Hash Brown Bruschetta

Preparation time: 5 minutes
Cooking time: 8 minutes
Servings: 4
Ingredients:
- 4 frozen hash brown patties
- 1 tablespoon olive oil
- 1/3 cup chopped cherry tomatoes
- 3 tablespoons diced fresh Mozzarella
- 2 tablespoons grated Parmesan cheese
- 1 tablespoon balsamic vinegar
- 1 tablespoon minced fresh basil

Directions:
1. Put the hash brown patties in your air fryer in a single layer. Air Fry at 400F for 6 to 8 minutes, or until the potatoes are crisp, hot, and golden brown.
2. Meanwhile, combine the olive oil, tomatoes, Mozzarella, Parmesan, vinegar, and basil in a small bowl. When the potatoes are done, carefully remove from the basket and arrange it on a serving plate. Top with the tomato mixture and serve.

147. Breaded Beef Cubes
Preparation time: 10 minutes
Cooking time: 16 minutes
Servings: 4
Ingredients:
- 1-pound (454 g) sirloin tip, cut into 1-inch cubes
- 1 cup cheese pasta sauce
- 1½ cups soft bread crumbs
- 2 tablespoons olive oil
- ½ teaspoon dried marjoram

Directions:
1. Mix the beef with the pasta sauce to coat in a medium bowl. In a shallow bowl, combine the bread crumbs, oil, and marjoram, and mix well. Drop the beef cubes, one at a time, into the bread crumb mixture to coat thoroughly.
2. Air Fry at 360 F in two batches for 6 to 8 minutes, shaking the basket once during the cooking time until the beef is at least 145 F and the outside is crisp and brown. Serve hot.

148. Waffle Fries Poutine
Preparation time: 10 minutes
Cooking time: 17 minutes
Servings: 4
Ingredients:
- 2 cups frozen waffle cut fries
- 2 teaspoons olive oil
- 1 red bell pepper, chopped
- 2 green onions, sliced
- 1 cup shredded Swiss cheese
- ½ cup bottled chicken gravy

Directions:
1. Toss the waffle fries with the olive oil and place it in the air fryer basket. Air fry for 10 to 12 minutes, or until the fries are crisp and light golden brown, shaking the basket halfway through the cooking time.
2. Transfer the fries to a nonstick round baking pan and top with the pepper, green onions, and cheese. Detach the rotating blade of the air fryer basket. Place the baking pan in the air fryer.
3. Air Fry at 380 F for 3 minutes, or until the vegetables are crisp and tender. Remove the pan from the air fryer and drizzle the gravy over the fries. Air fry for 2 minutes, or until the gravy is hot. Serve immediately.

149. Endive in Curried Yogurt
Preparation time: 5 minutes
Cooking time: 10 minutes
Servings: 6
Ingredients:
- 6 heads endive
- ½ cup plain and fat-free yogurt
- 3 tablespoons lemon juice
- 1 teaspoon garlic powder
- ½ teaspoon curry powder
- Salt and ground black pepper, to taste

Directions:
1. Wash the endives and slice them in half lengthwise. Mix the yogurt, lemon juice, garlic powder, curry powder, salt, and pepper in the bowl.
2. Brush the endive halves with the marinade, coating them completely. Allow sitting for at least 30 minutes or up to 24 hours. Put the endives in the air fryer basket and Air Fry at 320F for 10 minutes. Serve hot.

150. Tortilla Chips
Preparation time: 5 minutes
Cooking time: 3 minutes
Servings: 2
Ingredients:
- 8 corn tortillas
- 1 tablespoon olive oil
- Salt, to taste

Directions:
1. Slice the corn tortillas into triangles. Coat with a light brushing of olive oil. Put the tortilla pieces in the air fryer basket and Air Fry at 390 F for 3 minutes. You may need to do this in batches. Season with salt before serving.

151. Panko Artichoke Hearts
Preparation time: 5 minutes
Cooking time: 18 minutes
Servings: 4
Ingredients:
- 14 whole artichoke hearts, packed in water
- 1 egg
- ½ cup all-purpose flour
- 1/3 cup panko bread crumbs
- 1 teaspoon Italian seasoning
- Cooking spray

Directions:
1. Squeeze excess water from the artichoke hearts and place them on paper towels to dry.
2. Beat the egg in a small bowl. In another small bowl, place the flour. In a third small bowl, combine the bread crumbs and Italian seasoning, and stir.
3. Spritz the air fryer basket with cooking spray. Soak the artichoke hearts in the flour, then the egg, and then the bread crumb mixture.
4. Place the breaded artichoke hearts in the air fryer basket. Spray them with cooking spray. Air Fry at 380F for 8 minutes, or until the artichoke hearts have browned and are crisp. Let cool for 5 minutes before serving.

152. Steak Fries
Preparation time: 5 minutes
Cooking time: 20 minutes
Servings: 5
Ingredients:
- 1 (28-ounce / 794-g) bag frozen steak fries
- Cooking spray
- Salt and pepper, to taste
- ½ cup beef gravy
- 1 cup shredded Mozzarella cheese
- 2 scallions, green parts only, chopped

Directions:
1. Place the frozen steak fries in the air fryer. Air Fry at 400F for 10 minutes. Sprinkle with salt and pepper. Air fry for an additional 8 minutes.
2. Pour the beef gravy into a medium, microwave-safe bowl. Microwave for 30 seconds, or until the gravy is warm. Sprinkle the fries with the cheese. Air fry for an additional 2 minutes until the cheese is melted.
3. Transfer the fries to a serving dish. Drizzle the fries with gravy and sprinkle the scallions on top for a green garnish. Serve.

153. Breaded Green Olives
Preparation time: 5 minutes
Cooking time: 8 minutes
Servings: 4
Ingredients:
- 1 (5½-ounce / 156-g) jar pitted green olives
- ½ cup all-purpose flour
- Salt and pepper, to taste
- ½ cup bread crumbs
- 1 egg
- Cooking spray

Directions:
1. Remove the olives from the jar, then dry thoroughly with paper towels. In a small bowl, combine the flour with salt and pepper to taste. Place the bread crumbs in another small bowl. In a third small bowl, beat the egg.
2. Spritz the air fryer basket with cooking spray. Soak the olives in the flour, then the egg, and then the bread crumbs.
3. Place the breaded olives in the air fryer. Spray the olives with cooking spray. Air Fry at 400°F for 8 minutes or until brown and crisp. Cool before serving.

154. Apple Rolls
Preparation time: 5 minutes
Cooking time: 5 minutes
Servings: 8
Ingredients:
- 8 slices whole-wheat sandwich bread
- 4 ounces (113 g) Colby Jack cheese, grated
- ½ small apple, chopped
- 2 tablespoons butter, melted

Directions:
1. Flatten crusts from the bread with a rolling pin. Don't be gentle. Press hard so that the bread will be very thin.
2. Top bread slices with cheese and chopped apple, dividing the ingredients evenly. Roll up each slice tightly and secure each with one or two toothpicks. Brush outside of rolls with melted butter.
3. Put in air fryer basket and Air Fry at 390°F for 4 to 5 minutes, or until outside is crisp and nicely browned. Serve hot.

155. Pita Chips
Preparation time: 5 minutes
Cooking time: 5 minutes
Servings: 6
Ingredients:
- ¼ teaspoon dried basil
- ¼ teaspoon marjoram
- ¼ teaspoon ground oregano
- ¼ teaspoon garlic powder
- ¼ teaspoon ground thyme
- ¼ teaspoon salt
- 2 whole 6-inch pitas, whole grain or white
- Cooking spray

Directions:
1. Mix all the seasonings. Cut each pita half into 4 wedges. Break apart wedges at the fold. Mist one side of pita wedges with oil. Sprinkle with half of the seasoning mix.
2. Turn pita wedges over, mist the other side with oil, and sprinkle with remaining seasonings. Place pita wedges in air fryer basket and Air Fry at 330°F for 5 to 6 minutes or until crisp. Serve hot.

156. Mozzarella Eggroll Sticks
Preparation time: 5 minutes
Cooking time: 7 minutes
Servings: 8
Ingredients:
- 1 egg
- 1 tablespoon water
- 8 eggroll wraps
- 8 Mozzarella string cheese "sticks."

Directions:
1. Mix egg plus water in a small bowl. Layout eggroll wraps and moistens edges with egg wash. Place one piece of string cheese on each wrap near one end.
2. Fold in sides of eggroll wrap over ends of cheese, and then roll-up. Brush outside of wrap with egg wash and press gently to seal well.
3. Put in air fryer basket in a single layer and Air Fry at 390°F for 5 minutes. Air fry for an additional 1 or 2 minutes, if necessary, or until they are golden brown and crispy. Serve immediately.

157. Crab and Spinach Cups
Preparation time: 10 minutes
Cooking time: 10 minutes
Servings: 30 cups
Ingredients:
- 1 (6-ounce / 170-g) can crab meat, drained to yield 1/3 cup meat
- ¼ cup frozen spinach, thawed, drained, and chopped
- 1 clove garlic, minced
- ½ cup grated Parmesan cheese
- 3 tablespoons plain yogurt
- ¼ teaspoon lemon juice
- ½ teaspoon Worcestershire sauce
- 30 mini frozen phyllo shells, thawed

- Cooking spray

Directions:
1. Mix the crab meat, spinach, garlic, and cheese. Stir in the yogurt, lemon juice, and Worcestershire sauce and mix well.
2. Spoon a teaspoon of filling into each phyllo shell. Spritz the air fryer basket with cooking spray and arrange half the shells in the basket. Air Fry at 390°F for 5 minutes. Repeat with the remaining shells. Serve immediately.

158. Cajun Dill Pickle Chips

Preparation time: 5 minutes
Cooking time: 10 minutes
Servings: 16
Ingredients:
- ¼ cup all-purpose flour
- ½ cup panko bread crumbs
- 1 large egg, beaten
- 2 teaspoons Cajun seasoning
- 2 large dill pickles, sliced into 8 rounds each
- Cooking spray

Directions:
1. Place the all-purpose flour, panko bread crumbs, and egg into 3 separate shallow bowls, then stir the Cajun seasoning into the flour.
2. Dredge each pickle chip in the flour mixture, then the egg, and finally the bread crumbs. Shake off any excess, then place each coated pickle chip on a plate.
3. Spritz the air fryer basket with cooking spray, then place 8 pickle chips in the basket and Air Fry at 390°F for 5 minutes, or until crispy and golden brown. Repeat this process with the remaining pickle chips. Remove the chips and allow to slightly cool on a wire rack before serving.

159. Sriracha Wings

Preparation time: 5 minutes
Cooking time: 30 minutes
Servings: 4
Ingredients:
- 1 tablespoon Sriracha hot sauce
- 1 tablespoon honey
- 1 garlic clove, minced
- ½ teaspoon kosher salt
- 16 chicken wings and drumettes
- Cooking spray

Directions:
1. Mix the Sriracha hot sauce, honey, minced garlic, and kosher salt in a large bowl, then add the chicken and toss to coat.
2. Spray the air fryer basket using a cooking spray, then place 8 wings in the basket and Air Fry at 360°F for 15 minutes. Repeat this process with the remaining wings. Remove the wings and allow to cool on a wire rack for 10 minutes before serving.

160. Rosemary Cashews

Preparation time: 5 minutes
Cooking time: 3 minutes
Servings: 2
Ingredients:
- 2 sprigs of fresh rosemary (1 chopped and 1 whole)
- 1 teaspoon olive oil
- 1 teaspoon kosher salt
- ½ teaspoon honey
- 2 cups roasted and unsalted whole cashews
- Cooking spray

Directions:
1. Mix the chopped rosemary, olive oil, kosher salt, and honey in a medium bowl. Set aside.
2. Oiled the air fryer basket using a cooking spray, then place the cashews and the whole rosemary sprig in the basket and Air Fry at 300°F for 3 minutes.
3. Remove the cashews and rosemary from the air fryer, then discard the rosemary and add the cashews to the olive oil mixture, tossing to coat. Allow to cool for 15 minutes before serving.

161. Beef Enchilada Dip

Preparation time: 5 minutes
Cooking time: 23 minutes
Servings: 8
Ingredients:
- 2 lbs. ground beef
- ½ onion, chopped fine
- 2 cloves garlic, chopped fine
- 2 cups enchilada sauce
- 2 cups Monterrey Jack cheese, grated
- 2 tbsp.. sour cream

Directions:
1. Heat a large skillet over med-high heat. Put beef, then cook until it starts to brown. Drain off fat.
2. Stir in onion and garlic and cook until tender, about 3 minutes. Stir in enchilada sauce and transfer mixture to a small casserole dish and top with cheese.
3. Set your air fryer to bake at 325°F for 10 minutes. After 5 minutes, add casserole to it and bake 3-5 minutes until cheese is melted and the mixture is heated through. Serve warm topped with sour cream.

162. Cheesy Stuffed Sliders

Preparation time: 15 minutes
Cooking time: 10 minutes
Servings: 10
Ingredients:
- 2 tbsp.. garlic powder
- 1 ½ tsp. salt
- 2 tsp. pepper
- 2 lbs. ground beef
- 8 oz. Mozzarella slices, cut into 20 small pieces
- 20 potato slider rolls

Directions:
1. Mix garlic powder, salt, plus pepper in a small bowl.

2. Use 1 ½ tablespoon ground beef per patty. Roll it into a ball, then press an indentation in the ball with your thumb.
3. Place a piece of cheese into beef and fold over sides to cover it completely. Flatten to ½-inch thick by 3-inches wide. Season both sides with garlic mixture.
4. Place patties in the fryer basket in a single layer and place it on the baking pan. Air fry on 350°F for 10 minutes. Turn patties over halfway through cooking time. Repeat with any remaining patties. Place patties on bottoms of rolls and top with your favorite toppings. Serve immediately.

163. Philly Egg Rolls
Preparation time: 10 minutes
Cooking time: 10 minutes
Servings: 6
Ingredients:
- ½ lb. lean ground beef
- ¼ tsp. garlic powder
- ¼ tsp. onion powder
- ¼ tsp. salt
- ¼ tsp. pepper
- ¾ cup green bell pepper, chopped
- ¾ cup onion, chopped
- 2 slices provolone cheese, torn into pieces
- 3 tbsp.. cream cheese
- 6 square egg roll wrappers

Directions:
1. Lightly spray fryer basket with cooking spray. Heat a large skillet over med-high heat. Add beef, garlic powder, onion powder, salt, and pepper. Stir to combine.
2. Add in bell pepper and onion and cook, occasionally stirring, until beef is no longer pink, and vegetables are tender, about 6-8 minutes.
3. Remove from heat and drain fat. Add provolone and cream cheese and stir until melted and combined. Transfer to a large bowl.
4. Lay egg roll wrappers, one at a time, on a dry work surface. Spoon about 1/3 cup mixture in a row just below the center of the wrapper. Moisten edges with water. Fold the sides in towards the middle and roll up around filling.
5. Place egg rolls, seam side down in fryer basket. Spray lightly with cooking spray. Air fry on 400°F for 10 minutes. Cook until golden brown, turning over halfway through cooking time. Serve immediately.

164. Mozzarella Cheese Sticks
Preparation time: 10 minutes
Cooking time: 10 minutes
Servings: 6
Ingredients:
- Nonstick cooking spray
- 12 Mozzarella cheese sticks, halved
- 2 eggs
- ½ cup flour
- 1 ½ cups Italian panko bread crumbs
- ½ cup marinara sauce

Directions:
1. Blot cheese sticks with paper towels to soak up excess moisture. In a shallow dish, beat eggs. Place flour in a separate shallow dish.
2. Place bread crumbs in a third shallow dish. Line a baking sheet with parchment paper. One at a time, dip cheese sticks in egg, then flour, back in the egg, and finally in bread crumbs. Place on prepared pan. Freeze 1-2 hours until completely frozen.
3. Lightly spray fryer basket with cooking spray. Place cheese sticks in a single layer in the basket. Air fry at 375°F for 8 minutes. Cook until nicely browned and crispy, turning over halfway through cooking time. Serve with a marinara sauce for dipping.

165. Crispy Sausage Bites
Preparation time: 5 minutes
Cooking time: 20 minutes
Servings: 12
Ingredients:
- Nonstick cooking spray
- 2 lbs. spicy pork sausage
- 1 ½ cups Bisquick
- 4 cups sharp cheddar cheese, grated
- ½ cup onion diced fine
- 2 tsp. pepper
- 2 tsp. garlic, chopped fine

Directions:
1. Oiled baking pan using a cooking spray. In a large bowl, combine all ingredients. Form into 1-inch balls, then put on a baking pan; these will need to be cooked in batches.
2. Set the air fryer to bake at 375°F for 20 minutes. In 5 minutes of baking, place the baking pan in position 2 and continue baking until golden brown. Repeat with remaining sausage bites. Serve immediately.

166. Puffed Asparagus Spears
Preparation time: 15 minutes
Cooking time: 20 minutes
Servings: 10
Ingredients:
- Nonstick cooking spray
- 3 oz. prosciutto, sliced thin & cut into 30 long strips
- 30 asparagus spears, trimmed
- 10 (14 x 9-inch) sheets phyllo dough, thawed

Directions:
1. Wrap each asparagus spear using a piece of prosciutto, like a barber pole. One at a time, place a sheet of phyllo on a work surface and cut into 3 4 1/2x9-inch rectangles.
2. Place an asparagus spear across a short end and roll-up. Put in a single layer in your fryer basket. Spray with cooking spray.
3. Put the air fryer basket in your air fryer and set to air fry at 450°F for 10 minutes. Air fry until phyllo is crisp and golden, about 8-10 minutes, turning over halfway through cooking time. Repeat with the remaining ingredients. Serve warm.

167. Wonton Poppers

Preparation time: 15 minutes
Cooking time: 10 minutes
Servings: 10
Ingredients:
- Nonstick cooking spray
- 1 package refrigerated square wonton wrappers
- 1 8-ounce package cream cheese, softened
- 3 jalapenos, seeds and ribs removed, finely chopped
- 1/2 cup shredded cheddar cheese

Directions:
1. Lightly spray fryer basket with cooking spray. Mix all fixing except the wrappers in a large bowl.
2. Lay wrappers in a single layer on a baking sheet. Spoon a teaspoon of filling in the center. Moisten the edges with water and fold wrappers over the filling, pinching edges to seal. Place in a single layer in the basket.
3. Put the air fryer basket in your air fryer and air fry at 375°F for 10 minutes. Cook until golden brown and crisp, turning over halfway through cooking time. Repeat with the remaining ingredients. Serve immediately.

168. Party Pull Apart

Preparation time: 15 minutes
Cooking time: 20 minutes
Servings: 10
Ingredients:
- 5 cloves garlic
- 1/3 cup fresh parsley
- 2 tbsp.. olive oil
- 4 oz.. Mozzarella cheese, sliced
- 3 tbsp. butter
- 1/8 tsp. salt
- 1 loaf sourdough bread

Directions:
1. In a food processor, add garlic, parsley, and oil and pulse until garlic is chopped fine. Stack the Mozzarella cheese and cut into 1-inch squares.
2. Heat the butter in a small saucepan over medium heat. Add the garlic mixture and salt and cook 2 minutes, stirring occasionally. Remove from heat.
3. Use a sharp, serrated knife to make 1-inch diagonal cuts across the bread, being careful not to cut all the way through.
4. With a spoon, drizzle garlic butter into the cuts in the bread. Stack 3-4 cheese squares and place them in each of the cuts.
5. Place the bread on a sheet of foil and fold up the sides. Cut a second piece of foil just big enough to cover the top.
6. Set an air fryer to 350°F for 25 minutes. After 5 minutes, place the bread and bake 10 minutes. Remove the top piece of foil and bake 10 minutes more until the cheese has completely melted. Serve immediately.

Chapter 6. Side Dishes

169. Ranch Seasoned Air Fryer Chickpeas
Preparation time: 5 minutes
Cooking time: 17 minutes
Servings: 8
Ingredients:
- 1 tablespoon Lemon juice
- 1 can chickpeas (not rinsed but drained) save the liquid from the can
- 1 tablespoon Olive oil
- 2 teaspoons Garlic powder
- 2 teaspoons Onion powder
- 4 teaspoons dried dill
- 3/4 teaspoon Sea salt

Directions:
1. In a bowl, add chickpeas, 1 tbsp. of its liquid. Air fry for 12 minutes at 400 F. Then, in a bowl, add fried chickpeas with olive oil, lemon juice, onion powder, dill, salt, garlic powder, coat the chickpeas well. Put back these chickpeas to the air fryer and air fry for 5 minutes at 350 F. Serve hot or cold.

170. Spanakopita Bites
Preparation time: 10 minutes
Cooking time: 12 minutes
Servings: 4
Ingredients:
- 4 sheets phyllo dough
- 2 cups baby spinach leaves
- 2 tablespoons grated Parmesan cheese
- 1/4 cup Low-fat cottage cheese
- 1 teaspoon dried oregano
- 6 tbsp. Feta cheese, crumbled
- 2 tablespoons Water
- 1 egg white only
- 1 teaspoon Lemon zest
- 1/8 teaspoon Cayenne pepper
- 1 tablespoon Olive oil
- 1/4 teaspoon Kosher salt
- 1/4 teaspoon ground black pepper

Directions:
1. Put water and spinach in a pot over high heat, cook until wilted. Drain it and cool for ten minutes. Squeeze out excess moisture.
2. In a bowl, mix cottage cheese, Parmesan cheese, oregano, salt, cayenne pepper, egg white, freshly ground black pepper, feta cheese, spinach, and zest. Mix it well or in the food processor.
3. Put 1 phyllo sheet on a flat surface. Spray with oil. Add the second sheet of phyllo on top—spray oil. Add a total of 4 oiled sheets. Form 16 strips from these four oiled sheets. Add 1 tbsp. of filling in one strip. Roll it around filling.
4. Spray the air fryer basket with oil. Put eight bites in the basket, spray with oil. Air fry for 12 minutes at 375 F until crispy and golden brown. Flip halfway through. Serve with leaner protein.

171. Cheesy Spinach Wontons
Preparation time: 15 minutes
Cooking time: 6 minutes
Servings: 6
Ingredients:
- 1/4 cup Low-fat cream cheese, softened
- 16-20 Wonton wrappers
- 1 and 1/2 cups baby spinach, chopped

Directions:
1. In a small bowl, mix spinach and soften cream cheese, mix well Lay wonton wrappers on a flat surface, add one tsp. of the cream cheese mix in the center.
2. With the help of water, fold over corners to press the edges together. Give it a wonton shape. Air Fry for 6 minutes at 400 degrees. Serve.

172. Onion Rings
Preparation time: 20 minutes
Cooking time: 12 minutes
Servings: 4
Ingredients:
- 1 egg whisked
- 1 large onion
- 1 and 1/2 cup Whole-wheat breadcrumbs

- 1 teaspoon smoked paprika
- 1 cup Flour
- 1 teaspoon Garlic powder
- 1 cup Buttermilk
- Kosher salt and pepper, to taste

Directions:
1. Cut the stems of the onion. Then cut into half-inch-thick rounds. In a bowl, add flour, pepper, garlic powder, smoked paprika, and salt. Then add egg and buttermilk. Mix to combine.
2. In another bowl, add the breadcrumbs. Coat the onions in buttermilk mix, then in breadcrumbs mix. Freeze these breaded onions for 15 minutes. Spray the fryer basket with oil spray.
3. Put onions in the air fryer basket in one single layer. Spray the onion with cooking oil. Air fry at 370 degrees for 10-12 minutes. Flip only, if necessary.

173. Delicata Squash
Preparation time: 5 minutes
Cooking time: 10 minutes
Servings: 2
Ingredients:
- 1/2 tablespoon Olive oil
- 1 delicata squash
- 1/2 teaspoon salt
- 1/2 teaspoon rosemary

Directions:
1. Chop the squash in slices of 1/4 thickness. Discard the seeds. In a bowl, add olive oil, salt, rosemary with squash slices. Mix well. Air fries the squash for ten minutes at 400 F. Flip the squash halfway through. Make sure it is cooked thoroughly.

174. Egg Rolls
Preparation time: 10 minutes
Cooking time: 15 minutes
Servings: 3
Ingredients:
- ½ pack Coleslaw mix
- 1/2 onion
- 1/2 teaspoon salt
- 1/2 cup of mushrooms
- 2 cups Lean ground pork
- 1 stalk of celery
- Wrappers (egg roll)

Directions:
1. Put a skillet over medium flame, add onion and lean ground pork and cook for 5-7 minutes. Add coleslaw mixture, salt, mushrooms, and celery to skillet and cook for almost five minutes.
2. Lay egg roll wrapper flat and add filling (1/3 cup), roll it up, seal with water. Spray with oil the rolls. Put in the air fry for 6-8 minutes at 400F, flipping once halfway through. Serve hot.

175. Crispy Fried Okra
Preparation time: 15 minutes
Cooking time: 15 minutes
Servings: 4

Ingredients:
- 1 cup Water
- 1 1/4 cups Okra
- 1/2 cup Rice flour
- 1/2 tsp. Fennel Seeds
- 1/2 tsp. red chili powder
- 1 tsp. Kosher salt
- 1/4 cup Semolina: fine
- 1/2 tsp. Ground Turmeric

Directions:
1. Wash and completely dry okra. Slice in half. In a bowl, add semolina, fennel seeds, flour, turmeric, chili, salt, powder, mix well, and add water to make the batter. It should be should.
2. Coat the okra in the batter. Place okra slices in the air fryer basket in a single layer. Spray with some oil. Air fry for ten minutes at 330 F. Toss the okra, then air fry again for 2-5 minutes, at 350 F or until crispy. Serve hot

176. Baked Sweet Potato Cauliflower Patties
Preparation time: 15 minutes
Cooking time: 20 minutes
Servings: 7
Ingredients:
- 2 tbsp... Organic ranch seasoning mix
- 1 sweet potato
- 1 diced green onion
- 1/2 tsp. Chili powder
- 1 tsp. minced garlic
- 1 cup packed cilantro
- 2 cups Cauliflower florets
- 1/4 tsp. Cumin
- Gluten-free flour
- Kosher salt and pepper
- 1/4 cup ground flaxseed

Directions:
1. Preheat the air fryer at 370 F. Peel the sweet potato and cut into bite-size pieces. Pulse in the food processor along with onion, garlic, and cauliflower. Pulse it again.
2. Then add flaxseed, cilantro, flour, remaining seasoning, and pulse again until thick batter forms. Make medium thick patties.
3. Place them on a baking sheet and put them in the freezer for 10 minutes. Put them in the air fryer in one layer and air fry for 18 minutes or 20. Serve with any dipping sauce.

177. Falafel
Preparation time: 15 minutes
Cooking time: 14 minutes
Servings: 6
Ingredients:
- 1 teaspoon Paprika
- 2 cans of chickpeas drained and rinsed
- Cloves of garlic
- 1 chopped large onion

- 1/4 cup fresh parsley
- 3 tablespoons Gluten-free flour:
- 2 tablespoons sesame seeds
- 2 teaspoons ground cumin
- 1/4 cup Cilantro
- 1/2 lemon, juice only
- 1 teaspoon salt

Directions:
1. In a food processor, add sesame seeds, lemon, chickpeas, cumin, garlic, cilantro, shallot, parsley, paprika, salt, and flour. Pulse on high, so everything comes together, but it should not be a smooth paste.
2. Make one-inch diameter, tablespoon full balls, or form into discs Spray olive oil on the air fryer basket and then add the falafel to the basket in one layer and air fry for 8 minutes at 350 F. Toss and then air fry again for 6 minutes. Serve in warm pita bread, with vegetables' slices and your favorite sauce

178. Zucchini Parmesan Chips

Preparation time: 15 minutes
Cooking time: 8 minutes
Servings: 6
Ingredients:
- ½ cup Seasoned, whole Wheat Breadcrumbs
- 2 thinly slices of zucchinis
- ½ cup Parmesan Cheese, grated
- 1 egg whisked
- Kosher salt and pepper, to taste

Directions:
1. Pat dries the zucchini slices, so no moisture remains. In a bowl, whisk the egg with a few tsp. of water and salt, pepper.
2. In another bowl, mix the grated cheese, smoked paprika(optional), and breadcrumbs. Coat zucchini slices in egg mix then in breadcrumbs. Put all in a rack and spray with olive oil.
3. In a single layer, add in the air fryer, and air fry for 8 minutes at 350 F. Add kosher salt and pepper on top if needed, serve.

179. Lemony Green Beans

Preparation time: 15 minutes
Cooking time: 12 minutes
Servings: 6
Ingredients:
- Salt, to taste
- ground black pepper, to taste
- 4 cups green beans, trimmed
- 1 lemon
- 1/4 teaspoon oil

Directions:
1. Add the green beans to the air fryer basket, top with oil, salt, pepper, and lemon juice. Air fry for 10-12 minutes at 400 F. Serve.

180. Roasted Corn

Preparation time: 5 minutes
Cooking time: 10 minutes
Servings: 4
Ingredients:
- 4 corn ears
- 2 to 3 teaspoons Olive oil:
- Kosher salt and pepper to taste

Directions:
1. Clean the corn, wash, and pat dry. Fit in the basket of air fryer, cut if need to. Top with olive oil, kosher salt, and pepper. Air fry for 10 minutes at 400 F.

181. Spinach Frittata

Preparation time: 15 minutes
Cooking time: 8 minutes
Servings: 4
Ingredients:
- 1/3 cup of packed spinach
- 1 small chopped red onion
- Shredded Mozzarella cheese
- 3 eggs
- Salt, pepper

Directions:
1. Let the air fryer preheat to 180 F. In a skillet over a medium flame, add oil, onion, cook until translucent, add spinach and sauté until half cooked.
2. Beat eggs and season with kosher salt and pepper—mix spinach mixture in it. Air fry in the air fryer for 8 minutes or until cooked. Slice and serve hot.

182. Pecan Crusted Eggplant

Preparation time: 15 minutes
Cooking time: 8 minutes
Servings: 4
Ingredients:
- 1 eggplant
- 2 tablespoons egg replacer
- 1 cup whole-wheat breadcrumbs
- 1/4 teaspoon Marjoram
- 1/4 teaspoon Kosher salt
- 1/4 teaspoon pepper
- 1/4 teaspoon Dry mustard
- 4 tablespoons Water
- 1/2 cup Pecans
- 6 tablespoons Almond milk

Directions:
1. In a bowl, add water, almond milk, and egg replacer, mix, and set it aside.
2. In a food processor, add 1/4 teaspoon of pepper and kosher salt, marjoram, crumbs, pecans, and mustard. Pulse until well combined and chopped. Do not over mix.
3. Let the air fryer preheat to 390 F. Cut the eggplants into half-inch slices and season with kosher salt and pepper.
4. Coat slices in egg mix then in crumbs mix. Add coated slices in the air fryer in an even layer—Air fries for 6-8 minutes at 390 F. Serve.

183. Buffalo Cauliflower

Preparation time: 15 minutes
Cooking time: 10 minutes
Servings: 4

Ingredients:
- 1 egg
- 1/2 head of cauliflower
- 1 cup Whole wheat breadcrumbs:
- 1/2 teaspoon Salt:
- 1/2 teaspoon Garlic powder:
- 1 cup of low-fat ranch dressing
- Freshly ground black pepper
- 1/2 cup Hot sauce:

Directions:
1. Cut cauliflower into floret. In a bowl, mix the egg with garlic powder, salt, and pepper. Coat floret in eggs then in breadcrumbs.
2. Add them to the air fryer and air fry for 8-10 minutes at 400 F. Mix hot sauce with ranch and serve with fried cauliflower.

184. Roasted Waldorf Salad
Preparation time: 15 minutes
Cooking time: 14 minutes
Servings: 4
Ingredients:
- 2 Granny Smith apples, chunks
- 2 teaspoons olive oil, divided
- 1½ cups red grapes
- ½ cup mayonnaise
- 2 tablespoons freshly squeezed lemon juice
- 1 tablespoon honey
- 3 celery stalks, sliced
- ½ cup coarsely chopped pecans

Directions:
1. Put the chopped apples in the air fryer basket and drizzle with 1 teaspoon olive oil; toss to coat.
2. Set or preheat the air fryer to 400°F. Place the basket in the air fryer and roast for 4 minutes. Remove the basket.
3. Add the grapes to the basket and drizzle with the remaining 1 teaspoon of olive oil; toss again. Return the air fryer basket to your air fryer and roast for 8 to 10 minutes longer, shaking the basket halfway through cooking time, until tender.
4. Meanwhile, whisk together the mayonnaise, lemon juice, and honey in a medium bowl. Add the celery and pecans to the dressing and stir to combine.
5. Place the roasted apples and grapes in the bowl and stir gently to coat the fruit with the dressing. Serve or refrigerate for 2 hours before serving.

185. Melting Baby Potatoes
Preparation time: 15 minutes
Cooking time: 27 minutes
Servings: 4
Ingredients:
- 10 to 12 baby Yukon Gold potatoes
- 1 tablespoon olive oil
- 1 tablespoon butter, melted
- ½ teaspoon of sea salt
- 1/8 teaspoon freshly ground black pepper
- ½ teaspoon dried thyme
- 1/3 cup vegetable broth

Directions:
1. Slice the potatoes in half. Put the olive oil, then butter in a 7-inch round pan and swirl to coat the bottom. Add the potatoes, cut side down, in a single layer.
2. You may have to use more or fewer potatoes, depending on how many will fit in the pan. The cut side must sit flat on the pan bottom.
3. Put the pan in the air fryer basket. Set or preheat to 400°F and roast the potatoes for 12 minutes. Remove the pan from the basket and shake to loosen the potatoes.
4. Sprinkle the potatoes with the salt, pepper, and thyme and pour the vegetable broth into the pan around the potatoes.
5. Return to the air fryer and roast for another 10 to 15 minutes or until the liquid is absorbed and the potatoes are tender when pierced with a fork. Serve.

186. Roasted Spicy Corn
Preparation time: 5 minutes
Cooking time: 15 minutes
Servings: 4
Ingredients:
- 2 cups frozen corn kernels, drained
- 1 small onion, diced
- 2 garlic cloves, sliced
- 2 tablespoons butter, melted
- 1 teaspoon chili powder
- ½ teaspoon cayenne pepper
- ½ teaspoon of sea salt
- 1/8 teaspoon freshly ground black pepper
- ¼ cup heavy (whipping) cream

Directions:
1. Combine the corn, onion, garlic, butter, chili powder, cayenne pepper, salt, and black pepper in a 6-inch metal bowl that fits into your air fryer basket.
2. Set or preheat the air fryer to 400°F. Place the bowl in the basket and roast for 10 minutes, shaking the basket once during the cooking time until some of the kernels start to turn gold around the edges.
3. Remove the basket and pour the cream over the corn; stir to mix. Return it to the air fryer and roast for another 5 minutes or until the cream has thickened slightly. Serve.

187. Cauliflower Quesadillas
Preparation time: 15 minutes
Cooking time: 24 minutes
Servings: 4
Ingredients:
- 1 cup frozen cauliflower rice or fresh riced cauliflower
- 3 tablespoons vegetable broth
- 3 scallions, sliced
- 4 (10-inch) flour tortillas
- 1 cup shredded Havarti cheese

- 1 teaspoon dried oregano
- ½ cup shredded Parmesan cheese
- 1 tablespoon olive oil

Directions:
1. Combine the cauliflower rice, vegetable broth, and scallions in a 6-inch metal bowl. Put the bowl in the air fryer basket and the basket in the air fryer.
2. Set or preheat the air fryer to 375°F and cook the cauliflower mixture until tender, 7 to 8 minutes. Drain if necessary.
3. Put the tortillas on the work surface. Put ¼ cup of Havarti cheese on one side of each tortilla, then sprinkle with the oregano.
4. Divide the cauliflower rice mixture over the Havarti and oregano, then sprinkle with the Parmesan cheese. Fold the tortillas in half, folding in the edges about 1½ inches.
5. Brush both sides of the tortillas with olive oil. Place the quesadillas, two at a time, in the air fryer basket. Air Fry for 6 to 8 minutes, turning the quesadillas over once during the cooking time until crisp and the cheese is melted.
6. Repeat with remaining quesadillas. Cut each quesadilla into halves to serve.

188. Sweet Potato Hash Browns

Preparation time: 15 minutes
Cooking time: 22 minutes
Servings: 4
Ingredients:
- 2 medium sweet potatoes, peeled
- 2 tablespoons olive oil
- 2 teaspoons chili powder
- ½ teaspoon ground cumin
- ½ teaspoon of sea salt
- 1/8 teaspoon cayenne pepper

Directions:
1. Shred the sweet potatoes on the large side of your grater. Place the shredded potatoes in a bowl of cool water for 10 minutes, then drain well. Pat dry using paper towels.
2. In a large bowl, combine the sweet potatoes, olive oil, chili powder, cumin, salt, and cayenne pepper and toss to coat.
3. Put the seasoned potatoes in the air fryer basket. Set or preheat the air fryer to 400°F. Air Fry for 10 minutes, then remove the basket and shake the potatoes.
4. Return the basket and continue cooking for another 10 to 12 minutes or until the potatoes are crunchy and tender. Serve.

189. Roasted Five-Spice Broccoli

Preparation time: 10 minutes
Cooking time: 15 minutes
Servings: 4
Ingredients:
- 1 bunch fresh broccoli, cut into florets
- 2 tablespoons olive oil
- 1 teaspoon five-spice powder
- ¼ teaspoon onion powder
- ¼ teaspoon of sea salt
- 1/8 teaspoon freshly ground black pepper

Directions:
1. Drizzle the broccoli into a bowl with the olive oil. Toss to coat. Sprinkle with the five-spice powder, onion powder, salt, and pepper and toss again.
2. Put the broccoli into the air fryer basket and place the basket in the air fryer. Set or preheat the air fryer to 400°F. Roast the broccoli for 8 minutes.
3. Remove the basket and shake it to redistribute the broccoli. Return the basket and roast for another 5 to 7 minutes until the broccoli is tender with slightly browned edges. Serve immediately.

190. Mediterranean Style Veggies

Preparation time: 15 minutes
Cooking time: 20 minutes
Servings: 4
Ingredients:
- 1½ cups cherry tomatoes
- 1 yellow bell pepper, sliced
- 1 small zucchini, sliced
- 1½ cups button mushrooms halved lengthwise
- 2 tablespoons olive oil
- 1 teaspoon dried basil
- ½ teaspoon dried oregano
- ½ teaspoon dried thyme
- ½ teaspoon garlic powder
- ½ teaspoon of sea salt
- 1/8 teaspoon freshly ground black pepper

Directions:
1. Put the tomatoes, bell pepper, zucchini, and mushrooms in the air fryer basket, drizzle using olive oil.
2. Then sprinkle with the basil, oregano, thyme, garlic powder, salt, and pepper and toss again. Put the basket in the air fryer.
3. Set or preheat the air fryer to 375°F and roast for 15 to 20 minutes, tossing twice during cooking time, until the vegetables are tender. Serve.

191. Corn Fritters

Preparation time: 15 minutes
Cooking time: 15 minutes
Servings: 4
Ingredients:
- ½ cup all-purpose flour
- 1 teaspoon chili powder
- ½ teaspoon baking powder
- ½ teaspoon of sea salt
- 1/8 teaspoon freshly ground black pepper
- 1¼ cups frozen corn kernels, thawed and drained
- 1 large egg, beaten
- 1 tablespoon honey
- 1 garlic clove, minced

Directions:

1. In a medium bowl, combine the flour, chili powder, baking powder, salt, and pepper and mix well. In a small bowl, combine the corn, egg, honey, and garlic and mix well.
2. Put the corn batter to the flour batter and stir just until combined.
3. Line the air fryer basket using parchment paper. Drop two to four ¼-cup measures of the fritter batter onto the paper, 1½ inches apart. Place the basket in the air fryer.
4. Set or preheat the air fryer to 375°F and air fry for 10 to 15 minutes, until they are golden brown and hot. Repeat with the remaining batter, if needed. Serve.

192. Roasted Italian Bell Peppers

Preparation time: 10 minutes
Cooking time: 11 minutes
Servings: 4
Ingredients:
- 1 red bell pepper, sliced
- 1 yellow bell pepper, sliced
- 1 orange bell pepper, sliced
- 1 tablespoon olive oil
- 1 teaspoon freshly squeezed lemon juice
- 1 teaspoon dried Italian seasoning
- ½ teaspoon of sea salt
- 1/8 teaspoon freshly ground black pepper
- ¼ cup chopped fresh flat-leaf parsley

Directions:
1. Combine the bell peppers in the air fryer basket. Drizzle with the olive oil and lemon juice, and sprinkle with the Italian seasoning, salt, and pepper. Toss to coat. Place the basket in the air fryer.
2. Set or preheat the air fryer to 350°F. Roast for 8 to 11 minutes, shaking once during the cooking time until the peppers are tender and brown around the edges. Sprinkle with the parsley and serve.

193. Tex-Mex Corn and Beans

Preparation time: 10 minutes
Cooking time: 10 minutes
Servings: 4
Ingredients:
- 1 can black beans, drained and rinsed
- 1 cup frozen corn kernels
- 1 red bell pepper, seeded and chopped
- 1 jalapeño pepper, sliced
- 2 garlic cloves, sliced
- 1 tablespoon olive oil
- 1 tablespoon freshly squeezed lime juice
- 2 teaspoons chili powder
- ½ teaspoon of sea salt
- 1/8 teaspoon cayenne pepper

Directions:
1. Combine the black beans, corn, bell pepper, jalapeño pepper, and garlic in the air fryer basket.
2. Drizzle with the olive oil plus lime juice, then toss to coat. Sprinkle with the chili powder, salt, and cayenne pepper and toss again. Place the basket in the air fryer.
3. Set or preheat the air fryer to 350°F. Roast the vegetables for 10 minutes, shaking the basket halfway through cooking time, until hot and tender. Serve.

194. Mushroom Veggie Kabobs

Preparation time: 15 minutes
Cooking time: 11 minutes
Servings: 4
Ingredients:
- 1 (8-ounce) package button mushrooms, rinsed
- 1 green bell pepper, sliced
- 1 yellow bell pepper, sliced
- 1 cup cherry tomatoes
- 1 tablespoon freshly squeezed lemon juice
- 1 tablespoon olive oil
- 2 teaspoons Dijon mustard
- ½ teaspoon dried marjoram
- ½ teaspoon of sea salt
- 1/8 teaspoon freshly ground black pepper

Directions:
1. Build the skewers with the mushrooms, bell peppers, and cherry tomatoes, alternating vegetables for a nice appearance.
2. Mix the lemon juice, olive oil, mustard, marjoram, salt, and pepper in a small bowl. Brush this mixture onto the vegetables. Put the skewers in your air fryer basket and put the basket in the air fryer.
3. Set or preheat the air fryer to 400°F. Roast the skewers for 8 to 11 minutes, turning once halfway through cooking time, until the vegetables are tender and starting to brown. Serve.

195. Potatoes Au Gratin

Preparation time: 15 minutes
Cooking time: 15 minutes
Servings: 6
Ingredients:
- ½ cup whole milk
- ½ cup cream
- ½ cup Parmesan cheese
- 1 garlic clove, diced
- ½ teaspoon freshly grated nutmeg
- ½ teaspoon kosher salt
- 1 teaspoon freshly ground black pepper
- 3 medium russet potatoes, thinly sliced (1/8-inch thick or thinner)
- Canola oil cooking spray
- ½ cup grated Gruyère cheese

Directions:
1. In a large bowl, whisk together the milk, cream, Parmesan, garlic, nutmeg, salt, and pepper. Add the potato slices and mix well to coat.
2. Spray the bottom of the air fryer pan with canola oil. Put the potato batter into the pan.

3. Air fry at 390° F for 10 minutes, then top with the Gruyère. Continue frying until cheese is bubbly and begins to brown, about 5 minutes.

196. Perfect Potato Pancakes

Preparation time: 15 minutes
Cooking time: 30 minutes
Servings: 4
Ingredients:
- 2 medium or large russet potatoes, peeled
- 1 small onion
- 1 large egg, beaten
- 1 teaspoon kosher salt
- ½ teaspoon freshly ground pepper
- 3 tablespoons all-purpose flour

Directions:
1. Put the potatoes in a pot, then cover with water. Bring to a boil and cook potatoes until you can just sink a fork into them—they should still be firm—about 10 minutes.
2. Drain and let them cool enough to handle. Using a box grater, grate the onion and potatoes and toss together to combine. Place the grated mixture in a tight mesh strainer and press to release excess liquid. Blot the mixture with a paper towel and place in a large bowl.
3. Add the egg, salt, and pepper and stir with a fork to mix. Add the flour 1 tablespoon at a time, mixing thoroughly between each addition.
4. Scoop about ¼ of the mixture into the palm of your hand and form it into a patty. Repeat with the remaining mixture. Place 1 patty at a time in the air fryer basket. Air fry in batches at 400° F for 20 minutes. Serve.

197. String Bean Fries

Preparation time: 30 minutes
Cooking time: 10 minutes
Servings: 4
Ingredients:
- ½ pound fresh string (green) beans, trimmed
- 1 large egg
- ¼ cup 2% or whole milk
- 1 cup Italian-seasoned Breadcrumbs
- ½ teaspoon chili powder
- ½ teaspoon garlic powder
- ½ teaspoon onion powder
- ½ cup all-purpose flour

Directions:
1. Blanch the string beans by heating them in boiling water for 2–3 minutes, then immediately rinsing with cold water to stop the cooking process. Drain, then pat dry with paper towels and refrigerate for 30 minutes.
2. In a shallow bowl, whisk together the egg and the milk. In a separate shallow bowl, combine the breadcrumbs, chili powder, garlic powder, and onion powder and mix well.
3. Dredge each string bean in the flour, then dip into the beaten egg, then coat evenly with the breadcrumb mixture.
4. Put the beans in your air fryer basket, leaving space between each one. Air fry at 400° F until golden brown, about 10 minutes.

198. Four-Cheese Phyllo Triangles

Preparation time: 30 minutes
Cooking time: 15 minutes
Servings: 4
Ingredients:
- 2 cups crumbled feta cheese
- 1 1/3 cups freshly grated Parmesan cheese
- 1 cup shredded Gruyère cheese
- ½ cup ricotta cheese
- ¾ cup heavy cream
- ½ teaspoon freshly ground black pepper
- 8 (14 x 18 inch) sheets of frozen phyllo (filo) dough, thawed
- ¼ cup extra virgin olive oil, divided
- 2 large eggs, beaten

Directions:
1. In a large bowl, mix the cheeses, cream, plus pepper. Fridge for 30 minutes. Put 4 of the phyllo dough sheets on your work surface, then brush the tops with oil.
2. Top each of these sheets with another sheet and brush it with oil. Get both sheets, fold the dough in half lengthwise, so you have a long sheet with one of the short ends closest to you.
3. Brush a small amount of the beaten egg to all the edges of one of the dough sheets, like a frame.
4. Spoon 2 heaping tbsp. of the cheese batter onto the dough, at the top right. Fold the top left part or corner of the dough diagonally, making a triangle with the filling underneath. Press the edges to seal the dough.
5. Fold this filled triangle straight down, then diagonally down to the left, then straight down, then diagonally down to the right, repeating until you have used the rest of the dough sheet. Repeat process with remaining dough sheets.
6. Brush the outside of the filled triangles using the rest of the olive oil. Place it in the air fryer basket, leaving space between each one.
7. Air fry at 360° F for 15 minutes. Let the triangles cool for 20 minutes before serving to allow the cheese to set.

199. Summer Vegetable Gratin

Preparation time: 15 minutes
Cooking time: 25 minutes
Servings: 4
Ingredients:
- 1 medium zucchini
- 1 medium yellow squash
- 1 small eggplant, peeled
- 1 tablespoon salt

- 2 tablespoons olive oil
- ½ cup shredded Cheddar cheese
- ½ cup Italian-seasoned Breadcrumbs
- 1 garlic clove, minced
- ½ teaspoon freshly ground black pepper
- ¼ cup freshly grated Parmesan cheese
- Olive oil cooking spray
- 2 tablespoons chopped fresh Italian flat-leaf parsley

Directions:
1. With a box grater, grate the zucchini, yellow squash, and eggplant. Toss with the salt and let sit in a colander to sweat out moisture for at least 30 minutes and up to 90 minutes. Rinse with cool water to get rid of excess salt, then pat dry with paper towels.
2. Toss with the olive oil and Cheddar cheese. In a small bowl, combine the breadcrumbs, garlic, pepper, and Parmesan cheese and toss to combine.
3. Spray the air fryer pan with olive oil, then add the vegetable mixture. Top with breadcrumb mixture. Air fry at 350° F until vegetables are tender, about 25 minutes. Top with parsley.

200. Polenta Pie

Preparation time: 15 minutes
Cooking time: 35 minutes
Servings: 6
Ingredients:
- 1-piece Egg, slightly beaten
- 2 cups Water
- 3/4 cup Monterey Jack cheese, w/ jalapeno peppers, shredded
- 3/4 cup Cornmeal
- 1/4 teaspoon salt
- 15 ounces Chili beans, drained
- 1/3 cup Tortilla chips/crushed corn

Directions:
1. Warm air fryer at 350 F. Mist cooking sprays onto a pie plate.
2. In saucepan heated on medium-high, combine water, salt, and cornmeal. Let the mixture boil, then cook on medium heat for 6 minutes. Stir in egg and let sit for 5 minutes.
3. Pour cornmeal mixture into the pie plate and spread evenly. Air-fry for 15 minutes and top with beans, corn chips, and cheese. Air-fry for another 20 minutes.

201. Bean and Rice Dish

Preparation time: 15 minutes
Cooking time: 1 hour & minutes
Servings: 4
Ingredients:
- 1 ½ cups Boiling water
- 15 ounces Kidney beans, dark red, undrained
- 1/2 teaspoon Marjoram leaves, dried
- 1/2 cup Cheddar cheese, shredded
- 1 cup White rice, long-grain, uncooked
- 1 tablespoon Bouillon, chicken/vegetable, granulated
- 1 Onion, medium, chopped
- 9 ounces baby lima beans, frozen, thawed, drained

Directions:
1. Preheat the air fryer at 325 degrees Fahrenheit. Combine all ingredients, save for cheese, in casserole. Cover and air-fry for 1 hour and 15 minutes. Stir the dish before topping with cheese.

202. Cheesy Potato Mash Casserole

Preparation time: 15 minutes
Cooking time: 58 minutes
Servings: 24
Ingredients:
- 1 teaspoon Chives, fresh, chopped
- 3 ounces Cream cheese, reduced fat, softened
- 1 cup Yogurt, plain, fat-free
- 1 cup Cheddar cheese, reduced fat, shredded
- 1/4 teaspoon Paprika
- 5 pounds white potatoes, peeled, cubed
- 1/4 cup blue cheese, crumbled
- 1/4 cup Parmesan cheese, shredded
- 1 teaspoon Garlic salt

Directions:
1. Put the potatoes in your saucepan filled with water. Heat to boiling, then cook on simmer for 15 to 18 minutes. Beat together parmesan cheese, cheddar cheese, cream cheese, and blue cheese until smooth. Beat in garlic salt and yogurt.
2. Preheat air fryer to 325 degrees Fahrenheit. Mash cooked potatoes until smooth. Stir in cheese mixture. Add to a baking dish and air-fry for 35 to 40 minutes.

203. Simple Squash Casserole

Preparation time: 15 minutes
Cooking time: 42 minutes
Servings: 6
Ingredients:
- 1 Yellow summer squash, medium, sliced thinly
- 1 tablespoon Thyme leaves, fresh, chopped
- 1/2 teaspoon salt
- 1/2 cup Italian cheese blend, gluten-free, shredded
- 1 tablespoon Olive oil, extra virgin
- 1 Zucchini, medium, sliced thinly
- 1/2 cup Onion, diced
- 1 cup Brown rice, cooked
- 1 Plum tomato, diced
- 1/8 teaspoon Pepper

Directions:
1. Preheat air fryer to 375 degrees Fahrenheit. Mist cooking sprays onto a gratin dish.
2. Combine rice, onion, tomato, pepper, 1/4 teaspoon salt, oil, and ½ thyme leaves. Spread evenly into the gratin dish and layer on top with squash and zucchini.

3. Sprinkle with remaining 1/4 teaspoon salt and thyme. Cover and air-fry for 20 minutes. Top with cheese and air-fry for another 10 to 12 minutes.

204. Ginger Pork Lasagna

Preparation time: 15 minutes
Cooking time: 57 minutes
Servings: 8
Ingredients:
- 2 tablespoons Thai basil leaves, fresh, sliced thinly
- 1 tablespoon butter
- 2 Garlic cloves, minced
- 15 oz. Ricotta cheese, part-skim
- 48 Wonton wrappers, square
- 4 Green onion greens & whites, separated, sliced thinly
- 1 tbsp. Fish sauce
- 1 tbsp. Parmesan cheese, shredded
- 1 tbsp. Sesame oil, toasted
- 1-pound ground pork
- 1 tbsp. Ginger root, fresh, minced
- 15 oz. Tomato sauce
- 1 tbsp. Chili garlic sauce
- ½ cup Coconut milk

Directions:
1. Preheat the air fryer at 325 degrees Fahrenheit. Mist cooking sprays onto a baking dish.
2. In a skillet heated on medium, cook pork in butter and sesame oil for 8 to 10 minutes. Stir in garlic, green onion whites, and ginger root and cook for 1 to 2 minutes.
3. Stir in fish sauce, chili garlic sauce, and tomato sauce. Cook on a gentle simmer. Combine coconut milk, ricotta cheese, and 1 cup Parmesan cheese.
4. Arrange 8 overlapping wonton wrappers in a baking dish to line bottom, then top with a second layer of eight wrappers. Spread on top 1/3 of cheese mixture, and layer with 1/3 of pork mixture. Repeat layering twice and finish by topping with Parmesan cheese.
5. Cover dish with foil and air-fry for 30 minutes. Remove foil and air-fry for another 10 to 15 minutes. Serve topped with basil and green onion greens.

205. Scrambled Basil and Potato

Preparation time: 15 minutes
Cooking time: 30 minutes
Servings: 4
Ingredients:
- 8 eggs, large, beaten
- ½ cup Onion, minced
- ½ tsp. Salt
- 2 White potatoes, medium, peeled, cubed
- 1 Red bell pepper, small, chopped
- 2 tbsp. basil leaves, fresh, chopped
- 1/8 tsp. red pepper, ground

Directions:
1. Warm air fryer at 350 degrees Fahrenheit. Put the potatoes in your saucepan filled with water and heat to boiling. Continue cooking, covered, on simmer for 10 to 15 minutes.
2. Drain and toss with bell pepper and onion in a baking dish. Coat with cooking spray and air-fry for 5 to 10 minutes. Combine all other ingredients and add them to the pan. Air-fry for 3 to 5 minutes. Serve right away.

206. Sweet Pea Wontons

Preparation Time: 20 minutes
Cooking time: 25 minutes
Servings: 40
Ingredients:
- 2 tbsp. Mint, fresh
- 8 oz. Cream cheese, soft
- 10 oz. sweet peas
- 1 Egg mixed + 2 tbsp. water to make the egg wash
- ½ tsp. Kosher salt
- 40 Wonton wrappers, square

Directions:
1. Preheat the air fryer at 350 degrees Fahrenheit. Use parchment to line a baking sheet. Mash sweet peas together with salt and mint.
2. Make the egg wash by whisking eggs with water. Fill each wonton wrapper with 1 teaspoon cream cheese and 1 teaspoon pea mixture, then fold up ends to form a triangle and seal by folding corners under. Brush egg wash on all filled wontons. Air-fry for 15 to 20 minutes. Serve.

207. Onion Bread Pudding

Preparation time: 15 minutes
Cooking time: 1 hour & 8 minutes
Servings: 12
Ingredients:
- 1 tsp. Thyme leaves, dried
- 2 Sweet onions, large, diced
- 4 Eggs
- 3 cups zucchini, shredded
- 1 tsp. salt
- 1 tbsp. Olive oil
- 1-pound Rustic bread, whole grain, cubed
- 2 cups Swiss cheese, shredded
- 2 cups milk
- ¼ tsp. Pepper

Directions:
1. Preheat the air fryer at 325 degrees Fahrenheit. In a skillet heated on medium-high, cook onions in oil for 20 to 25 minutes.
2. Mist cooking sprays into a baking dish. Fill with layered of 4 cups bread, 1 ½ cups zucchini, and ¾ cup cheese; repeat layering once.
3. Beat together all other ingredients and pour on top of bread mixture. Sprinkle with onions before covering with foil and air-frying for 30 to 40 minutes. Top with ½ cup cheese and air-fry for another 2 to 3 minutes. Serve.

208. Spicy Acorn Squash with Feta

Preparation time: 15 minutes
Cooking time: 20 minutes
Servings: 4
Ingredients:
- 2 small acorn squash (about 2 pounds), halved, seeded, and sliced (¾ inch thick)
- 1½ tablespoons olive oil
- ½ teaspoon smoked paprika
- 1/8 teaspoon ground red (cayenne) pepper
- ¼ teaspoon salt
- 3 fresh sage leaves, finely chopped
- ¼ cup crumbled feta cheese (about 1 ounce)

Directions:
1. Preheat air fryer to 380°F. In a large bowl, toss squash, oil, paprika, red pepper, and salt.
2. Place squash in the air fryer basket. Air-fry for 20 minutes, turning slices with tongs a few times, or until tender and lightly browned. Transfer squash to a serving platter; sprinkle with sage and feta.

209. Herb-Roasted Root Vegetables

Preparation time: 15 minutes
Cooking time: 35 minutes
Servings: 4
Ingredients:
- 1-pound mixed baby potatoes, cut into halves
- ½ pound thin baby carrots (halved, if large)
- 4 large radishes, trimmed, cut into halves
- 2 tablespoons olive oil
- ½ teaspoon salt
- ¼ teaspoon pepper
- 1 tablespoon chopped fresh thyme
- 2 tablespoons chopped fresh parsley

Directions:
1. Preheat air fryer to 350°F.
2. Mix potatoes, carrots, and radishes with 1 tablespoon oil, salt, and pepper in a large bowl. Place coated vegetables in basket and air-fry for 20 minutes.
3. Place air fried vegetables back in the bowl and toss with the remaining tablespoon of oil and the thyme. Return to the basket and air-fry until golden brown and tender, 15 minutes more, shaking basket. Sprinkle with parsley and serve.

210. Crispy Roasted Potatoes with Caper Vinaigrette

Preparation time: 15 minutes
Cooking time: 26 minutes
Servings: 4
Ingredients:
- 1¼ pounds Yukon gold potatoes, unpeeled, cut into 1-inch chunks
- ¾ pound sweet potatoes, unpeeled, cut into 1-inch chunks
- 1 tablespoon salt, plus ¼ teaspoon
- 3 tablespoons olive oil
- 2 tablespoons flat-leaf parsley leaves, chopped
- 2 tablespoons sherry vinegar
- 1½ tablespoons capers, drained and chopped
- 1½ teaspoons anchovy paste
- ½ clove garlic, crushed with press

Directions:
1. In a 4- to 5-quart saucepot, cover Yukon gold and sweet potatoes with cold water. Stir in 1 tablespoon salt. Partially cover, then heat to boiling on high. Reduce heat to maintain a simmer; cook 6 minutes, stirring occasionally. Drain well; return to pot.
2. Potatoes can be parboiled and kept at room temperature up to 2 hours before air frying. Preheat air fryer to 390°F. Vigorously toss potatoes with 2 tablespoons oil.
3. Place potatoes in the air fryer basket. Air-fry for 20 minutes, shaking the basket occasionally until potatoes are browned and crisp.
4. Meanwhile, in a large bowl, whisk parsley, vinegar, capers, anchovy paste, garlic, remaining 1 tablespoon oil, and ¼ teaspoon salt. Toss potatoes with vinaigrette until well coated. Serve at once while crispy and hot.

211. Roasted Beet & Pistachio Salad

Preparation time: 15 minutes
Cooking time: 30 minutes
Servings: 4
Ingredients:
- 2 medium-size beets (about 6 ounces each)
- 2 tablespoons shelled, unsalted pistachios
- 1 tablespoon balsamic vinegar
- ½ teaspoon Dijon mustard
- 1/8 teaspoon salt
- 1/8 teaspoon pepper
- 2 tablespoons extra-virgin olive oil
- 8 cups lightly packed baby greens and herbs mix (about 4 ounces)
- 3 tablespoons crumbled blue cheese
- 2 tablespoons packed fresh mint leaves

Directions:
1. Peel beets and cut into ½-inch chunks. Pile beets on a doubled sheet of foil and wrap to enclose tightly.
2. Preheat air fryer to 390°F. Place foil-wrapped beets in basket and air-fry for 25 to 30 minutes, or until tender. Carefully open the foil and let beets cool. Place pistachios in the basket and air-fry for 1 minute, or until toasted; let cool.
3. Prepare dressing, in a small bowl, with a fork or a wire whisk, mix vinegar, mustard, salt, and pepper until blended. In a thin, steady stream, whisk in olive oil until blended.
4. In a medium-size bowl, combine beets and 2 teaspoons dressing. Mix greens with remaining dressing in a large serving bowl. Top with blue cheese, pistachios, and beets. Tear mint leaves over salad.

212. Roasted Sweet & Sour Brussels Sprouts
Preparation time: 15 minutes
Cooking time: 22 minutes
Servings: 4
Ingredients:
- 1-pound Brussels sprouts, trimmed and halved
- 1 tablespoon olive oil
- 2 tablespoons low-sodium soy sauce
- 2 tablespoons balsamic vinegar
- 1 tablespoon brown sugar
- ¼ teaspoon ground ginger
- 1/8 teaspoon pepper
- 2 tablespoons loosely packed fresh parsley leaves, finely chopped

Directions:
1. Toss together Brussels sprouts, oil, and 3 tablespoons water.
2. Preheat air fryer to 350°F. Line air fryer basket with a piece of foil cut to fit. Add Brussels sprouts to the basket. Air-fry for 15 to 20 minutes, tossing a few times, until tender and browned.
3. Meanwhile, in a 2-cup glass measuring cup, combine soy sauce, vinegar, brown sugar, ginger, and pepper. Microwave on High, 2 to 2½ minutes, or until syrupy.
4. Toss sprouts with parsley and enough sauce to coat. Serve the remaining sauce on the side.

213. Chimichurri Cauliflower "Steaks"
Preparation time: 15 minutes
Cooking time: 16 minutes
Servings: 4
Ingredients:
- 1 large head cauliflower (about 2 pounds)
- 1 teaspoon ground cumin
- 3 tablespoons canola oil
- 3/8 teaspoon salt
- ¼ cup loosely packed cilantro, finely chopped
- ¼ cup loosely packed parsley, finely chopped
- 3 tablespoons red wine vinegar
- 1 small clove garlic, crushed with press
- 1 jalapeño, seeded and finely chopped

Directions:
1. Quarter the cauliflower and slice into ¾-inch slabs. Combine cumin, 1 tablespoon oil, and ¼ teaspoon salt in a large bowl. Toss in cauliflower until evenly coated.
2. Preheat air fryer to 390°F. Place cauliflower in basket and air-fry until tender and browned, 16 minutes, shaking basket twice during cooking.
3. Meanwhile, stir together cilantro, parsley, vinegar, garlic, jalapeño, remaining 2 tablespoons oil, and 1/8 teaspoon salt. Serve cauliflower with herb sauce.

214. Spice-Roasted Carrots
Preparation time: 15 minutes
Cooking time: 15 minutes
Servings: 4
Ingredients:
- 6 carrots (about 1¼ pounds), peeled, halved crosswise and lengthwise
- 1 tablespoon olive oil
- 1 tablespoon packed fresh oregano leaves, chopped
- ½ teaspoon smoked paprika
- ¼ teaspoon ground nutmeg
- ¼ teaspoon salt
- 1/8 teaspoon pepper
- 1 tablespoon butter, melted
- 1 tablespoon red wine vinegar
- 2 tablespoons roasted, salted, shelled pistachios, chopped

Directions:
1. Toss together carrots, oil, oregano, paprika, nutmeg, salt, and pepper. Preheat air fryer to 370°F. Place carrots in the air fryer basket. Air-fry for 15 minutes, tossing a few times, until lightly browned and tender. Transfer to a serving platter. Drizzle with butter and vinegar, and sprinkle with pistachios.

215. Summer Veggie Roast
Preparation time: 15 minutes
Cooking time: 25 minutes
Servings: 4
Ingredients:
- 1 medium zucchini, cut into ½-inch-thick slices
- 1 medium yellow or summer squash, halved lengthwise and cut into ½-inch-thick slices
- 1 large orange or red pepper, slice into 1-inch pieces
- ½ red onion, cut into thin wedges through root end
- 1 tablespoon olive oil
- ¼ teaspoon salt
- 2 ears corn, kernels cut from cobs
- ½ cup grape tomatoes halved
- ¼ cup packed fresh basil leaves, chopped
- 1 tablespoon butter

Directions:
1. Toss together zucchini, yellow squash, orange pepper, onion, olive oil, and salt.
2. Preheat air fryer to 380°F. Place vegetables in a basket. Air-fry for 15 minutes, tossing once. Stir in corn and tomatoes.
3. Air-fry for 8 to 10 minutes more, tossing once, or until vegetables are tender. Place vegetables in a serving bowl and stir in basil and butter.

216. Corn on the Cob
Preparation time: 15 minutes
Cooking time: 12 minutes
Servings: 4
Ingredients:
- 4 ears corn on the cob, shucked

Directions:
1. Preheat air fryer to 375°F. Trim corn, if needed, to fit air fryer and place in the basket. Air-fry 12 minutes, or until tender, turning over with tongs halfway through.

217. Twice-Baked Herb-Stuffed Potatoes
Preparation time: 15 minutes
Cooking time: 28 minutes
Servings: 6
Ingredients:
- 3 large russet potatoes (2¾ pounds), well-scrubbed
- 1 medium shallot
- ¼ cup packed fresh basil leaves
- 4 tablespoons Parmesan cheese
- 2 tablespoons butter
- ¼ teaspoon dried marjoram
- ½ teaspoon salt
- ½ teaspoon freshly ground black pepper
- 2 tablespoons low-fat sour cream
- 1/3 cup 2% milk

Directions:
1. Pierce each potato 3 times using a fork; place on a sheet of parchment paper in the microwave. Microwave on High for 15 minutes, or until tender, turning once. Cover with a kitchen towel; let cool.
2. Meanwhile, finely chop shallots and basil. Grate Parmesan. Combine butter and shallots in a small bowl, cover with plastic. Microwave on High for 1½ minutes, until shallots are softened. Place in a large bowl with marjoram, basil, 3 tablespoons Parmesan, salt, and pepper.
3. Cut potatoes crosswise in half. Trim off the rounded ends so that potatoes stand upright. With a spoon, scoop out potato flesh, leaving a ¼-inch shell; place the flesh in a bowl. Add sour cream and milk, mash well. Spoon mixture into shells. Top with remaining 1 tablespoon Parmesan.
4. Preheat air fryer to 375°F. Place potatoes in the basket using tongs, and air-fry until golden brown and heated through, 12 minutes.

Chapter 7. Poultry

218. Chicken Tenders
Preparation Time: 10 minutes
Cooking Time: 10 minutes
Serving: 3
Ingredients:
- 1 egg
- 1 lb. chicken breast, boneless & cut into strips
- 1 tsp. garlic powder
- 2 tsp. Italian seasoning
- 1/3 cup pecans, chopped
- 2/3 cup almond flour
- 1 tbsp. water
- 1/2 tsp. sea salt

Directions:
1. Mix egg plus 1 tablespoon of water in a small bowl. In a shallow bowl, mix almond flour, pecans, Italian seasoning, garlic powder, and salt. Dip each chicken strip in egg, then coat with almond flour mixture.
2. Place the cooking tray in the air fryer basket. Air fry to 10 minutes and temperature 350 F.
3. Once the temperature is reached, then place coated chicken strips in the air fryer basket. Turn chicken strips halfway through. Serve and enjoy.

219. Sweet & Tangy Chicken
Preparation Time: 10 minutes
Cooking Time: 15 minutes
Servings: 3
Ingredients:
- 1 lb. chicken breast, boneless and cut into bite-size pieces
- 1 tbsp. sesame seeds, toasted
- 2 garlic cloves, minced
- 1 tsp. fresh ginger, chopped
- 1 tsp. orange zest, grated
- 2 tbsp. orange juice
- 1 tbsp. sesame oil
- 2 tbsp. vinegar
- 1/4 cup coconut amino
- 1 tsp. garlic powder
- 3 1/2 tbsp. arrowroot

Directions:
1. Toss chicken with 3 tablespoons of arrowroot and garlic powder. Place the cooking tray in the air fryer basket.
2. Set temperature 370 F. Put chicken pieces in the air fryer basket. Spray chicken pieces with cooking spray. Air fry for 12 minutes. Toss chicken halfway through.
3. Meanwhile, in a small saucepan, for sauce, whisk together vinegar, garlic, ginger, orange zest, sesame oil, orange juice, and coconut aminos.
4. Whisk in remaining arrowroot and cook over medium heat until sauce thicken. Remove from heat. Once the chicken is done, toss in a mixing bowl with sauce. Sprinkle with sesame seeds and serve.

220. Parmesan Chicken Breast
Preparation Time: 10 minutes
Cooking Time: 14 minutes
Servings: 4
Ingredients:
- 2 eggs, lightly beaten
- 1 lb. chicken breast, skinless & boneless
- 1 cup parmesan cheese, grated
- 1/2 cup almond flour
- 1/2 tsp. garlic powder
- 1 tsp. Italian seasoning
- Pepper
- Salt

Directions:
1. Beat eggs in a shallow bowl. In a separate shallow dish, mix parmesan cheese, Italian seasoning, garlic powder, almond flour, pepper, and salt.
2. Dip chicken breast into the egg mixture and coat with parmesan cheese mixture. Place the cooking tray in the air fryer basket.
3. Set temperature 360 F. Place coated chicken breasts in the air fryer basket, then air fry for 12 minutes. Serve and enjoy.

221. Garlic Herb Turkey Breast
Preparation Time: 10 minutes
Cooking Time: 40 minutes
Servings: 6
Ingredients:

- 3 lbs. turkey breast, boneless & thawed
- 2 garlic cloves, minced
- 1 tbsp. fresh parsley, chopped
- 1 tbsp. fresh rosemary, chopped
- 1 tsp. pepper
- 1 tsp. salt

Directions:
1. Mix garlic, parsley, rosemary, pepper, and salt in a small bowl and rub all over turkey breast. Place the cooking tray in the air fryer basket. Set temperature at 350 F.
2. Place turkey breast in the air fryer basket, then air fry for 40 minutes. Remove turkey breast from the air fryer and let it cool for 10 minutes. Slice and serve.

222. Simple & Juicy Chicken Breasts

Preparation Time: 10 minutes
Cooking Time: 30 minutes
Servings: 2
Ingredients:
- 2 chicken breasts, skinless & boneless
- 1/2 tsp. garlic powder
- 1 tbsp. olive oil
- 1/4 tsp. pepper
- 1/2 tsp. salt

Directions:
1. Massage chicken breasts with oil and season with garlic powder, pepper, and salt. Place the cooking tray in the air fryer basket. Set to and temperature at 360 F.
2. Place chicken breasts in the air fryer basket, then air fry for 30 minutes. Turn chicken after 20 minutes. Serve and enjoy.

223. Cauliflower Chicken Casserole

Preparation Time: 10 minutes
Cooking Time: 30 minutes
Servings: 4
Ingredients:
- 1 lb. cooked chicken, shredded
- 4 oz. cream cheese, softened
- 4 cups cauliflower florets
- 1/8 tsp. black pepper
- 1/4 cup Greek yogurt
- 1 cup cheddar cheese, shredded
- 1/2 cup salsa
- 1/2 tsp. kosher salt

Directions:
1. Put cauliflower florets into the baking dish, then microwave for 10 minutes. Add cream cheese and microwave for 30 seconds more. Mix well. Add chicken, yogurt, cheddar cheese, salsa, pepper, and salt, and stir everything well.
2. Set the air fryer at temperature 375 F. Place the baking dish in the air fryer basket, then bake for 20 minutes. Serve and enjoy.

224. Greek Chicken

Preparation Time: 10 minutes
Cooking Time: 30 minutes
Servings: 4
Ingredients:
- 1 lb. chicken breasts, skinless & boneless

For marinade:
- 1 tsp. onion powder
- 1/4 tsp. basil
- 1/4 tsp. oregano
- 3 garlic cloves, minced
- 1 tbsp. lemon juice
- 3 tbsp. olive oil
- 1/2 tsp. dill
- 1/4 tsp. pepper
- 1/2 tsp. salt

Directions:
1. Add all marinade ingredients into the bowl and mix well. Add chicken into the marinade and coat well. Cover and place in the refrigerator overnight. Arrange marinated chicken into the baking dish. Cover dish with foil.
2. Set the air fryer at 400 F. Place baking dish in the air fryer basket, then bake for 30 minutes. Serve and enjoy.

225. Baked Chicken Breast

Preparation Time: 10 minutes
Cooking Time: 25 minutes
Servings: 6
Ingredients:
- 6 chicken breasts, skinless & boneless
- 1/4 tsp. pepper
- 1/4 tsp. paprika
- 1 tsp. Italian seasoning
- 2 tbsp. olive oil
- 1/2 tsp. garlic salt

Directions:
1. Brush chicken with oil. Mix Italian seasoning, garlic salt, paprika, and pepper and rub all over the chicken. Arrange chicken breasts into the baking dish. Wrap dish with foil. Set the air fryer at 400 F, then bake for 25 minutes, then serve and enjoy.

226. Baked Chicken Thighs

Preparation Time: 10 minutes
Cooking Time: 35 minutes
Servings: 6
Ingredients:
- 6 chicken thighs
- 2 tsp. poultry seasoning
- 2 tbsp. olive oil
- Pepper
- Salt

Directions:
1. Brush chicken with oil and rub with poultry seasoning, pepper, and salt. Arrange chicken into the baking dish. Cover dish with foil. Set the air fryer at 400 F. Bake for 35 minutes. Serve and enjoy.

227. Tasty Chicken Wings

Preparation Time: 10 minutes

Cooking Time: 45 minutes
Serving: 6
Ingredients:
- 3 lbs. chicken wings
- 2 tbsp. olive oil
- 1/2 cup dry BBQ spice rub

Directions:
1. Massage chicken wings with olive oil and place in a large bowl. Add BBQ spice over chicken wings and toss well. Set the air fryer at 400 F. Bake for 45 minutes, serve and enjoy.

228. Italian Turkey Tenderloin
Preparation Time: 10 minutes
Cooking Time: 45 minutes
Servings: 4
Ingredients:
- 1 1/2 lbs. turkey breast tenderloin
- 1/2 tbsp. olive oil
- 1 tsp. Italian seasoning
- 1/4 tsp. pepper
- 1/2 tsp. salt

Directions:
1. Massage turkey tenderloin with olive oil and rub with Italian seasoning, pepper, and salt. Set the air fryer at 390 F. Place turkey tenderloin in the air fryer basket, then bake for 45 minutes. Serve and enjoy.

229. Pesto Parmesan Chicken
Preparation Time: 10 minutes
Cooking Time: 25 minutes
Servings: 4
Ingredients:
- 4 chicken breasts, skinless & boneless
- 1/2 cup Parmesan cheese, shredded
- 1/2 cup basil pesto
- Pepper
- Salt

Directions:
1. Flavor the chicken with pepper and salt and place it into the baking dish. Spread pesto on top of the chicken and sprinkle with shredded cheese. Set the air fryer at 400 F. Bake for 25 minutes, serve.

230. Lemon Chicken Breasts
Preparation Time: 10 minutes
Cooking Time: 30 minutes
Servings: 4
Ingredients:
- 4 chicken breasts, skinless and boneless
- 4 tsp. butter, sliced
- 1/2 tsp. paprika
- 1 tsp. garlic powder
- 1 tsp. lemon pepper seasoning
- 4 tsp. lemon juice
- Pepper
- Salt

Directions:
1. Flavor chicken with pepper and salt and place it into the baking dish. Pour lemon juice over chicken. Mix paprika, garlic powder, and lemon pepper seasoning and sprinkle over chicken. Add butter slices on top of the chicken. Set the air fryer at 350 F. Bake for 30 minutes, serve.

231. Spicy Chicken Wings
Preparation Time: 10 minutes
Cooking Time: 20 minutes
Servings: 4
Ingredients:
- 12 chicken wings
- 1 tbsp. chili powder
- 1/2 tbsp. baking powder
- 1 tsp. granulated garlic
- 1/2 tsp. sea salt

Directions:
1. Put the chicken wings into the large bowl and toss with the remaining ingredients. Set the air fryer at 400 F. Place chicken wings in the air fryer basket, then air fryer for 20 minutes, serve and enjoy.

232. Fajita Chicken
Preparation Time: 10 minutes
Cooking Time: 15 minutes
Servings: 4
Ingredients:
- 4 chicken breasts, make horizontal cuts on each piece
- 2 tbsp. fajita seasoning
- 2 tbsp. olive oil
- 1 onion, sliced
- 1 bell pepper, sliced

Directions:
1. Brush chicken with oil and season with fajita seasoning. Set the air fryer at 375 F. Put the chicken, onion, and bell pepper in the air fryer basket, then bake for 15 minutes. Serve and enjoy.

233. One-Dish Chicken & Rice
Preparation time: 15 minutes
Cooking time: 40 minutes
Servings: 4
Ingredients:
- 1 cup long-grain white rice
- 1 cup cut frozen green beans
- 1 tablespoon minced fresh ginger
- 3 cloves garlic, minced
- 1 tablespoon toasted sesame oil
- 1 teaspoon kosher salt
- 1 teaspoon black pepper
- 1 pound chicken wings

Directions:
1. In a 6 × 3-inch round heatproof pan, combine the rice, green beans, ginger, garlic, sesame oil, salt, and pepper. Stir to combine.
2. Place the chicken wings on top of the rice mixture. Cover the pan with foil. Make a long slash in the foil to allow the pan to vent steam.

3. Put the pan in the air fryer basket. Set the air fryer to 375 F to air fry for 30 minutes. Remove the foil. Set the air fryer to 400°F to air fry again for 10 minutes, or until the wings have browned and rendered fat into the rice and vegetables, turning the wings halfway through the cooking time. Serve.

234. Lebanese Turkey Burgers with Feta & Tzatziki

Preparation time: 15 minutes
Cooking time: 12 minutes
Servings: 4
Ingredients:
For the Tzatziki:
- 1 large cucumber, peeled and grated
- 2 to 3 cloves garlic, minced
- 1 cup plain Greek yogurt
- 1 tablespoon tahini (sesame paste)
- 1 tablespoon fresh lemon juice
- ½ teaspoon kosher salt

For the Burgers:
- 1-pound ground turkey, chicken, or lamb
- 1 small yellow onion, finely diced
- 1 clove garlic, minced
- 2 tablespoons chopped fresh parsley
- 2 teaspoons Lebanese Seven-Spice Mix
- ½ teaspoon kosher salt
- Vegetable oil spray

For Serving:
- 4 lettuce leaves or 2 whole-wheat pita bread, halved
- 8 slices ripe tomato
- 1 cup baby spinach
- 1/3 cup crumbled feta cheese

Directions:
1. For the tzatziki, in a medium bowl, stir together all the ingredients until well combined. Cover and chill until ready to serve.
2. For the burgers, mix the ground turkey, onion, garlic, parsley, spice mix, and salt in a large bowl. Mix gently until well combined. Divide the turkey into four portions and form into round patties.
3. Spray the air fryer basket using a vegetable oil spray. Put the patties in the air fryer basket. Set the air fryer to 400°F to air fry for 12 minutes. Place one burger in each lettuce leaf or pita half. Tuck in 2 tomato slices, spinach, cheese, and some tzatziki.

235. Sweet and Sour Chicken

Preparation time: 15 minutes
Cooking time: 20 minutes
Servings: 6
Ingredients:
- 3 Chicken Breasts, cubed
- 1/2 Cup Flour
- 1/2 Cup Cornstarch
- 2 Red Peppers, sliced
- 1 Onion, chopped
- 2 Carrots, julienned
- 3/4 Cup Sugar
- 2 tbsp. Cornstarch
- 1/3 Cup Vinegar
- 2/3 Cup Water
- 1/4 cup Soy sauce
- 1 tbsp. Ketchup

Directions:
1. Preheat the air fryer to 375 F. Combine the flour, cornstarch, and chicken in an airtight container and shake to combine. Remove chicken from the container and shake off any excess flour.
2. Add chicken to the Air Fryer tray and air fry for 20 minutes. In a saucepan, whisk together sugar, water, vinegar, soy sauce, and ketchup. Bring to a boil over medium heat, reduce the heat, then simmer for 2 minutes.
3. After cooking the chicken for 20 minutes, add the vegetables and sauce mixture to the Air fryer and air fry for another 5 minutes. Serve over hot rice.

236. Lemon Chicken Thighs

Preparation time: 15 minutes
Cooking time: 10 minutes
Servings: 4
Ingredients:
- 1 teaspoon salt
- 1 teaspoon freshly ground black pepper
- 2 tablespoons olive oil
- 2 tablespoons Italian seasoning
- 2 tablespoons freshly squeezed lemon juice
- 1 lemon, sliced

Directions:
1. Put the chicken thighs in a medium mixing bowl and season them with salt and pepper. Add the olive oil, Italian seasoning, and lemon juice and toss until the chicken thighs are thoroughly coated with oil. Add the sliced lemons.
2. Place the chicken thighs into the air fryer basket in a single layer. Set the air fryer to 350°F. Set the timer and air fry for 10 minutes.
3. Using tongs, flip the chicken. Reset the timer and air fry for 10 minutes more. Once the chicken is fully cooked, plate, serve and enjoy.

237. Southern Fried Chicken

Preparation time: 1 hour & 15 minutes
Cooking time: 26 minutes
Servings: 4
Ingredients:
- ½ cup buttermilk
- 2 teaspoons salt, plus 1 tablespoon
- 1 teaspoon freshly ground black pepper
- 1-pound chicken thighs and drumsticks
- 1 cup all-purpose flour
- 2 teaspoons onion powder
- 2 teaspoons garlic powder
- ½ teaspoon sweet paprika

Directions:

1. Mix the buttermilk, 2 teaspoons of salt, and pepper in a large mixing bowl. Add the chicken pieces to the bowl, and let the chicken marinate for at least an hour, covered, in the refrigerator. About 5 minutes before the chicken is done marinating, prepare the dredging mixture.
2. Mix the flour, 1 tablespoon of salt, onion powder, garlic powder, and paprika in a large mixing bowl. Oil the air fryer basket with olive oil.
3. Remove the chicken from the buttermilk mixture and dredge it in the flour mixture. Shake off any excess flour.
4. Place the chicken pieces into the greased air fryer basket in a single layer, leaving space between each piece. Spray the chicken generously with olive oil.
5. Set your air fryer to 390°F. Set the timer and air fry for 13 minutes. Using tongs, flip the chicken. Spray generously with olive oil. Reset the timer and air fry for 13 minutes more. Once the chicken is fully cooked, plate, serve, and enjoy!

238. Buffalo Chicken Wings

Preparation time: 15 minutes
Cooking time: 30 minutes
Servings: 8
Ingredients:
- 1 tsp.. salt
- 1-2 tbsp.. brown sugar
- 1 tbsp.. Worcestershire sauce
- ½ cup vegan butter
- ½ cup cayenne pepper sauce
- 4 pounds of chicken wings

Directions:
1. Mix salt, brown sugar, Worcestershire sauce, butter, plus hot sauce and set aside. Pat dry wings, then put to the air fryer basket.
2. Set temperature to 380°F and air fry to 25 minutes. Cook halfway through. Shake wings and adjust to 400 degrees, and air fry again for 5 minutes.
3. Take out wings and place them into a big bowl. Add sauce and toss well. Serve alongside celery sticks.

239. Chicken Parmesan with Provolone Cheese

Preparation time: 15 minutes
Cooking time: 25 minutes
Servings: 2
Ingredients:
- 2 large white meat chicken breasts
- 1 cup of breadcrumbs
- 2 medium-sized eggs
- Pinch of salt and pepper
- 1 tablespoon of dried oregano
- 1 cup of marinara sauce
- 2 slices of provolone cheese
- 1 tablespoon of parmesan cheese

Directions:
1. Wrap the basket of the Air fryer using a lining of tin foil, leaving the edges uncovered.
2. Preheat the air fryer to 350 degrees. Mix the eggs until the yolks and whites in a mixing bowl are thoroughly combined and set aside.
3. Mix the breadcrumbs, oregano, salt, and pepper in a separate mixing bowl and set aside. One by one, dip the raw chicken breasts into the bowl with dry ingredients, coating both sides.
4. Submerge into the bowl with wet ingredients, then dip again into the dry ingredients. This double coating will ensure an extra crisp-and-delicious air-fry. Lay the coated chicken breasts on the foil covering the Air fryer basket in a single flat layer.
5. Set to air fry for 10 minutes. Flip chicken over using tongs to ensure a full all-over fry. Air fry again to 320 degrees for another 10 minutes. While the chicken is cooking, pour half the marinara sauce into a 7-inch heat-safe pan.
6. After 15 minutes, when the air fryer shuts off, remove the fried chicken breasts using tongs and set in the marinara-covered pan.
7. Drizzle the rest of the marinara sauce over the fried chicken, then place the slices of provolone cheese atop both and sprinkle the parmesan cheese over the entire pan.
8. Air fry again to 350 degrees for 5 minutes. Remove the dish from the air fryer using tongs. The chicken will be perfectly crisped, and the cheese melted and lightly toasted. Serve while hot!

240. Zingy & Nutty Chicken Wings

Preparation time: 15 minutes
Cooking time: 18 minutes
Servings: 4
Ingredients:
- 1 tablespoon fish sauce
- 1 tablespoon fresh lemon juice
- 1 teaspoon sugar
- 12 chicken middle wings, cut into half
- 2 fresh lemongrass stalks, chopped finely
- ¼ cup unsalted cashews, crushed

Directions:
1. Mix fish sauce, lime juice plus sugar in a bowl, mix. Add wings ad coat with mixture generously. Refrigerate to marinate for about 1-2 hours.
2. Warm air fryer to 355 degrees F. In the Air fryer pan, place lemongrass stalks. Air fry for about 2-3 minutes. Remove the cashew mixture from Air fryer and transfer it into a bowl. Now, Set the air fryer to 390 degrees F.
3. Place the chicken wings in the air fryer pan. Air fry for about 13-15 minutes further. Transfer the wings into serving plates. Sprinkle with cashew mixture and serve.

241. Pesto-Cream Chicken with Cherry Tomatoes

Preparation time: 15 minutes
Cooking time: 15 minutes
Servings: 4
Ingredients:
- Vegetable oil spray

- ½ cup prepared pesto
- ¼ cup half-and-half
- ¼ grated Parmesan cheese
- ½ to 1 teaspoon red pepper flakes
- 1-pound boneless, skinless chicken thighs, halved crosswise
- 1 small onion, sliced
- ½cup sliced red or green bell peppers
- ½ cup halved cherry tomatoes

Directions:
1. Spray a 6 × 3-inch round heatproof pan with vegetable oil spray; set aside. In a large bowl, combine the pesto, half-and-half, cheese, and red pepper flakes.
2. Whisk until well combined. Add the chicken and turn to coat. Transfer the sauce and chicken to the prepared pan. Scatter the onion, bell pepper, and tomatoes on top. Put the pan in the air fryer basket. Set your air fryer to 350F to air fry for 15 minutes. Serve.

242. Peanut Chicken

Preparation time: 45 minutes
Cooking time: 20 minutes
Servings: 4
Ingredients:
- ¼ cup creamy peanut butter
- 2 tablespoons sweet chili sauce
- 2 tablespoons fresh lime juice
- 1 tablespoon sriracha
- 1 tablespoon soy sauce
- 1 teaspoon minced fresh ginger
- 1 clove garlic, minced
- ½ teaspoon kosher salt
- ½ cup hot water
- 1-pound bone-in chicken thighs
- 2 tablespoons chopped fresh cilantro, for garnish
- ¼ cup chopped green onions, for garnish
- 2 to 3 tablespoons crushed roasted and salted peanuts, for garnish

Directions:
1. In a small bowl, combine the peanut butter, sweet chili sauce, lime juice, sriracha, soy sauce, ginger, garlic, and salt. Add the hot water and whisk until smooth. Place the chicken in a resealable plastic bag and pour in half of the sauce.
2. Reserve the remaining sauce for serving. Seal the bag and massage until all the chicken is well coated. Marinate at room temperature for 30 minutes. Remove the chicken from the bag and discard the marinade.
3. Put the chicken in the air fryer basket. Set the air fryer to 350°F to air fry for 20 minutes. Transfer the chicken to a serving platter. Sprinkle with the cilantro, green onions, and peanuts. Serve with the reserved sauce for dipping.

243. Basil-Garlic Breaded Chicken Bake

Preparation time: 15 minutes
Cooking time: 25 minutes
Servings: 2
Ingredients:
- 2 boneless skinless chicken breast halves
- 1 tablespoon butter, melted
- 1 large tomato, seeded and chopped
- 2 garlic cloves, minced
- 1 1/2 tablespoons minced fresh basil
- 1/2 tablespoon olive oil
- 1/2 teaspoon salt
- 1/4 cup all-purpose flour
- 1/4 cup egg substitute
- 1/4 cup grated Parmesan cheese
- 1/4 cup dry bread crumbs
- 1/4 teaspoon pepper

Directions:
1. In a shallow bowl, whisk well egg substitute and place flour in a separate bowl. Put the chicken in flour, then egg, and then flour.
2. In a small bowl, whisk well butter, bread crumbs, and cheese. Sprinkle over chicken. Lightly grease the baking pan of the air fryer with cooking spray. Place breaded chicken on the bottom of the pan. Cover with foil.
3. Bake for 20 minutes at 390°F. Meanwhile, in a bowl, whisk well the remaining ingredient. Remove foil from pan and then pour over chicken the remaining ingredients. Bake for 8 minutes. Serve and enjoy.

244. Crispy Butter Chicken

Preparation time: 15 minutes
Cooking time: 14 minutes
Servings: 2
Ingredients:
- 2 (8-ounce) boneless, skinless chicken breasts
- 1 sleeve Ritz crackers
- 4 tablespoons (½ stick) cold unsalted butter, cut into 1-tablespoon slices

Directions:
1. Oiled the air fryer basket with olive oil or spray an air fryer–sized baking sheet with olive oil or cooking spray.
2. Dip the chicken breasts in water. Put the crackers in a resealable plastic bag. Using a mallet or your hands, crush the crackers. Place the chicken breasts inside the bag one at a time and coat them with the cracker crumbs.
3. Place the chicken in the greased air fryer basket or on the greased baking sheet set into the air fryer basket. Put 1 to 2 dabs of butter onto each piece of chicken. Set the temperature of your AF to 370°F. Set the timer and bake for 7 minutes.
4. Using tongs, flip the chicken. Spray the chicken generously with olive oil to avoid uncooked breading. Reset the timer and bake for 7 minutes

more. Using tongs, remove the chicken from the air fryer and serve.

245. South Indian Pepper Chicken

Preparation time: 45 minutes
Cooking time: 15 minutes
Servings: 4
Ingredients:
For the Spice Mix:
- 1 dried red chili or ½ teaspoon dried red pepper flakes
- 1-inch piece cinnamon or cassia bark
- 1½ teaspoons coriander seeds
- 1 teaspoon fennel seeds
- 1 teaspoon cumin seeds
- 1 teaspoon black peppercorns
- ½ teaspoon cardamom seeds
- ¼ teaspoon ground turmeric
- 1 teaspoon kosher salt

For the Chicken:
- 1 pound boneless, skinless chicken thighs, cut crosswise into thirds
- 2 medium onions, cut into ½-inch-thick slices
- ¼ cup olive oil
- Cauliflower rice, steamed rice, or naan bread, for serving

Directions:
1. For the spice mix, combine the dried chili, cinnamon, coriander, fennel, cumin, peppercorns, and cardamom in a clean coffee or spice grinder.
2. Grind, shaking the grinder lightly, so all the seeds and bits get into the blades until the mixture is broken down to a fine powder. Stir in the turmeric and salt.
3. For the chicken, place the chicken and onions in a resealable plastic bag. Add the oil and 1½ tablespoons of the spice mix.
4. Seal the bag and massage the chicken, marinate at room temperature for 30 minutes.
5. Place the chicken and onions in the air fryer basket. Set the air fryer at 350°F to air fry for 10 minutes, stirring once halfway through the cooking time.
6. Increase the temperature to 400°F to air fry for 5 minutes. Serve with steamed rice, cauliflower rice, or naan.

246. Honey and Wine Chicken Breasts

Preparation time: 15 minutes
Cooking time: 15 minutes
Servings: 4
Ingredients:
- 2 chicken breasts, rinsed and halved
- 1 tablespoon melted butter
- 1/2 tsp. ground pepper
- 3/4 tsp. sea salt
- 1 tsp. paprika
- 1 teaspoon dried rosemary
- 2 tablespoons dry white wine
- 1 tablespoon honey

Directions:
1. Firstly, pat the chicken breasts dry. Lightly coat them with the melted butter. Then, add the remaining ingredients. Transfer them to the air fryer basket; bake about 15 minutes at 330 degrees F. Serve warm and enjoy.

247. Roasted Veggie Chicken Salad

Preparation time: 10 minutes
Cooking time: 13 minutes
Servings: 4
Ingredients:
- 3 boneless chicken breasts, skinless, cut into 1-inch cubes
- 1 small red onion, sliced
- 1 orange bell pepper, sliced
- 1 cup sliced yellow summer squash
- 4 tablespoons of honey mustard salad dressing, divided
- ½ teaspoon dried thyme
- ½ cup mayonnaise
- 2 tablespoons lemon juice

Directions:
1. Place the chicken, onion, pepper, and squash in the air fryer basket. Drizzle with 1 tablespoon of the honey mustard salad dressing, add the thyme and toss.
2. Roast for 10 to 13 minutes or until the chicken is 165°F on a food thermometer, tossing the food once during cooking.
3. Put the chicken plus vegetables to a bowl and mix in the remaining 3 tablespoons of honey mustard salad dressing, the mayonnaise, and lemon juice. Serve on lettuce leaves, if desired.

248. Asian Turkey Meatballs

Preparation time: 10 minutes
Cooking time: 14 minutes
Servings: 4
Ingredients:
- 2 tablespoons peanut oil, divided
- 1 small onion, minced
- ¼ cup water chestnuts, finely chopped
- ½ teaspoon ground ginger
- 2 tablespoons low-sodium soy sauce
- ¼ cup panko bread crumbs
- 1 egg, beaten
- 1-pound ground turkey

Directions:
1. In a 6-by-6-by-2-inch pan, combine the peanut oil and onion. Air fry for 1 to 2 minutes or until crisp and tender. Transfer the onions to a medium bowl.
2. Add the water chestnuts, ground ginger, soy sauce, and bread crumbs to the onions and mix well. Add egg and stir well. Mix in the ground turkey until combined.
3. Form the mixture into 1-inch meatballs. Put the rest of the 1 tablespoon of oil over the meatballs. Bake the meatballs in the 6-by-6-by-2-inch pan in your air

fryer by batches for 10 to 12 minutes or until they are 165°F on a meat thermometer.

249. Stir-Fried Chicken with Pineapple
Preparation time: 10 minutes
Cooking time: 15 minutes
Servings: 4
Ingredients:
- 2 boneless, skinless chicken breasts
- 2 tablespoons cornstarch
- 1 egg white, lightly beaten
- 1 tablespoon olive or peanut oil
- 1 onion, sliced
- 1 red bell pepper, chopped
- 1 can pineapple tidbits, juice reserved
- 2 tablespoons reduced-sodium soy sauce

Directions:
1. Slice the chicken breasts into cubes, then put them into a medium bowl. Add the cornstarch and egg white and mix thoroughly. Set aside.
2. In a 6-inch metal bowl, combine the oil and the onion. Air fry in the air fryer for 2 to 3 minutes or until the onion is crisp and tender.
3. Drain the chicken and add to the bowl with the onions; stir well. Air fry for 7 to 9 minutes or until the chicken is thoroughly cooked to 165°F.
4. Stir the chicken mixture, then add the pepper, pineapple tidbits, 3 tablespoons of the reserved pineapple liquid, and the soy sauce, and stir again. Air fry for 2 to 3 minutes or until the food is cooked, and the sauce is slightly thickened.

250. Sweet and Sour Drumsticks
Preparation time: 5 minutes
Cooking time: 25 minutes
Servings: 4
Ingredients:
- 6 chicken drumsticks
- 3 tablespoons lemon juice, divided
- 3 tablespoons low-sodium soy sauce, divided
- 1 tablespoon peanut oil
- 3 tablespoons honey
- 3 tablespoons brown sugar
- 2 tablespoons ketchup
- ¼ cup pineapple juice

Directions:
1. Sprinkle the drumsticks with 1 tablespoon of lemon juice and 1 tablespoon of soy sauce. Place in the air fryer basket and drizzle with the peanut oil. Toss to coat. Bake for 18 minutes or until the chicken is almost done.
2. Meanwhile, in a 6-inch bowl, combine the remaining 2 tablespoons of lemon juice, the remaining 2 tablespoons of soy sauce, honey, brown sugar, ketchup, and pineapple juice.
3. Put the cooked chicken in the bowl and stir to coat the chicken well with the sauce. Place the metal bowl in the basket. Bake for 5 to 7 minutes or until the chicken is glazed and registers 165°F on a meat thermometer.

251. Chicken Satay
Preparation time: 12 minutes
Cooking time: 18 minutes
Servings: 4
Ingredients:
- ½ cup crunchy peanut butter
- 1/3 cup chicken broth
- 3 tablespoons low-sodium soy sauce
- 2 tablespoons lemon juice
- 2 cloves garlic, minced
- 2 tablespoons olive oil
- 1 teaspoon curry powder
- 1-pound chicken tenders

Directions:
1. Mix the peanut butter, chicken broth, soy sauce, lemon juice, garlic, olive oil, and curry powder in a medium bowl, and mix well with a wire whisk until smooth.
2. Remove 2 tablespoons of this batter to a small bowl. Put the remaining sauce into a serving bowl and set aside.
3. Add the chicken tenders to the bowl with the 2 tablespoons sauce and stir to coat. Let stand for a few minutes to marinate, then run a bamboo skewer through each chicken tender lengthwise.
4. Put the chicken in your air fryer basket, then grill in batches for 6 to 9 minutes or until the chicken reaches 165°F on a meat thermometer. Serve the chicken with the reserved sauce.

252. Orange Curried Chicken Stir-Fry
Preparation time: 10 minutes
Cooking time: 19 minutes
Servings: 4
Ingredients:
- ¾ pound chicken thighs, cut into 1-inch pieces
- 1 yellow bell pepper, cut into 1½-inch pieces
- 1 small red onion, sliced
- Olive oil for misting
- ¼ cup chicken stock
- 2 tablespoons honey
- ¼ cup of orange juice
- 1 tablespoon cornstarch
- 2 to 3 teaspoons curry powder

Directions:
1. Put the chicken thighs, pepper, and red onion in the air fryer basket and mist with olive oil.
2. Air fry for 12 to 14 minutes or until the chicken is cooked to 165°F, shaking the basket halfway through cooking time. Remove the chicken and vegetables from the air fryer basket and set aside.
3. In a 6-inch metal bowl, combine the stock, honey, orange juice, cornstarch, curry powder, and mix well. Add the chicken and vegetables, stir, and put the bowl in the basket.

4. Return the basket to the air fryer and air fry for 2 minutes. Remove and stir, then air fry for 2 to 3 minutes or until the sauce is thickened and bubbly.

253. Tex-Mex Turkey Burgers

Preparation time: 10 minutes
Cooking time: 16 minutes
Servings: 4
Ingredients:
- 1/3 cup finely crushed corn tortilla chips
- 1 egg, beaten
- ¼ cup of salsa
- 1/3 cup shredded pepper Jack cheese
- Pinch salt
- Freshly ground black pepper
- 1-pound ground turkey
- 1 tablespoon olive oil
- 1 teaspoon paprika

Directions:
1. In a medium bowl, combine the tortilla chips, egg, salsa, cheese, salt, pepper, and mix well. Add the turkey and mix gently but thoroughly with clean hands.
2. Form the meat mixture into patties about ½ inch thick. Make an indentation in the center of each patty with your thumb, so the burgers don't puff up while cooking.
3. Brush the patties on both sides with the olive oil and sprinkle with paprika. Put in the air fryer basket. Grill for 14 to 16 minutes or until the meat registers at least 165°F.

254. Barbecued Chicken Thighs

Preparation time: 10 minutes
Cooking time: 18 minutes
Servings: 4
Ingredients:
- 6 boneless, skinless chicken thighs
- ¼ cup store-bought gluten-free barbecue sauce
- 2 cloves garlic, minced
- 2 tablespoons lemon juice

Directions:
1. Mix the chicken, barbecue sauce, cloves, and lemon juice in a medium bowl. Let marinate for 10 minutes.
2. Remove the chicken thighs from the bowl and shake off excess sauce. Put the chicken pieces in the air fryer, leaving a bit of space between each one. Grill for 15 to 18 minutes or until the chicken is 165°F on an instant-read meat thermometer.

255. Garlic-Roasted Chicken with Creamer Potatoes

Preparation time: 10 minutes
Cooking time: 25 minutes
Servings: 4
Ingredients:
- 1 (2½- to 3-pound) broiler-fryer whole chicken
- 2 tablespoons olive oil
- ½ teaspoon garlic salt
- 8 cloves garlic, peeled
- 1 slice lemon
- ½ teaspoon dried thyme
- ½ teaspoon dried marjoram
- 12 to 16 creamer potatoes, scrubbed

Directions:
1. Do not wash the chicken before cooking. Remove it from its packaging and pat the chicken dry. Combine the olive oil and salt in a small bowl.
2. Rub half of this mixture on the inside of the chicken, under the skin, and on the chicken skin. Place the garlic cloves and lemon slice inside the chicken. Sprinkle the chicken with the thyme and marjoram.
3. Put the chicken in the air fryer basket. Surround with the potatoes and drizzle the potatoes with the remaining olive oil mixture.
4. Roast for 25 minutes, then test the temperature of the chicken. It should be 160°F. Test at the thickest part of the breast, making sure the probe doesn't touch bone.
5. When the chicken is done, transfer it and the potatoes to a serving platter and cover with foil. Let the chicken rest for 5 minutes before serving.

256. Ham and Cheese Stuffed Chicken Burgers

Preparation time: 12 minutes
Cooking time: 16 minutes
Servings: 4
Ingredients:
- 1/3 cup soft bread crumbs
- 3 tablespoons milk
- 1 egg, beaten
- ½ teaspoon dried thyme
- Pinch salt
- Freshly ground black pepper
- 1¼ pounds ground chicken
- ¼ cup finely chopped ham
- 1/3 cup grated Havarti cheese
- Olive oil for misting

Directions:
1. Mix the bread crumbs, milk, egg, thyme, salt, and pepper in a medium bowl. Add the chicken and mix gently but thoroughly with clean hands.
2. Form the chicken into eight thin patties and place on waxed paper. Top four of the patties with the ham and cheese. Top with the remaining four patties and gently press the edges together to seal, so the ham and cheese mixture is in the middle of the burger.
3. Place the burgers in the basket and mist with olive oil. Grill in your air fryer for 13 to 16 minutes or until the chicken is thoroughly cooked to 165°F as measured with a meat thermometer.

257. Mustard Chicken Tenders

Preparation time: 5 minutes
Cooking time: 20 minutes
Servings: 4
Ingredients:
- ½ cup coconut flour
- 1 tbsp.. spicy brown mustard

- 2 beaten eggs
- 1 pound of chicken tenders

Directions:
1. Season tenders with pepper and salt. Place a thin layer of mustard onto tenders and then dredge in flour and dip in egg. Add to the Air Fryer, then Air Fry at 390°F, and set timer to 20 minutes. Serve.

258. Almond Flour Coco-Milk Battered Chicken

Preparation time: 5 minutes
Cooking time: 30 minutes
Servings: 4
Ingredients:
- ¼ cup of coconut milk
- ½ cup almond flour
- 1 ½ tablespoon old bay Cajun seasoning
- 1 egg, beaten
- 4 small chicken thighs
- Salt and pepper to taste

Directions:
1. Preheat the air fryer for 5 minutes. Mix the egg and coconut milk in a bowl. Soak the chicken thighs in the beaten egg mixture. In a mixing bowl, combine the almond flour, Cajun seasoning, salt, and pepper.
2. Dredge the chicken thighs in the almond flour mixture. Place in the Air Fryer basket. Set to Air Fry and cook for 30 minutes at 350°F. Serve.

259. Ricotta and Parsley Stuffed Turkey Breasts

Preparation time: 5 minutes
Cooking time: 25 minutes
Servings: 4
Ingredients:
- 1 turkey breast, quartered
- 1 cup Ricotta cheese
- 1/4 cup fresh Italian parsley, chopped
- 1 teaspoon garlic powder
- 1/2 teaspoon cumin powder
- 1 egg, beaten
- 1 teaspoon paprika
- Salt and ground black pepper, to taste
- Crushed tortilla chips
- 1 ½ tablespoon extra-virgin olive oil

Directions:
1. Firstly, flatten out each piece of turkey breast with a rolling pin. Prepare three mixing bowls. In a shallow bowl, combine Ricotta cheese with the parsley, garlic powder, and cumin powder.
2. Place the Ricotta/parsley mixture in the middle of each piece. Repeat with the remaining pieces of the turkey breast and roll them up.
3. In another shallow bowl, whisk the egg together with paprika. In the third shallow bowl, combine the salt, pepper, and crushed tortilla chips. Dip each roll in the whisked egg, then roll them over the tortilla chips mixture.
4. Transfer prepared rolls to the Air Fryer basket. Drizzle olive oil overall. Air Fry at 350 degrees F and cook for 25 minutes, working in batches. Serve warm.

260. Bacon Lovers' Stuffed Chicken

Preparation time: 10 minutes
Cooking time: 20 minutes
Servings: 4
Ingredients:
- 4 (5-ounce) boneless, skinless chicken breasts, pounded to ¼ inch thick
- 2 packages Boursin cheese
- 8 slices thin-cut bacon or beef bacon
- A sprig of fresh cilantro, for garnish

Directions:
1. Oiled the Air Fryer basket with avocado oil. Preheat the air fryer to 400°F.
2. Put one of the chicken breasts on a cutting board. With a sharp knife held parallel to the cutting board, make a 1-inch-wide incision at the top of the breast.
3. Carefully cut into the breast to form a large pocket, leaving a ½-inch border along the sides and bottom. Repeat with the other 3 chicken breasts. Snip the corner of a large resealable plastic bag to form a ¾-inch hole.
4. Place the Boursin cheese in the bag and pipe the cheese into the chicken breasts' pockets, dividing the cheese evenly among them. Wrap 2 slices of bacon around each chicken breast and secure the ends with toothpicks.
5. Place the bacon-wrapped chicken in your Air Fryer basket. Air Fry at 400°F and cook until the bacon is crisp, and the chicken's internal temperature reaches 165°F, about 18 to 20 minutes, flipping after 10 minutes. Garnish with a sprig of cilantro before serving, if desired.

261. Crusted Chicken Tenders

Preparation time: 5 minutes
Cooking time: 15 minutes
Servings: 3
Ingredients:
- ½ cup all-purpose flour
- 2 eggs, beaten
- ½ cup seasoned breadcrumbs
- Salt
- Ground black pepper
- 2 tablespoons olive oil
- ¾ pound chicken tenders

Directions:
1. In a bowl, place the flour. In a second bowl, place the eggs. In a third bowl, mix breadcrumbs, salt, black pepper, and oil. Coat the chicken tenders in the flour, then dip into the eggs, and finally coat with the bread crumbs mixture evenly.
2. Preheat the Air fryer to 330 degrees F. Arrange the chicken tenderloins in the Air fryer basket. Air Fry at 330°F for about 10 minutes. Now, set the Air fryer to 390 degrees F. Air fry for about 5 minutes further. Serve.

262. Harissa-Rubbed Cornish Game Hens

Preparation time: 40 minutes
Cooking time: 20 minutes
Servings: 4
Ingredients:
For the Harissa:
- ½ cup olive oil
- 6 cloves garlic, minced
- 2 tablespoons smoked paprika
- 1 tablespoon ground coriander
- 1 tablespoon ground cumin
- 1 teaspoon ground caraway
- 1 teaspoon kosher salt
- ½ to 1 teaspoon cayenne pepper

For the Hens:
- ½ cup yogurt
- Cornish game hens, any giblets removed, split in half lengthwise

Directions:
1. For the harissa, in a medium microwave-safe bowl, combine the oil, garlic, paprika, coriander, cumin, caraway, salt, and cayenne. Microwave on high for 1 minute, stirring halfway through the cooking time.
2. For the hens, in a small bowl, combine 1 to 2 tablespoons harissa and the yogurt. Whisk until well combined. Place the hen halves in a resealable plastic bag and pour the marinade over.
3. Seal the bag and massage until all the pieces are thoroughly coated. Marinate at room temperature for 30 minutes.
4. Arrange the hen halves in a single layer in the Air Fryer basket. Air Fry at 400°F for 20 minutes. Use a meat thermometer to ensure the game hens have reached an internal temperature.

263. Parmesan Chicken Tenders

Preparation time: 5 minutes
Cooking time: 8 minutes
Servings: 4
Ingredients:
- 1-pound chicken tenderloins
- 3 large egg whites
- ½ cup Italian-style bread crumbs
- ¼ cup grated Parmesan cheese

Directions:
1. Oil the Air Fryer basket with olive oil. Trim off any white fat from the chicken tenders. In a small bowl, beat the egg whites until frothy.
2. In a separate small mixing bowl, combine the bread crumbs and Parmesan cheese. Mix well. Dip the chicken tenders into the egg mixture, then into the Parmesan and bread crumbs. Shake off any excess breading.
3. Place the chicken tenders in the greased Air Fryer basket in a single layer. Generously spray the chicken with olive oil to avoid powdery, uncooked breading.
4. Bake at 370°F for 4 minutes. Using tongs, flip the chicken tenders and bake for 4 minutes more. Serve, and enjoy.

264. Grilled Chicken Fajitas

Preparation time: 10 minutes
Cooking time: 14 minutes
Servings: 4
Ingredients:
- 1-pound chicken tenders
- 1 onion, sliced
- 1 yellow bell pepper, diced
- 1 red bell pepper, diced
- 1 orange bell pepper, diced
- 2 tablespoons olive oil
- 1 tablespoon fajita seasoning mix

Directions:
1. Slice the chicken into thin strips. Mix the chicken, onion, and peppers in a large mixing bowl. Add the olive oil and fajita seasoning and mix well so that the chicken and vegetables are thoroughly covered with oil.
2. Place the chicken and vegetable mixture into the Air Fryer basket in a single layer. Grill at 350°F for 7 minutes. Shake the air fryer basket and use tongs to flip the chicken.
3. Reset the timer and grill for 7 minutes more, or until the chicken is cooked through and the juices run clear. Once the chicken is fully cooked, transfer it to a platter and serve.

265. Thai Basil Chicken

Preparation time: 5 minutes
Cooking time: 25 minutes
Servings: 4
Ingredients:
- 4 chicken breasts
- 1 onion
- 2 bell peppers
- 2 hot peppers
- 1 tbsp. olive oil
- 3 tbsp. fish sauce
- 2 tbsp. oyster sauce
- 3 tbsp. sweet chili sauce
- 1 tbsp. soy sauce
- 1-quart chicken broth
- 1 tbsp. garlic powder
- 1 tbsp. chili powder
- 1 cup Thai basil

Directions:
1. Wash the breasts and boil them in the chicken broth for 10 minutes, then lower to simmer for another 10 minutes until tender. Take them out of the broth and allow it to cool.
2. Using two forks, tear the chicken into shreds. Toss the shreds with the garlic powder, chili powder, and salt and pepper to taste
3. Warm Air fryer to 390 degrees and air fry the chicken shreds for 20 minutes, at which point they will get

dark brown and crispy. They will soften up as they absorb the juices from cooking with the veggies.
4. While the chicken is cooking, cut the onions and peppers into thin slices. Add the olive oil to a wok and heat for a minute on medium-high heat. Toss in all the veggies and sauté for 5 minutes.
5. Add in the fish sauce, oyster sauce, soy sauce, sweet chili sauce, and stir well for 1 minute. Add the chicken and basil leaves and stir until the leaves have wilted. Serve over jasmine rice.

266. French Garlic Chicken
Preparation time: 40 minutes
Cooking time: 27 minutes
Servings: 4
Ingredients:
- 2 tablespoon extra-virgin olive oil
- 1 tablespoon Dijon mustard
- 1 tablespoon apple cider vinegar
- 3 cloves garlic, minced
- 2 teaspoons herbes de Provence
- ½ teaspoon kosher salt
- 1 teaspoon black pepper
- 1pound boneless, skinless chicken thighs, halved crosswise
- 2 tablespoons butter
- 8 cloves garlic, chopped
- ¼ cup heavy whipping cream

Directions:
1. Mix the olive oil, mustard, vinegar, minced garlic, herbes de Provence, salt, and pepper in a small bowl. Use a wire whisk to emulsify the mixture.
2. Pierce the chicken all over with a fork to allow the marinade to penetrate better. Place the chicken in a resealable plastic bag, pour the marinade over, and seal.
3. Massage until the chicken is well coated. Marinate at room temperature for 30 minutes or in the refrigerator for up to 24 hours.
4. When you are ready to cook, place the butter and chopped garlic in a baking pan and place it in the air fryer rack. Air fry at 400°F for 5 minutes, or until the butter has melted and the garlic is sizzling. Put the chicken and the marinade in the seasoned butter.
5. Set the Air Fryer at 350°F to air fry for 15 minutes. Transfer the chicken to a plate and cover lightly with foil to keep warm.
6. Add the cream to the pan, stirring to combine with the garlic, butter, and cooking juices. Put the pan in your Air Fryer basket. Air fry at 350°F for 7 minutes. Pour the thickened sauce over the chicken and serve.

267. Chicken Strips with Satay Sauce
Preparation time: 5 minutes
Cooking time: 10 minutes
Servings: 4
Ingredients:
- 4 (6-ounce) boneless, skinless chicken breasts, sliced into 16 (1-inch) strips
- 1 teaspoon fine sea salt
- 1 teaspoon paprika

Sauce:
- ¼ cup creamy almond butter
- 2 tablespoons chicken broth
- 1½ tablespoons coconut vinegar or unseasoned rice vinegar
- 1 clove garlic, minced
- 1 teaspoon peeled and minced fresh ginger
- ½ teaspoon hot sauce
- 1/8 teaspoon stevia glycerite or 2 to 3 drops liquid stevia

For garnish/serving (optional):
- ¼ cup chopped cilantro leaves
- Red pepper flakes
- Sea salt flakes
- red, orange, plus yellow bell peppers, sliced
- Special equipment:
- 16 wooden or bamboo skewers, soaked in water for 15 minutes

Directions:
1. Oiled the Air Fryer basket using avocado oil. Preheat the air fryer to 400°F. Thread the chicken strips onto the skewers. Season on all sides with the salt and paprika.
2. Place the chicken skewers in the Air Fryer basket. Air Fry at 400°F for 5 minutes, flip, and cook for another 5 minutes until the chicken is cooked through and the internal temperature reaches 165°F.
3. While the chicken skewers cook, for the sauce, in a medium-sized bowl, stir together all the sauce ingredients until well combined. Taste and adjust the sweetness and heat to your liking.
4. Garnish the chicken with cilantro, red pepper flakes, and salt flakes, if desired, and serve with sliced bell peppers, if desired. Serve the sauce on the side.

268. Chicken Pesto Parmigiana
Preparation time: 10 minutes
Cooking time: 23 minutes
Servings: 4
Ingredients:
- 2 large eggs
- 1 tablespoon water
- Fine sea salt and ground black pepper
- 1 cup powdered Parmesan cheese
- 2 teaspoons Italian seasoning
- 4 (5-ounce) boneless, skinless chicken breasts or thighs, pounded to ¼ inch thick
- 1 cup pesto
- 1 cup shredded Mozzarella cheese
- Finely chopped fresh basil, for garnish
- Grape tomatoes, halved, for serving

Directions:
1. Oil Air Fryer basket with avocado oil. Preheat the air fryer to 400°F. Put the cracked eggs into a baking

dish, put the water plus a pinch each of salt, pepper, and combine.
2. Mix the Parmesan and Italian seasoning in another shallow baking dish. Flavor the chicken breasts well on both sides with salt and pepper.
3. Dip one chicken breast in the eggs, let any excess drip off and then dredge both sides of the breast in the Parmesan mixture.
4. Spray the breast with avocado oil and place it in the Air Fryer basket. Repeat with the remaining 3 chicken breasts.
5. Air Fry at 400°F for 20 minutes, or until the internal temperature reaches 165F, and the breading is golden brown, flipping halfway through.
6. Dollop each chicken breast with ¼ cup of the pesto and top with the Mozzarella. Return the breasts to the Air Fryer, then air fry again for 3 minutes, or until the cheese is melted. Garnish with basil and serve with halved grape tomatoes on the side, if desired

269. Ginger Chicken
Preparation time: 40 minutes
Cooking time: 10 minutes
Servings: 4
Ingredients:
- ¼ cup julienned peeled fresh ginger
- 2 tablespoons vegetable oil
- 1 tablespoon honey
- 1 tablespoon soy sauce
- 1 tablespoon ketchup
- 1 teaspoon Garam Masala
- 1 teaspoon ground turmeric
- ¼ teaspoon kosher salt
- ½ teaspoon cayenne pepper
- Vegetable oil spray
- 1pound boneless, skinless chicken thighs, cut crosswise into thirds
- ¼ cup chopped fresh cilantro, for garnish

Directions:
1. In a small bowl, combine the ginger, oil, honey, soy sauce, ketchup, garam masala, turmeric, salt, and cayenne. Whisk until well combined.
2. Place the chicken in a resealable plastic bag and pour the marinade over. Seal the bag and massage to cover all the chicken with the marinade. Marinate at room temperature for 30 minutes or in the refrigerator for up to 24 hours.
3. Spray the Air Fryer basket with vegetable oil spray and add the chicken and as much of the marinade and julienned ginger as possible. Air Fry at 350°F for 10 minutes. To serve, garnish with cilantro.

270. Chicken Jalfrezi
Preparation time: 15 minutes
Cooking time: 16 minutes
Servings: 4
Ingredients:
For the Chicken:
- 1pound boneless, skinless chicken thighs, cut into 2 or 3 pieces each
- 1 medium onion, chopped
- 1 large green bell pepper, chopped
- 2 tablespoons olive oil
- 1 teaspoon ground turmeric
- 1 teaspoon Garam Masala
- 1 teaspoon kosher salt
- ½ to 1 teaspoon cayenne pepper

For the Sauce:
- ¼ cup tomato sauce
- 1 tablespoon water
- 1 teaspoon Garam Masala
- ½ teaspoon kosher salt
- ½ teaspoon cayenne pepper
- Side salad, rice, or naan bread, for serving

Directions:
1. For the chicken, mix the chicken, onion, bell pepper, oil, turmeric, garam masala, salt, and cayenne in a large bowl. Stir and toss until well combined.
2. Place the chicken and vegetables in the Air Fryer basket. Air Fry at 350°F for 15 minutes, stirring and tossing halfway through the cooking time. Meanwhile, for the sauce, in a small microwave-safe bowl, combine the tomato sauce, water, garam masala, salt, and cayenne. Microwave on high for 1 minute. Remove and stir. Microwave for another minute; set aside.
3. Remove the chicken and place chicken and vegetables in a large bowl. Pour the sauce overall. Stir and toss to coat the chicken and vegetables evenly. Serve with rice, naan, or a side salad.

271. Sweet Rub Chicken Drumsticks
Preparation time: 5 minutes
Cooking time: 20 minutes
Servings: 4
Ingredients:
- ¼ cup brown sugar
- 1 tablespoon salt
- ½ teaspoon freshly ground black pepper
- 1 teaspoon chili powder
- 1 teaspoon smoked paprika
- 1 teaspoon dry mustard
- 1 teaspoon garlic powder
- 1 teaspoon onion powder
- 4 to 6 chicken drumsticks
- 2 tablespoons olive oil

Directions:
1. Mix the brown sugar, salt, pepper, chili powder, paprika, mustard, garlic powder, and onion powder in a small mixing bowl.
2. Using a paper towel, wipe any moisture off the chicken. Put the chicken drumsticks into a large resealable plastic bag, then pour in the dry rub. Seal the bag. Shake the bag to coat the chicken.

3. Put the drumsticks in your Air Fryer basket. Brush the drumsticks with olive oil. Bake at 390°F for 10 minutes. Using tongs, flip the drumsticks, and brush them with olive oil. Reset the timer and bake for 10 minutes more. Once the chicken is fully cooked, transfer it to a platter and serve.

272. Buttermilk Marinated Chicken

Preparation Time: 10 minutes
Cooking Time: 25 minutes
Servings: 6
Ingredients:
- 3-lb. whole chicken
- 1 tablespoon salt
- 1-pint buttermilk

Directions:
1. Place the whole chicken in a large bowl and drizzle salt on top. Pour the buttermilk over it and leave the chicken soaking overnight. Cover the chicken bowl and refrigerate overnight.
2. Remove the chicken from the marinade and fix it on the rotisserie rod in your Air fryer. Roast for 25 minutes at 370 degrees F. Serve warm.

273. Thyme Turkey Breast

Preparation Time: 10 minutes
Cooking Time: 40 minutes
Servings: 4
Ingredients:
- 2 lb. turkey breast
- Salt, to taste
- Black pepper, to taste
- 4 tablespoon butter, melted
- 3 cloves garlic, minced
- 1 teaspoon thyme, chopped
- 1 teaspoon rosemary, chopped

Directions:
1. Mix butter with salt, black pepper, garlic, thyme, and rosemary in a bowl. Rub this seasoning over the turkey breast liberally and place in the Air Fryer basket. Preheat at 375 degrees F. Air fry for 40 minutes. Slice and serve fresh.

274. Roasted Duck

Preparation Time: 10 minutes
Cooking Time: 3 hours
Servings: 12
Ingredients
- 6 lb. whole Pekin duck
- Salt
- 5 garlic cloves chopped
- 1 lemon, chopped

Glaze:
- 1/2 cup balsamic vinegar
- 1 lemon, juiced
- 1/4 cup honey

Directions:
1. Place the Pekin duck in a baking tray and add garlic, lemon, and salt on top. Whisk honey, vinegar, and honey in a bowl. Brush this glaze over the duck liberally. Marinate overnight in the refrigerator.
2. Remove the duck from the marinade and fix it on the rotisserie rod in the air fryer. Roast at 350 degrees F for 3 hours. Serve warm.

275. Blackened Chicken Bake

Preparation Time: 10 minutes
Cooking Time: 18 minutes
Servings: 4
Ingredients:
- 4 chicken breasts
- 2 teaspoon olive oil
- Seasoning:
- 1 1/2 tablespoon brown sugar
- 1 teaspoon paprika
- 1 teaspoon dried oregano
- 1/4 teaspoon garlic powder
- 1/2 teaspoon salt and pepper

Garnish:
- Chopped parsley

Directions:
1. Mix olive oil with brown sugar, paprika, oregano, garlic powder, salt, and black pepper in a bowl. Place the chicken breasts in the baking tray of the air fryer.
2. Pour and rub this mixture liberally over all the chicken breasts. Preheat at 425 F. Once preheated, place the baking tray inside the air fryer. Bake for 18 minutes. Serve warm.

276. Crusted Chicken Drumsticks

Preparation Time: 10 minutes
Cooking Time: 10 minutes
Servings: 4
Ingredients:
- 1 lb. chicken drumsticks
- 1/2 cup buttermilk
- 1/2 cup panko breadcrumbs
- 1/2 cup flour
- 1/4 teaspoon baking powder

Spice Mixture:
- 1/2 teaspoon salt
- 1/2 teaspoon celery salt
- 1/4 teaspoon oregano
- 1/4 teaspoon cayenne
- 1 teaspoon paprika
- 1/4 teaspoon garlic powder
- 1/4 teaspoon dried thyme
- 1/2 teaspoon ground ginger
- 1/2 teaspoon white pepper
- 1/2 teaspoon black pepper
- 3 tablespoons butter melted

Directions:
1. Soak chicken in the buttermilk and cover to marinate overnight in the refrigerator. Mix spices with flour, breadcrumbs, and baking powder in a shallow tray.
2. Remove the chicken from the milk and coat them well with the flour spice mixture. Place the chicken

drumsticks in the air fryer basket. Pour the melted butter over the drumsticks.
3. Preheat at 425 degrees F. Once preheated, place the baking tray inside the air fryer. Air fry for 10 minutes. Flip the drumsticks and resume air frying for another 10 minutes. Serve warm.

277. Roasted Turkey Breast
Preparation Time: 10 minutes
Cooking Time: 50 minutes
Servings: 6
Ingredients:
- 3 lb. boneless turkey breast
- ¼ cup mayonnaise
- 2 teaspoon poultry seasoning
- 1 teaspoon salt
- ½ teaspoon garlic powder
- ¼ teaspoon black pepper

Directions:
1. Whisk all the ingredients, including turkey, in a bowl, and coat it well. Place the boneless turkey breast in the air fryer basket. Preheat at 350 degrees F. Once preheated, place the air fryer basket. Bake for 50 minutes. Slice and serve.

278. Brine Soaked Turkey
Preparation Time: 10 minutes
Cooking Time: 45 minutes
Servings: 8
Ingredients
- 7 lb. bone-in, skin-on turkey breast

Brine:
- 1/2 cup salt
- 1 lemon
- 1/2 onion
- 3 cloves garlic, smashed
- 5 sprigs fresh thyme
- 3 bay leaves
- Black pepper

Turkey Breast:
- 4 tablespoon butter, softened
- 1/2 teaspoon black pepper
- 1/2 teaspoon garlic powder
- 1/4 teaspoon dried thyme
- 1/4 teaspoon dried oregano

Directions:
1. Mix the turkey brine ingredients in a pot and soak the turkey in the brine overnight. The following morning, remove the soaked turkey from the brine.
2. Whisk the butter, black pepper, garlic powder, oregano, and thyme. Brush the butter mixture over the turkey, then place it in a baking tray.
3. Preheat at 370 degrees F. Once preheated, place the turkey in the air fryer baking tray, roast for 45 minutes. Slice and serve warm.

279. Lemon Pepper Turkey
Preparation Time: 10 minutes
Cooking Time: 45 minutes
Servings: 6
Ingredients:
- 3 lbs. turkey breast
- 2 tablespoons oil
- 1 tablespoon Worcestershire sauce
- 1 teaspoon lemon pepper
- 1/2 teaspoon salt

Directions:
1. Whisk everything in a bowl and coat the turkey liberally. Place the turkey in the air fryer basket. Preheat at 375 degrees F. Once preheated, place the air fryer basket inside, then air fry for 45 minutes. Serve warm.

280. Ground Chicken Meatballs
Preparation Time: 10 minutes
Cooking Time: 10 minutes
Servings: 4
Ingredients:
- 1-lb. ground chicken
- 1/3 cup panko
- 1 teaspoon salt
- 2 teaspoons chives
- 1/2 teaspoon garlic powder
- 1 teaspoon thyme
- 1 egg

Directions:
1. Toss all the fixing in a bowl and mix well, form small meatballs, and place them in the air fryer basket.
2. Preheat at 350 degrees F. Once preheated, place the air fryer basket inside, then air fry for 10 minutes. Serve warm.

281. Parmesan Chicken Meatballs
Preparation Time: 10 minutes
Cooking Time: 12 minutes
Servings: 4
Ingredients:
- 1-lb. ground chicken
- 1 large egg, beaten
- ½ cup Parmesan cheese, grated
- ½ cup pork rinds, ground
- 1 teaspoon garlic powder
- 1 teaspoon paprika
- 1 teaspoon kosher salt
- ½ teaspoon pepper

Crust:
- ½ cup pork rinds, ground

Directions:
1. Toss all the meatball listed fixing in a bowl and mix well. Make small meatballs out of this batter and roll them in the pork rinds. Place the coated meatballs in the air fryer basket. Preheat at 400 degrees F. Bake for 12 minutes. Serve warm.

282. Italian Meatballs

Preparation Time: 10 minutes
Cooking Time: 13 minutes
Servings: 4
Ingredients:
- 2-lb. lean ground turkey
- ¼ cup onion, minced
- 2 cloves garlic, minced
- 2 tablespoons parsley, chopped
- 2 eggs
- 1½ cup parmesan cheese, grated
- ½ teaspoon red pepper flakes
- ½ teaspoon Italian seasoning
- Salt and black pepper to taste

Directions:
1. Toss all the fixing listed in a bowl and mix well, form small meatballs out of this mixture and place them in the air fryer basket.
2. Warm your air fryer at 350 degrees F. Air fry for 13 minutes. Flip the meatballs when cooked halfway through. Serve warm.

283. Oregano Chicken Breast

Preparation Time: 10 minutes
Cooking Time: 25 minutes
Servings: 6
Ingredients:
- 2 lbs. chicken breasts, minced
- 1 tablespoon avocado oil
- 1 teaspoon smoked paprika
- 1 teaspoon garlic powder
- 1 teaspoon oregano
- 1/2 teaspoon salt
- Black pepper, to taste

Directions:
1. Toss all the meatball ingredients in a bowl and mix well. Form small meatballs out of this mixture and put them in the air fryer basket. Preheat your air fryer at 375 degrees F. Air fry for 25 minutes. Serve warm.

284. Maple Chicken Thighs

Preparation Time: 10 minutes
Cooking Time: 30 minutes
Servings: 4
Ingredients:
- 4 large chicken thighs, bone-in
- 2 tablespoons French mustard
- 2 tablespoons Dijon mustard
- 1 clove minced garlic
- 1/2 teaspoon dried marjoram
- 2 tablespoons maple syrup

Directions:
1. Mix chicken with everything in a bowl and coat it well. Place the chicken along with its marinade in the baking pan. Preheat your air fryer at 370 degrees F. Bake for 30 minutes; serve warm.

285. Orange Chicken Rice

Preparation Time: 10 minutes
Cooking Time: 55 minutes
Servings: 4
Ingredients:
- 3 tablespoons olive oil
- 1 medium onion, chopped
- 1 3/4 cups chicken broth
- 1 cup brown basmati rice
- Zest and juice of 2 oranges
- Salt to taste
- 4 (6-oz.) boneless, skinless chicken thighs
- Black pepper, to taste
- 2 tablespoons fresh mint, chopped
- 2 tablespoons pine nuts, toasted

Directions:
1. Spread the rice in a casserole dish and place the chicken on top. Toss the rest of the ingredients in a bowl and liberally pour over the chicken. Preheat the air fryer at 350 degrees F. Bake for 55 minutes. Serve warm.

286. Deviled Chicken

Preparation Time: 10 minutes
Cooking Time: 40 minutes
Servings: 8
Ingredients:
- 2 tablespoons butter
- 2 cloves garlic, chopped
- 1 cup Dijon mustard
- 1/2 teaspoon cayenne pepper
- 1 1/2 cups panko breadcrumbs
- 3/4 cup Parmesan, freshly grated
- 1/4 cup chives, chopped
- 2 teaspoons paprika
- 8 small bone-in chicken thighs, skin removed

Directions:
1. Toss the chicken thighs with crumbs, cheese, chives, butter, and spices in a bowl and mix well to coat. Transfer the chicken along with its spice mix to a baking pan. Warm your air fryer at 350 degrees F. Once preheated, air fry for 40 minutes. Serve warm.

Chapter 8. Beef

287. Air Fried Grilled Steak
Preparation time: 15 minutes
Cooking time: 45 minutes
Servings: 2
Ingredients:
- 2 top sirloin steaks
- 3 tablespoons butter, melted
- 3 tablespoons olive oil
- Salt and pepper to taste

Directions:
1. Preheat the air fryer for 5 minutes. Season the sirloin steaks with olive oil, salt, and pepper. Put the beef in the air fryer basket. Air fry for 45 minutes at 350°F. Once cooked, serve with butter.

288. Texas Beef Brisket
Preparation time: 15 minutes
Cooking time: 1 hour & 30 minutes
Servings: 8
Ingredients:
- 1 ½ cup beef stock
- 1 bay leaf
- 1 tablespoon garlic powder
- 1 tablespoon onion powder
- 2 pounds beef brisket, trimmed
- 2 tablespoons chili powder
- 2 teaspoons dry mustard
- 4 tablespoons olive oil
- Salt and pepper to taste

Directions:
1. Preheat the air fryer for 5 minutes. Place all fixing in a deep baking dish that will fit in the air fryer. Bake for 1 hour and 30 minutes at 400°F. Stir the beef every after 30 minutes to soak in the sauce. Serve.

289. Savory Beefy Poppers
Preparation time: 15 minutes
Cooking time: 15 minutes
Servings: 8
Ingredients:
- 8 medium jalapeño peppers, stemmed, halved, and seeded
- 1 (8-ounce) package cream cheese softened
- 2 pounds ground beef (85% lean)
- 1 teaspoon fine sea salt
- ½ teaspoon ground black pepper
- 8 slices thin-cut bacon
- Fresh cilantro leaves, for garnish

Directions:
1. Oiled the air fryer basket with avocado oil. Preheat the air fryer to 400°F. Stuff each jalapeño half with a few tablespoons of cream cheese. Place the halves back again to form 8 jalapeños.
2. Season the ground beef with the salt and pepper and mix with your hands to incorporate. Flatten about ¼ pound of ground beef in the palm of your hand and place a stuffed jalapeño in the center.
3. Fold the beef around the jalapeño, forming an egg shape. Wrap the beef-covered jalapeño with a slice of bacon and secure it with a toothpick.
4. Place the jalapeños in the air fryer basket, leaving space between them (if you're using a smaller air fryer, work in batches if necessary), and air fry for 15 minutes, or until the beef is cooked through, and the bacon is crispy. Garnish with cilantro before serving.

290. Juicy Cheeseburgers
Preparation time: 15 minutes
Cooking time: 15 minutes
Servings: 4
Ingredients:
- 1 pound 93% lean ground beef
- 1 teaspoon Worcestershire sauce
- 1 tablespoon burger seasoning
- Salt
- Pepper
- Cooking oil
- 4 slices cheese
- 2 buns

Directions:
1. Mix the ground beef, Worcestershire, burger seasoning, and salt and pepper in a large bowl. Oiled

the air fryer basket with cooking oil. You will need only a quick spritz.
2. The burgers will produce oil as they cook. Shape the mixture into 4 patties. Place the burgers in the air fryer. The burgers should fit without the need to stack, but stacking is okay if necessary.
3. Air fry for 8 minutes, then flips the burgers. Air fry for an additional 3 to 4 minutes.
4. Put each burger with a slice of cheese. Cook for an additional minute, or until the cheese has melted. Serve on buns with any additional toppings of your choice.

291. Copycat Taco Bell Crunch Wraps
Preparation time: 15 minutes
Cooking time: 2 minutes
Servings: 6
Ingredients:
- 6 wheat tostadas
- 2 cups of sour cream
- 2 cups of Mexican blend cheese
- 2 cups of shredded lettuce
- 12 ounces low-sodium nacho cheese
- 3 Roma tomatoes
- 6 12-inch wheat tortillas
- 1 1/3 cup of water
- 2 packets low-sodium taco seasoning
- 2 pounds of lean ground beef

Directions:
1. Ensure your air fryer is preheated to 400 degrees.
2. Make beef according to taco seasoning packets. Place 2/3 cup of prepared beef, 4 tbsp. cheese, 1 tostada, 1/3 cup of sour cream, 1/3 cup of lettuce, 1/6 of tomatoes, and 1/3 cup of cheese on each tortilla.
3. Fold up tortillas edges and repeat with remaining ingredients. Lay the folded sides of tortillas down into the air fryer and spray with olive oil. Set temperature to 400°F and air fry for 2 minutes until browned.

292. Swedish Meatloaf
Preparation time: 15 minutes
Cooking time: 45 minutes
Servings: 8
Ingredients:
- 1½ pounds ground beef (85% lean)
- ¼ pound ground pork or ground beef
- 1 large egg (omit for egg-free)
- ½ cup minced onions
- ¼ cup tomato sauce
- 2 tablespoons dry mustard
- 2 cloves garlic, minced
- 2 teaspoons fine sea salt
- 1 tsp. ground black pepper, + more for garnish

Sauce:
- ½ cup (1 stick) unsalted butter
- ½ cup shredded Swiss or mild cheddar cheese (about 2 ounces)
- 2 ounces cream cheese (¼ cup), softened
- 1/3 cup beef broth
- 1/8 teaspoon ground nutmeg
- Halved cherry tomatoes, for serving (optional)

Directions:
1. Preheat the air fryer to 390°F.
2. Mix the ground beef, ground pork, egg, onions, tomato sauce, dry mustard, garlic, salt, and pepper in a large bowl. Using your hands, mix until well combined.
3. Place the meatloaf mixture in a 9 by 5-inch loaf pan and place it in the air fryer. Air fry for 35 minutes, or until cooked through and the internal temperature reaches 145°F. Check the meatloaf after 25 minutes; if it's getting too brown on the top, cover it loosely with foil to prevent burning.
4. While the meatloaf cooks, heat the butter in a saucepan over medium-high heat until it sizzles and brown flecks appear, continually stirring to keep the butter from burning; adjust the heat to low and whisk in the Swiss cheese, cream cheese, broth, and nutmeg. Simmer for at least 10 minutes.
5. When the meatloaf is done, transfer it to a serving tray and pour the sauce over it. Garnish with ground black pepper and serve with cherry tomatoes, if desired. Allow the meatloaf to rest for 10 minutes before slicing, so it doesn't crumble apart.

293. Carne Asada
Preparation time: 2 hours
Cooking time: 8 minutes
Servings: 4
Ingredients:
- 1-pound skirt steak, cut into 4 equal portions

Marinade:
- 1 cup cilantro leaves and stems, plus more for garnish if desired
- 1 jalapeño pepper, seeded and diced
- ½ cup lime juice
- 2 tablespoons avocado oil
- 2 tbsp. coconut vinegar or apple cider vinegar
- 2 teaspoons orange extract
- 1 teaspoon stevia glycerite or 1/8 teaspoon liquid stevia
- 2 teaspoons ancho chili powder
- 2 teaspoons fine sea salt
- 1 teaspoon coriander seeds
- 1 teaspoon cumin seeds

For serving (optional):
- Chopped avocado
- Lime slices
- Sliced radishes

Directions:
1. Place all the fixing for the marinade in a blender and puree until smooth. Put the steak in a dish, then pour the marinade over it, making sure the meat is covered completely. Wrap, then put in the fridge for 2 hours or overnight.

2. Oiled the air fryer basket with avocado oil. Preheat the air fryer to 400°F. Remove the steak from the marinade and place it in the air fryer basket in one layer. Air fry for 8 minutes, or until the internal temperature is 145F; do not overcook it.
3. Remove the steak, then place it on a cutting board to rest for 10 minutes before slicing it against the grain. Garnish with cilantro, if desired, and serve with chopped avocado, lime slices, or sliced radishes, if desired.

294. Spicy Thai Beef Stir-Fry
Preparation time: 15 minutes
Cooking time: 10 minutes
Servings: 4
Ingredients:
- 1 pound sirloin steaks, thinly sliced
- 2 tablespoons lime juice, divided
- 1/3 cup crunchy peanut butter
- ½ cup beef broth
- 1 tablespoon olive oil
- 1½ cups broccoli florets
- 2 cloves garlic, sliced
- 1 to 2 red chili peppers, sliced

Directions:
1. In a medium bowl, combine the steak with 1 tablespoon of the lime juice. Set aside. Combine the peanut butter and beef broth in a small bowl and mix well.
2. Drain the beef and add the juice from the bowl into the peanut butter mixture. In a 6-inch metal bowl, combine the olive oil, steak, and broccoli.
3. Air fry for 3 to 4 minutes or until the steak is almost cooked and the broccoli is crisp and tender, shaking the basket once during cooking time.
4. Add the garlic, chili peppers, and the peanut butter mixture and stir. Air fry again for 3 to 5 minutes or until the sauce is bubbling, and the broccoli is tender. Serve over hot rice.

295. Beef Casserole
Preparation time: 15 minutes
Cooking time: 30 minutes
Servings: 4
Ingredients:
- 1 green bell pepper, seeded and chopped
- 1 onion, chopped
- 1-pound ground beef
- 3 cloves of garlic, minced
- 3 tablespoons olive oil
- 6 cups eggs, beaten
- Salt and pepper to taste

Directions:
1. Preheat the air fryer for 5 minutes. Mix the ground beef, onion, garlic, olive oil, and bell pepper in a baking dish that will fit in the air fryer. Season with salt and pepper to taste.
2. Pour in the beaten eggs and give a good stir. Place the dish with the beef and egg mixture in the air fryer. Bake for 30 minutes at 325°F.

296. Fajita Meatball Lettuce Wraps
Preparation time: 15 minutes
Cooking time: 10 minutes
Servings: 4
Ingredients:
- 1 pound ground beef (85% lean)
- ½ cup salsa, plus more for serving if desired
- ¼ cup chopped onions
- ¼ cup diced green or red bell peppers
- 1 large egg, beaten
- 1 teaspoon fine sea salt
- ½ teaspoon chili powder
- ½ teaspoon ground cumin
- 1 clove garlic, minced

For serving (optional):
- 8 leaves Boston lettuce
- Pico de Gallo or salsa
- Lime slices

Directions:
1. Oiled the air fryer basket with avocado oil. Preheat the air fryer to 350°F. In a large bowl, mix all the ingredients until well combined. Shape the meat mixture into eight 1-inch balls.
2. Place the meatballs in the air fryer basket, leaving a little space between them. Air fry for 10 minutes, or until cooked through and no longer pink inside, and the internal temperature reaches 145°F. Serve each meatball on a lettuce leaf, topped with Pico de Gallo or salsa, if desired. Serve with lime slices if desired.

297. Chimichurri Skirt Steak
Preparation time: overnight & 30 minutes
Cooking time: 10 minutes
Servings: 2
Ingredients:
- 2 x 8 oz. Skirt Steak
- 1 cup Finely Chopped Parsley
- ¼ cup Finely Chopped Mint
- 2 tbsp. Fresh Oregano (Washed & finely chopped)
- 3 Finely Chopped Cloves of Garlic
- 1 tsp. Red Pepper Flakes (Crushed)
- 1 tbsp. Ground Cumin
- 1 tsp. Cayenne Pepper
- 2 tsp. Smoked Paprika
- 1 tsp. Salt
- ¼ tsp. Pepper
- ¾ cup Oil
- 3 tbsp. Red Wine Vinegar

Directions:
1. Put all the ingredients in a bowl except the steak and mix well. Put ¼ cup of the mixture in a plastic baggie with the steak and leave in the fridge overnight.
2. Leave the bag out at room temperature for at least 30 min before popping into the Air fryer. Preheat for a

minute or 2 to 390° F before air frying until med-rare for 8–10 minutes. Put 2 tbsp. of the chimichurri mix on top of each steak before serving.

298. Reuben Fritters
Preparation time: 15 minutes
Cooking time: 16 minutes
Servings: 12
Ingredients:
- 2 cups finely diced cooked corned beef
- 1 (8-ounce) package cream cheese, softened
- ½ cup finely shredded Swiss cheese (about 2 ounces)
- ¼ cup sauerkraut
- 1 cup pork dust or powdered Parmesan cheese
- Chopped fresh thyme for garnish
- Thousand Island Dipping Sauce for serving
- Cornichons, for serving (optional)

Directions:
1. Oiled the air fryer basket with avocado oil. Preheat the air fryer to 390°F. In a large bowl, mix the corned beef, cream cheese, Swiss cheese, and sauerkraut. Form the corned beef mixture into 12 1½-inch balls.
2. Place the pork dust in a shallow bowl. Roll the corned beef balls in the pork dust and use your hands to form it into a thick crust around each ball.
3. Put 6 balls in your air fryer basket, spaced about ½ inch apart, and air fry for 8 minutes, or until golden brown and crispy. Allow them to cool a bit before lifting them out of the air fryer.
4. Repeat with the remaining fritters. Garnish with chopped fresh thyme and serve with the dipping sauce and cornichons, if desired.

299. Charred Onions and Steak Cube BBQ
Preparation time: 15 minutes
Cooking time: 40 minutes
Servings: 3
Ingredients:
- 1 cup red onions, cut into wedges
- 1 tablespoon dry mustard
- 1 tablespoon olive oil
- 1-pound boneless beef sirloin, cut into cubes
- Salt and pepper to taste

Directions:
1. Preheat the air fryer to 390F. Toss all fixing in a bowl and mix until everything is coated with the seasonings. Place on the grill pan and air fry for 40 minutes. Halfway through the cooking time, give a stir to cook evenly.

300. Steak and Mushroom Gravy
Preparation time: 15 minutes
Cooking time: 15 minutes
Servings: 4
Ingredients:
- 4 cubed steaks
- 2 large eggs
- 1/2 dozen mushrooms
- 4 tablespoons unsalted butter
- 4 tablespoons black pepper
- 2 tablespoons salt
- 1/2 teaspoon onion powder
- 1/2 teaspoon garlic powder
- 1/4 teaspoon cayenne powder
- 1 1/4 teaspoons paprika
- 1 1/2 cups whole milk
- 1/3 cup flour
- 2 tablespoons vegetable oil

Directions:
1. Mix 1/2 flour and a pinch of black pepper in a shallow bowl or on a plate. Beat 2 eggs in a bowl and mix in a pinch of salt and pepper.
2. Mix the other half of the flour with pepper to taste, garlic powder, paprika, cayenne, and onion powder in a separate shallow bowl.
3. Chop mushrooms and set aside. Press your steak into the first flour bowl, then dip in egg, then press the steak into the second flour bowl until covered completely.
4. Air fries the steak 360 degrees for 15 minutes, flipping halfway through. While the steak cooks, warm the butter over medium heat and add mushrooms to sauté. Add 4 tablespoons of the flour and pepper mix to the pan and mix until there are no clumps of flour. Mix in whole milk and simmer. Serve over steak for breakfast, lunch, or dinner.

301. Country Fried Steak
Preparation time: 15 minutes
Cooking time: 15 minutes
Servings: 2
Ingredients:
- 1 tsp. pepper
- 2 cups of almond milk
- 2 tbsp. almond flour
- 6 ounces ground sausage meat
- 1 tsp. pepper
- 1 tsp. salt
- 1 tsp. garlic powder
- 1 tsp. onion powder
- 1 cup panko breadcrumbs
- 1 cup almond flour
- 3 beaten eggs
- 6 ounces sirloin steak, pounded till thin

Directions:
1. Season panko breadcrumbs with spices. Dredge steak in flour, then egg, and then seasoned panko mixture. Place into an air fryer basket. Set temperature to 370°F and air fry to 12 minutes.
2. To make sausage gravy, cook sausage and drain off fat, but reserve 2 tablespoons. Add flour to sausage and mix until incorporated.
3. Gradually mix in milk over medium to high heat till it becomes thick. Season mixture with pepper and cook 3 minutes longer. Serve steak topped with gravy and enjoy.

302. Spicy Grilled Steak

Preparation time: 15 minutes
Cooking time: 9 minutes
Servings: 4
Ingredients:
- 2 tbsp. low-Sodium salsa
- 1 tbsp. diced chipotle pepper
- 1 tbsp. apple cider vinegar
- 1 tsp. ground cumin
- 1/8 tsp. freshly ground black pepper
- 1/8 tsp. red pepper flakes
- ¾ pound sirloin tip steak, cut into 4 pieces and gently pounded to about 1/3 inch thick

Directions:
1. In a small bowl, thoroughly mix the salsa, chipotle pepper, cider vinegar, cumin, black pepper, and red pepper flakes. Rub this mixture into both sides of each steak piece. Let stand for 15 minutes at room temperature.
2. Grill the steaks in the Air Fryer, 2 at a time, for 6 to 9 minutes, or until they reach at least 145 F on a meat thermometer.

303. Toothsome Greek Vegetable Skillet

Preparation time: 20 minutes
Cooking time: 29 minutes
Servings: 4
Ingredients:
- ½ pound 96 percent lean ground beef
- 2 medium tomatoes, minced
- 1 onion, minced
- 2 garlic cloves, diced
- 2 cups fresh baby spinach
- 2 tbsp. freshly squeezed lemon juice
- 1/3 cup low-Sodium beef broth
- 2 tbsp. crumbled low-Sodium feta cheese

Directions:
1. In a 6-by-2-inch metal pan, crumble the beef. Air fry for 3 to 7 min, stirring once during cooking until browned. Drain off any fat or liquid.
2. Add the tomatoes, onion, and garlic to the pan. Air-fry for 4 to 8 min more or until the onion is tender. Add the spinach, lemon juice, and beef broth. Air-fry for 2 to 4 min more or until the spinach is wilted. Sprinkle with the feta cheese and serve immediately.

304. Light Herbed Meatballs

Preparation time: 10 minutes
Cooking time: 21 minutes
Servings: 24
Ingredients:
- 1 medium onion, diced
- 2 garlic cloves, diced
- 1 tsp. olive oil
- 1 slice low-sodium whole-wheat bread, crumbled
- 3 tbsp. 1 percent milk
- 1 tsp. dried marjoram
- 1 tsp. dried basil
- 1-pound 96 percent lean ground beef

Directions:
1. In a 6-by-2-inch pan, combine the onion, garlic, and olive oil. Air-fry for 2 to 4 min, or until the vegetables are crisp-tender.
2. Transfer the vegetables to a medium bowl and add the breadcrumbs, milk, marjoram, and basil. Mix well.
3. Add the ground beef. With your hands, work the mixture gently but thoroughly until combined. Form the meat mixture into about 24 (1-inch) meatballs.
4. Bake the meatballs, in batches, in the Air Fryer basket for 12 to 17 min, or until they reach 160°f on a meat thermometer. Serve immediately.

305. Sirloin Steak

Preparation time: 5 minutes
Cooking time: 15 minutes
Servings: 6
Ingredients:
- 2 sirloin steaks, grass-fed
- 1 tbsp. olive oil
- 2 tbsp. steak seasoning

Directions:
1. Switch on the Air Fryer, insert fryer basket, grease it with olive oil. Preheat the fryer at 392 F for 5 min.
2. Meanwhile, pat dries the steaks, brush with oil and then season well with steak seasoning until coated on both sides.
3. Open the fryer, add steaks in it, close with its lid, and air fry for 10 min until nicely golden and crispy, flipping the steaks halfway through the frying. Transfer steaks onto a serving plate.

306. Buttered Filet Mignon

Preparation time: 10 minutes
Cooking time: 14 minutes
Servings: 4
Ingredients:
- 2 (6-ounces) filet mignon steaks
- 1 tbsp. butter softened
- Salt and ground black pepper, as required

Directions:
1. Coat each steak evenly with butter and then season with salt and black pepper. Set Air Fryer to 390 degrees F. Grease an Air Fryer basket.
2. Arrange steaks into the prepared Air Fryer basket. Air fry for about 14 min, flipping once halfway through. Remove from the Air Fryer and transfer onto serving plates. Serve hot.

307. Savory Spiced & Herbed Skirt Steak

Preparation time: 24 hours & 30 minutes
Cooking time: 10 minutes
Servings: 4
Ingredients:
Directions:
- 3 garlic cloves, diced
- 1 cup fresh parsley leaves, finely minced

- 3 tbsp. fresh oregano, finely minced
- 3 tbsp. fresh mint leaves, finely minced
- 1 tbsp. ground cumin
- 2 tsp. smoked paprika
- 1 tsp. cayenne pepper
- 1 tsp. red pepper flakes, crushed
- Salt and ground black pepper, as required
- ¾ cup olive oil
- 3 tbsp. red wine vinegar
- 2 (8-ounces) skirt steaks

Directions:
1. In a bowl, mix the garlic, herbs, spices, oil, and vinegar. In a resealable bag, place ¼ cup of the herb mixture and steaks. Refrigerate for about 24 hours.
2. Reserve the remaining herb mixture in the refrigerator. Take out the steaks from the fridge and place it at room temperature for about 30 min.
3. Warm Air Fryer to 390 degrees F. Grease an Air Fryer basket, then arrange the steaks into the prepared Air Fryer basket.
4. Air fry for about 8-10 minutes. Remove from the Air Fryer and place the steaks onto a cutting board for about 10 min before slicing.
5. Cut each steak into desired size slices and transfer onto a serving platter. Top with reserved herb mixture and serve.

308. Steak with Bell Peppers

Preparation time: 20 minutes
Cooking time: 22 minutes
Servings: 4
Ingredients:
- 1 tsp. dried oregano, crushed
- 1 tsp. onion powder
- 1 tsp. garlic powder
- 1 tsp. red chili powder
- 1 tsp. paprika
- Salt, to taste
- 1¼ pounds beef steak, cut into thin strips
- 2 green bell peppers, seeded and cubed
- 1 red bell pepper, seeded and cubed
- 1 red onion, sliced
- 2 tbsp. olive oil

Directions:
1. In a large bowl, mix the oregano and spices. Add the beef strips, bell peppers, onion, and oil. Mix until well combined.
2. Set the Air Fryer at 390 degrees F. Grease an Air Fryer basket, then arrange steak strips mixture into the prepared Air Fryer basket in 2 batches.
3. Air fry for about 10-11 minutes. Remove from the Air Fryer and transfer the steak mixture onto serving plates.

309. Corned Beef

Preparation time: 10 minutes
Cooking time: 35 minutes
Servings: 6
Ingredients:
- 2 ¼ lbs. corned beef, minced
- 1 onion, minced
- 2 celery stalks, minced
- 1/2 tbsp. cumin
- 1 tbsp. garlic powder
- 3 cups chicken broth
- 1 tbsp. butter
- 2 bacon slices, diced
- 2 1/2 lbs. cabbage, minced
- 1 carrot, sliced
- 1/2 tbsp. salt

Directions:
1. Add butter into the Air Fryer and set the container on sauté mode. Add bacon to the pot and cook until bacon is crispy.
2. Add meat and cook until browned. Add remaining ingredients and stir. Seal fryer with lid and air fry for 35 minutes. Stir and serve.

310. Roasted Pepper Beef Prosciutto

Preparation time: 20 minutes
Cooking time: 30 minutes
Servings: 8
Ingredients:
- 24 ounces. Beef cutlets
- Olive oil spray
- 12 ounces. sliced thin prosciutto
- 4 slices Mozzarella cheese
- 22 ounces. roasted peppers
- 1 lemon
- 24 Spinach leaves
- 1 tbsp. olive oil
- 1/2 cup breadcrumbs
- Salt and fresh pepper

Directions:
1. First, wash and dry the Beef cutlets very thoroughly with paper towels. Add breadcrumbs in a bowl and another second bowl, stir the olive oil, lemon juice, and pepper.
2. Preheat the Air Fryer to 450°F. Slightly spray a baking dish with olive oil spray. Put each cutlet on a work surface such as a cutting board and lay 1/2 slice prosciutto, 1/2 slice cheese, 1 piece of roasted pepper, and 3 spinach leaves on 1 side of the Beef cutlet.
3. Roll it and put seam side down on a dish. Dip down the beef in the olive oil and lemon juice after that into the breadcrumbs. Do the same with the beef left. Bake it 25 to 30 min or until your desired crispness.

311. Honey Mustard Cheesy Meatballs

Preparation time: 15 minutes
Cooking time: 15 minutes
Servings: 8
Ingredients:
- 2 onions, minced
- 1-pound ground beef

- 4 tbsp. fresh basil, minced
- 2 tbsp. cheddar cheese, grated
- 2 tsp. garlic paste
- 2 tsp. honey
- Salt and black pepper, to taste
- 2 tsp. mustard

Directions:
1. Preheat the Air Fryer to 385 F and grease an Air Fryer basket. Mix all the ingredients in a bowl until well combined.
2. Shape the mixture into equal-sized balls gently and arrange the meatballs in the Air Fryer basket. Air fry for about 15 min and dish out to serve warm.

312. Garlic-Mustard Rubbed Roast Beef
Preparation time: 20 minutes
Cooking time: 2 hours
Servings: 12
Ingredients:
- ¼ cup Dijon mustard
- ¼ cup freshly parsley, minced
- ¼ cup unsalted butter
- 2 cups almond flour
- 2 tbsp. olive oil
- 3 ½ cups beef broth
- 3 pounds boneless beef eye round roast
- 4 cloves of garlic, minced
- Salt and pepper to taste

Directions:
1. In a mixing bowl, combine the garlic, almond flour, parsley, salt, and pepper. Heat butter and olive oil in a skillet and brown the beef on all sides.
2. Rub the almond flour mixture all over the beef. Brush with Dijon mustard. Place the crusted beef in a baking dish.
3. Pour the beef broth slowly. Place the baking dish with the bee in the Air Fryer. Roast for 2 hours at 400 F. Baste the beef with the sauce every 30 min.

313. Ginger Soy Beef
Preparation time: 5 minutes
Cooking time: 5 minutes
Servings: 3
Ingredients:
- 2 tbsp. soy sauce
- 1 green onion, minced
- 1 clove garlic, diced
- 1 tbsp. and 1-1/2 tsp. hoisin sauce
- 1 tbsp. and 1-1/2 tsp. sherry
- 1/2 tsp. barbeque sauce
- 1-1/2 tsp. diced fresh ginger root
- 3/4-pound flank steak, thinly sliced

Directions:
1. In a resealable bag, mix fresh ginger, garlic, green onions, barbecue sauce, soy sauce, sherry, and hoisin. Add steak and mix well. Remove excess air, seal, and marinate for at least 2 hours.
2. Thread steak into skewers and discard marinade. Air fry for 5 minutes on preheated a 390 F Air Fryer. Enjoy.

314. Ginger-Orange Beef Strips
Preparation time: 5 minutes
Cooking time: 25 minutes
Servings: 3
Ingredients:
- 1 ½ pound stir-fry steak slices
- 1 ½ tsp. sesame oil
- 1 navel oranges, segmented
- 1 tbsp. olive oil
- 1 tbsp. rice vinegar
- 1 tsp. grated ginger
- 2 scallions, minced
- 3 cloves of garlic, diced
- 3 tbsp. molasses
- 3 tbsp. soy sauce
- 6 tbsp. cornstarch

Directions:
1. Preheat the Air Fryer to 330F. Season the steak slices with soy sauce and dust with cornstarch. Put in the Air Fryer basket and air fry for 25 min.
2. Meanwhile, place in the skillet oil and heat over medium flame. Sauté the garlic and ginger until fragrant. Stir in the oranges, molasses, and rice vinegar. Season with salt and pepper to taste.
3. Once the meat is done, place in the skillet and stir to coat the sauce. Drizzle with oil and garnish with scallions.

315. Grilled Beef with Grated Daikon Radish
Preparation time: 10 minutes
Cooking time: 40 minutes
Servings: 2
Ingredients:
- ¼ cup grated daikon radish
- ½ cup of rice wine vinegar
- ½ cup of soy sauce
- 1 tbsp. olive oil
- 2 strip steaks
- Salt and pepper to taste

Directions:
1. Preheat the Air Fryer to 390F. Season the steak with salt and pepper. Brush with oil. Grill for 20 min per piece, and make sure to flip the beef halfway through the time to cook. Preparing the dipping sauce by combining the soy and vinegar. Serve the steak with the sauce and daikon radish.

316. Grilled Tri-Tip Over Beet Salad
Preparation time: 10 minutes
Cooking time: 45 minutes
Servings: 6
Ingredients:
- 1 bunch arugula, torn
- 1 bunch scallions, minced
- 1-pound tri-tip, sliced
- 2 tbsp. olive oil
- 3 beets, peeled and sliced thinly
- 3 tbsp. balsamic vinegar
- Salt and pepper to taste

Directions:
1. Preheat the Air Fryer to 390F. Season the tri-tip with salt and pepper. Drizzle with oil.
2. Grill in your air fryer for 15 minutes per batch. Meanwhile, prepare the salad by tossing the rest of the ingredients in a salad bowl. Toss in the grilled tri-trip and drizzle with more balsamic vinegar.

Chapter 9. Pork

317. Pork Taquitos
Preparation time: 15 minutes
Cooking time: 17 minutes
Servings: 8
Ingredients:
- 1 juiced lime
- 10 whole-wheat tortillas
- 2 ½ cups of shredded Mozzarella cheese
- 30 oz. of cooked and shredded pork tenderloin

Directions:
1. Preparing the Ingredients. Ensure your air fryer is preheated to 380 degrees. Drizzle pork with lime juice and gently mix. Heat tortillas in the microwave with a dampened paper towel to soften.
2. Add about 3 ounces of pork and ¼ cup of shredded cheese to each tortilla. Tightly roll them up. Spray the air fryer basket with a bit of olive oil.
3. Warm air fryer at 380°F and set time to 10 minutes. Air fry taquitos 7-10 minutes till tortillas turn a slight golden color, making sure to flip halfway through the cooking process.

318. Panko Breaded Pork Chops
Preparation time: 15 minutes
Cooking time: 12 minutes
Servings: 6
Ingredients:
- 5 (3½- to 5-ounce) pork chops (bone-in or boneless)
- Seasoning salt
- Pepper
- ¼ cup all-purpose flour
- 2 tablespoons panko bread crumbs
- Cooking oil

Directions:
1. Flavor the pork chops with the seasoning salt plus pepper to taste. Put the flour on both sides of the pork chops, then coat both sides with panko bread crumbs. Put the pork chops in the air fryer. Stacking them is okay.
2. Spray the pork chops with cooking oil. Air fry for 6 minutes, flip the pork chops. Air fry for an additional 6 minutes Cools before serving.

319. Apricot Glazed Pork Tenderloins
Preparation time: 15 minutes
Cooking time: 30 minutes
Servings: 3
Ingredients:
- 1 teaspoon salt
- 1/2 teaspoon pepper
- 1-lb pork tenderloin
- 2 tablespoons fresh rosemary, minced
- 2 tablespoons olive oil, divided
- 3 garlic cloves, minced

Apricot Glaze Ingredients:
- 1 cup apricot preserves
- 3 garlic cloves, minced
- 4 tablespoons lemon juice

Directions:
1. Mix well pepper, salt, garlic, oil, and rosemary. Brush all over pork. If needed, cut pork crosswise in half to fit in the air fryer. Lightly grease the baking pan of the air fryer with cooking spray. Add pork.
2. Air fry for 3 minutes per side, brown pork in a preheated 390°F air fryer. Meanwhile, mix well all glaze ingredients in a small bowl. Baste pork every 5 minutes. Air fry again for 20 minutes at 330°F. Serve and enjoy.

320. Pork Tenders with Bell Peppers
Preparation time: 15 minutes
Cooking time: 15 minutes
Servings: 4
Ingredients:
- 11 oz. Pork Tenderloin
- 1 Bell Pepper, in thin strips
- 1 Red Onion, sliced
- 2 tsp. Provencal Herbs
- Black Pepper to taste
- 1 tbsp. Olive Oil

- 1/2 tbsp. Mustard
- Needed: Round Oven Dish

Directions:
1. Preheat the air fryer to 390 degrees. In the oven dish, mix the bell pepper strips with the onion, herbs, and salt plus pepper to taste. Put half a tbsp. of olive oil into the mixture
2. Cut the pork tenderloin into four pieces and rub with salt, pepper, and mustard. Thinly coat the pieces with remaining olive oil and place them upright in the oven dish on top of the pepper mixture
3. Place the bowl into the air fryer. Set the timer to 15 minutes to "roast" the meat and the vegetables. Turn the meat and mix the peppers halfway through. Serve with a fresh salad

321. Barbecue Flavored Pork Ribs

Preparation time: 25 minutes
Cooking time: 13 minutes
Servings: 6
Ingredients:
- ¼ cup honey, divided
- ¾ cup BBQ sauce
- 2 tablespoons tomato ketchup
- 1 tablespoon Worcestershire sauce
- 1 tablespoon soy sauce
- ½ teaspoon garlic powder
- Freshly ground white pepper, to taste
- 1¾ pound pork ribs

Directions:
1. Mix 3 tablespoons of honey and remaining ingredients except pork ribs in a large bowl. Refrigerate to marinate for about 20 minutes.
2. Preheat the air fryer to 355 degrees F. Place the ribs in an Air fryer basket. Air fry for about 13 minutes. Remove the ribs from the air fryer and coat with remaining honey. Serve hot.

322. Balsamic Glazed Pork Chops

Preparation time: 2 hours
Cooking time: 30 minutes
Servings: 4
Ingredients:
- ¾ cup balsamic vinegar
- 1 ½ tablespoons sugar
- 1 tablespoon butter
- 3 tablespoons olive oil
- 3 tablespoons salt
- 3 pork rib chops

Directions:
1. Place all ingredients in a bowl and let the meat marinate in the fridge for 2 hours. Preheat the air fryer to 390°F. Place the grill pan accessory in the air fryer.
2. Grill the pork chops for 20 minutes, making sure to flip the meat every 10 minutes for even grilling. Meanwhile, pour the balsamic vinegar into a saucepan and allow to simmer for at least 10 minutes until the sauce thickens. Brush the meat with the glaze before serving.

323. Rustic Pork Ribs

Preparation time: 60 minutes
Cooking time: 25 minutes
Servings: 4
Ingredients:
- 1 rack of pork ribs
- 3 tablespoons dry red wine
- 1 tablespoon soy sauce
- 1/2 teaspoon dried thyme
- 1/2 teaspoon onion powder
- 1/2 teaspoon garlic powder
- 1/2 teaspoon ground black pepper
- 1 teaspoon smoked salt
- 1 tablespoon cornstarch
- 1/2 teaspoon olive oil

Directions:
1. Warm your air fryer to 390 degrees F. Place all ingredients in a mixing bowl and let them marinate at least 1 hour. Air fries the marinated ribs for approximately 25 minutes at 390 degrees F. Serve hot.

324. Keto Parmesan Crusted Pork Chops

Preparation time: 15 minutes
Cooking time: 15 minutes
Servings: 8
Ingredients:
- 3 tbsp.. grated parmesan cheese
- 1 cup of pork rind crumbs
- 2 beaten eggs
- ¼ tsp. chili powder
- ½ tsp. onion powder
- 1 tsp. smoked paprika
- ¼ tsp. pepper
- ½ tsp. salt
- 4-6 thick boneless pork chops

Directions:
2. Ensure your air fryer is preheated to 400 degrees. With pepper and salt, season both sides of pork chops.
3. In a food processor, pulse pork rinds into crumbs. Mix crumbs with other seasonings. Beat eggs and add to another bowl. Dip pork chops into eggs then into pork rind crumb mixture.
4. Spray down air fryer with olive oil and add pork chops to the basket. Set temperature to 400°F and air fry 15 minutes.

325. Crispy Fried Pork Chops the Southern Way

Preparation time: 60 minutes
Cooking time: 25 minutes
Servings: 4
Ingredients:
- ½ cup all-purpose flour
- ½ cup low-fat buttermilk
- ½ teaspoon black pepper

- ½ teaspoon Tabasco sauce
- teaspoon paprika
- 3 bone-in pork chops

Directions:
1. Put the buttermilk plus hot sauce in a Ziploc bag and add the pork chops. Allow marinating for an hour in the fridge.
2. In a bowl, combine the flour, paprika, and black pepper. Remove pork from the Ziploc bag and dredge in the flour mixture.
3. Preheat the air fryer to 390°F. Spray the pork chops with cooking oil. Put in the air fryer basket and air fry for 25 minutes.

326. Fried Pork Quesadilla

Preparation time: 15 minutes
Cooking time: 32 minutes
Servings: 2
Ingredients:
- 2 6-inch corn or flour tortilla shells
- 1 medium-sized pork shoulder, approximately 4 ounces, sliced
- ½ medium-sized white onion, sliced
- ½ medium-sized red pepper, sliced
- ½ medium-sized green pepper, sliced
- ½ medium-sized yellow pepper, sliced
- ¼ cup of shredded pepper-jack cheese
- ¼ cup of shredded Mozzarella cheese

Directions:
1. Preheat the air fryer to 350 degrees.
2. In the oven on a high heat for 20 minutes, grill the pork, onion, and peppers in foil in the same pan, allowing the moisture from the vegetables and the juice from the pork mingle. Remove pork and vegetables in foil from the oven.
3. While they're cooling, sprinkle half the shredded cheese over one of the tortillas, then cover with the pieces of pork, onions, peppers, and then layer on the rest of the shredded cheese. Top with the second tortilla. Place directly on the hot surface of the air fryer basket.
4. Air fry for 6 minutes. After 6 minutes, when the air fryer shuts off, flip the tortillas onto the other side with a spatula; the cheese should be melted enough that it won't fall apart, but be careful anyway not to spill any toppings!
5. Reset the air fryer to 350 degrees for another 6 minutes, air fry. When the air fryer shuts off, the tortillas should be browned and crisp, and the pork, onion, peppers, and cheese will be crispy and hot and delicious. Remove with tongs and let sit on a serving plate to cool for a few minutes before slicing.

327. Cilantro-Mint Pork BBQ Thai Style

Preparation time: 15 minutes
Cooking time: 15 minutes
Servings: 3
Ingredients:
- 1 minced hot chili
- 1 minced shallot
- 1-pound ground pork
- 2 tablespoons fish sauce
- 2 tablespoons lime juice
- 3 tablespoons basil
- 3 tablespoons chopped mint
- 3 tablespoons cilantro

Directions:
1. In a shallow dish, mix well all ingredients with hands. Form into 1-inch ovals. Thread ovals in skewers. Place on skewer rack in the air fryer.
2. Air Fry for 15 minutes, cook at 360°F. Halfway through cooking time, turnover skewers. If needed, cook in batches. Serve and enjoy.

328. Tuscan Pork Chops

Preparation time: 15 minutes
Cooking time: 15 minutes
Servings: 4
Ingredients:
- 1/4 cup all-purpose flour
- 1 teaspoon salt
- 3/4 teaspoons seasoned pepper
- 4 (1-inch-thick) boneless pork chops
- 1 tablespoon olive oil
- 3 to 4 garlic cloves
- 1/3 cup balsamic vinegar
- 1/3 cup chicken broth
- 3 plum tomatoes, seeded and diced
- 3 tablespoons capers

Directions:
1. Combine flour, salt, and pepper. Press pork chops into flour mixture on both sides until evenly covered. Air fry at 360 degrees for 14 minutes, flipping halfway through.
2. While the pork chops cook, warm olive oil in a medium skillet, add garlic and sauté for 1 minute, then mix in vinegar and chicken broth. Add capers and tomatoes and turn to high heat.
3. Bring the sauce to a boil, stirring regularly, then add pork chops, cooking for one minute. Remove, then cover for about 5 minutes to allow the pork to absorb some of the sauce; serve hot.

329. Italian Parmesan Breaded Pork Chops

Preparation time: 15 minutes
Cooking time: 12 minutes
Servings: 5
Ingredients:
- 5 (3½- to 5-ounce) pork chops (bone-in or boneless)
- 1 teaspoon Italian seasoning
- Seasoning salt
- Pepper
- ¼ cup all-purpose flour
- 2 tablespoons Italian bread crumbs
- 3 tablespoons finely grated Parmesan cheese
- Cooking oil

Directions:

1. Flavor the pork chops with the Italian seasoning and seasoning salt and pepper to taste. Sprinkle the flour on all sides of the pork chops, then coat with the bread crumbs and Parmesan cheese.
2. Place the pork chops in the air fryer. Stacking them is okay. Spray the pork chops with cooking oil. Air fry for 6 minutes, then open the air fryer and flip the pork chops. Air fry again for 6 minutes.
3. Cool before serving. Instead of seasoning salt, you can use either chicken or pork rub for additional flavor. You can find these rubs in the spice aisle of the grocery store.

330. Crispy Roast Garlic-Salt Pork

Preparation time: 15 minutes
Cooking time: 45 minutes
Servings: 4
Ingredients:
- 1 teaspoon Chinese five-spice powder
- 1 teaspoon white pepper
- 2 pounds of pork belly
- 2 teaspoons garlic salt

Directions:
1. Preheat the air fryer to 390°F. Mix all the listed spices in a bowl to create the dry rub. Slice or score the pork belly's skin using a knife and season the entire pork with the spice rub.
2. Put in the air fryer basket and air fry for 40 to 45 minutes until the skin is crispy. Chop before serving.

331. Peanut Satay Pork

Preparation time: 15 minutes
Cooking time: 20 minutes
Servings: 5
Ingredients:
- 11 oz. Pork Fillet, sliced into bite-sized strips
- 4 Cloves Garlic, crushed
- 1 tsp. Ginger Powder
- 2 tsp. Chili Paste
- 2 tbsp. Sweet Soy Sauce
- 2 tbsp. Vegetable Oil
- 1 Shallot, finely chopped
- 1 tsp. Ground Coriander
- 3/4 Cup Coconut Milk
- 1/3 Cup Peanuts, ground

Directions:
1. Mix half of the garlic, ginger, a tablespoon of sweet soy sauce, and a tablespoon of the oil in a dish. Combine the meat into the mixture and leave to marinate for 15 minutes
2. Preheat the air fryer to 390 F. Place the marinated meat into the air fryer. Roast for 12 minutes until brown and done. Turn once while roasting
3. In the meantime, make the peanut sauce by heating the remaining tablespoon of oil in a saucepan and gently sauté the shallot with the garlic. Add the coriander and fry until fragrant
4. Mix the coconut milk plus the peanuts with the chili paste and remaining soy sauce with the shallot mixture and gently boil for 5 minutes, while stirring. Drizzle over the cooked meat and serve with rice

332. Boozy Pork Loin Chops

Preparation time: 15 minutes
Cooking time: 18 minutes
Servings: 6
Ingredients:
- 2 tablespoons vermouth
- 6 center-cut loin pork chops
- 1/2 tablespoon fresh basil, minced
- 1/3 teaspoon ground black pepper, or more to taste
- 2 tablespoons whole-grain mustard
- 1 teaspoon fine kosher salt

Directions:
1. Toss pork chops with other ingredients until they are well coated on both sides. Air-fry your chops for 18 minutes at 405 degrees F, turning once or twice. Mound your favorite salad on a serving plate; top with pork chops and enjoy.

333. Pork Sausage with Mashed Cauliflower

Preparation time: 15 minutes
Cooking time: 27 minutes
Servings: 6
Ingredients:
- 1-pound cauliflower, chopped
- 1/2 teaspoon tarragon
- 1/3 cup Colby cheese
- 1/2 teaspoon ground black pepper
- 1/2 onion, peeled and sliced
- 1 teaspoon cumin powder
- 1/2 teaspoon sea salt
- 3 beaten eggs
- 6 pork sausages, chopped

Directions:
1. Boil the cauliflower until tender. Then, purée the cauliflower in your blender. Transfer to a mixing dish along with the other ingredients.
2. Divide the prepared mixture among six lightly greased ramekins; now, place ramekins in your air fryer. Bake in the preheated Air Fryer for 27 minutes at 365 degrees F. Eat warm.

334. Farmhouse Pork with Vegetables

Preparation time: 15 minutes
Cooking time: 45 minutes
Servings: 6
Ingredients:
- 1 ½ pound pork belly
- 2 bell peppers, sliced
- 2 cloves garlic, finely minced
- 4 green onions, quartered, white and green parts
- 1/4 cup cooking wine
- Kosher salt
- ground black pepper
- 1 teaspoon cayenne pepper
- 1 tablespoon coriander
- 1 teaspoon celery seeds

Directions:
1. Put the pork belly in boiled water for approximately 15 minutes. Then, cut it into chunks.
2. Arrange the pork chunks, bell peppers, garlic, and green onions in the Air Fryer basket. Drizzle everything with cooking wine of your choice.
3. Sprinkle with salt, black pepper, cayenne pepper, fresh coriander, and celery seeds. Toss to coat well.
4. Roast in the preheated Air Fryer at 330 degrees F for 30 minutes. Serve on individual serving plates. Bon appétit!

335. Spicy Pork Meatballs
Preparation time: 15 minutes
Cooking time: 15 minutes
Servings: 4
Ingredients:
- 1-pound ground pork
- 1 cup scallions, finely chopped
- 2 cloves garlic, finely minced
- 1 ½ tablespoon Worcester sauce
- 1 tablespoon oyster sauce
- 1 teaspoon turmeric powder
- 1/2 teaspoon freshly grated ginger root
- 1 small sliced red chili, for garnish

Directions:
1. Mix all the above fixings, apart from the red chili. Knead with your hands to ensure an even mixture.
2. Roll into equal balls and transfer them to the Air Fryer cooking basket. Air fry for 15 minutes at 350 degrees F. Sprinkle with sliced red chili; serve immediately with your favorite sauce for dipping. Enjoy!

336. 30-Minute Hoisin Pork Loin Steak
Preparation time: 20 minutes
Cooking time: 5 minutes
Servings: 4
Ingredients:
- 2 tablespoons dry white wine
- 1/3 cup hoisin sauce
- 2 teaspoons smoked cayenne pepper
- 3 garlic cloves, pressed
- 1/2-pound pork loin steak, cut into strips
- 3 teaspoons fresh lime juice
- Salt and ground black pepper, to taste

Directions:
1. Start by preheating your Air Fryer to 395 degrees F. Toss the pork with other ingredients; let it marinate at least 20 minutes in a fridge. Then, air-fry the pork strips for 5 minutes. Bon appétit!

337. Pork Kebabs with Serrano Pepper
Preparation time: 15 minutes
Cooking time: 18 minutes
Servings: 3
Ingredients:
- 2 tablespoons tomato puree
- 1/2 fresh serrano, minced
- 1/3 teaspoon paprika
- 1-pound pork, ground
- 1/2 cup green onions, finely chopped
- 3 cloves garlic, peeled and finely minced
- 1 teaspoon ground black pepper
- 1 teaspoon salt, or more to taste

Directions:
1. Thoroughly combine all ingredients in a mixing dish. Then, form your mixture into sausage shapes. Air fry for 18 minutes at 355 degrees F. Mound salad on a serving platter, top with air-fried kebabs, and serve warm. Bon appétit!

338. Bacon-Wrapped Hot Dogs
Preparation time: 15 minutes
Cooking time: 12 minutes
Servings: 5
Ingredients:
- 10 thin slices of bacon
- 5 pork hot dogs, halved
- 1 teaspoon cayenne pepper

Sauce:
- 1/4 cup mayo
- 4 tablespoons ketchup, low-carb
- 1 teaspoon rice vinegar
- 1 teaspoon chili powder

Directions:
1. Lay the slices of bacon on your working surface. Place a hot dog on one end of each slice; sprinkle with cayenne pepper and roll them over. Air fry in the preheated Air Fryer at 390 degrees F for 10 to 12 minutes.
2. Whisk all ingredients for the sauce in a mixing bowl and store in your refrigerator, covered, until ready to serve. Serve bacon-wrapped hot dogs with the sauce on the side. Enjoy!

339. Cheesy Ground Pork Casserole
Preparation time: 15 minutes
Cooking time: 10 minutes
Servings: 4
Ingredients:
- 1-pound lean ground pork
- 1/2-pound ground beef
- 1/4 cup tomato puree
- Sea salt
- ground black pepper
- 1 teaspoon smoked paprika
- 1/2 teaspoon dried oregano
- 1 teaspoon dried basil
- 1 teaspoon dried rosemary
- 2 eggs
- 1 cup Cottage cheese, crumbled, at room temperature
- 1/2 cup Cotija cheese, shredded

Directions:
1. Lightly grease a casserole dish with nonstick cooking oil. Add the ground meat to the bottom of your casserole dish. Add the tomato puree. Sprinkle with

salt, black pepper, paprika, oregano, basil, and rosemary.
2. In a mixing bowl, whisk the egg with cheese. Place on top of the ground meat mixture. Place a piece of foil on top.
3. Bake in the preheated Air Fryer at 350 degrees F for 10 minutes; remove the foil and cook an additional 6 minutes. Bon appétit!

340. Spicy Pork with Herbs and Candy Onions
Preparation time: 15 minutes
Cooking time: 50 minutes
Servings: 4
Ingredients:
- 1 rosemary sprig, chopped
- 1 thyme sprig, chopped
- 1 teaspoon dried sage, crushed
- Sea salt
- ground black pepper
- 1 teaspoon cayenne pepper
- 2 teaspoons sesame oil
- 2 pounds pork leg roast, scored
- 1/2-pound candy onions, peeled
- 2 chili peppers, minced
- 4 cloves garlic, finely chopped

Directions:
1. Start by warming or preheating your Air Fryer to 400 degrees F. Then, mix the seasonings with the sesame oil. Rub the seasoning batter all over the pork leg.
2. Air fry in the preheated Air Fryer for 40 minutes. Add the candy onions, peppers, and garlic and air fry an additional 12 minutes.
3. Slice the pork leg. Afterward, spoon the pan juices over the meat and serve with the candy onions. Bon appétit!

341. Pork Steak with Mustard and Herbs
Preparation time: 15 minutes
Cooking time: 14 minutes
Servings: 2
Ingredients:
- 1-pound porterhouse steak, cut meat from bones in 2 pieces
- 1/2 teaspoon ground black pepper
- 1 teaspoon cayenne pepper
- 1/2 teaspoon salt
- 1 teaspoon garlic powder
- 1/2 teaspoon dried thyme
- 1/2 teaspoon dried marjoram
- 1 teaspoon Dijon mustard
- 1 tablespoon butter, melted

Directions
1. Sprinkle the porterhouse steak with all the seasonings. Spread the mustard and butter evenly over the meat.
2. Air fry in the preheated Air Fryer at 390 degrees F for 12 to 14 minutes. Taste for doneness with a meat thermometer and serve immediately.

342. Spicy and Creamy Pork Gratin
Preparation time: 15 minutes
Cooking time: 22 minutes
Servings: 4
Ingredients:
- 2 tablespoons olive oil
- 2 pounds pork tenderloin, cut into serving-size pieces
- 1 teaspoon coarse sea salt
- 1/2 teaspoon freshly ground pepper
- 1/4 teaspoon chili powder
- 1 teaspoon dried marjoram
- 1 tablespoon mustard
- 1 cup Ricotta cheese
- 1 ½ cups chicken broth

Directions:
1. Warm your Air Fryer to 350 degrees F. Heat the olive oil in a pan over medium-high heat. Once hot, cook the pork for 6 to 7 minutes, flipping it to ensure even cooking.
2. Arrange the pork in a lightly greased casserole dish. Season with salt, black pepper, chili powder, and marjoram.
3. In a mixing dish, thoroughly combine the mustard, cheese, and chicken broth. Put the mixture over the pork chops in the casserole dish. Bake for 15 minutes or until bubbly and heated through. Bon appétit!

343. Pork Tenderloin with Herbs
Preparation time: 15 minutes
Cooking time: 17 minutes
Servings: 4
Ingredients:
- 1-pound pork tenderloin
- 4-5 garlic cloves, peeled and halved
- 1 teaspoon kosher salt
- 1/3 teaspoon ground black pepper
- 1 teaspoon dried basil
- 1/2 teaspoon dried oregano
- 1/2 teaspoon dried rosemary
- 1/2 teaspoon dried marjoram
- 2 tablespoons cooking wine

Directions:
1. Rub the pork with garlic halves; add the seasoning and drizzle with the cooking wine. Then, cut slits completely through pork tenderloin. Tuck the remaining garlic into the slits.
2. Wrap the pork tenderloin with foil; let it marinate overnight. Roast in your air fryer at 360 degrees F for 15 to 17 minutes. Serve warm with roasted potatoes. Bon appétit!

344. Family Pork Loin Roast
Preparation time: 15 minutes
Cooking time: 55 minutes
Servings: 6
Ingredients:

- 1 ½ pound boneless pork loin roast, washed
- 1 teaspoon mustard seeds
- 1 teaspoon garlic powder
- 1 teaspoon porcini powder
- 1 teaspoon shallot powder
- 3/4 teaspoon sea salt flakes
- 1 teaspoon red pepper flakes, crushed
- 2 dried sprigs thyme, crushed
- 2 tablespoons lime juice

Directions:
1. Firstly, score the meat using a small knife; make sure not to cut too deep. In a small-sized mixing dish, combine all seasonings in the order listed above; mix to combine well. Massage the spice mix into the pork meat to evenly distribute. Drizzle with lemon juice.
2. Then, set your Air Fryer to cook at 360 degrees F. Place the pork in the Air Fryer basket; roast for 25 to 30 minutes. Pause the machine, check for doneness, and roast for 25 minutes more.

345. Traditional Walliser Schnitzel

Preparation time: 15 minutes
Cooking time: 14 minutes
Servings: 2
Ingredients:
- 1/3 tablespoon cider vinegar
- 1/3 teaspoon ground black pepper
- 1 teaspoon garlic salt
- 1/2 teaspoon mustard
- 1/2 heaping tablespoon fresh parsley
- 1/2 cup pork rinds
- 2 eggs, beaten
- 1/2 teaspoon fennel seed
- 2 pork schnitzel, halved

Directions:
1. Blitz the vinegar, black pepper, garlic salt, mustard, fennel seeds, fresh parsley, and pork rinds in your food processor until uniform and smooth.
2. Dump the blended mixture into a shallow bowl. Add the beaten egg to another shallow bowl. Coat the pork schnitzel with the beaten egg; then, dredge it in the herb mixture.
3. Air fry in the preheated Air Fryer at 355 degrees F for about 14 minutes. Bon appétit!

346. Bolognese Sauce with a Twist

Preparation time: 15 minutes
Cooking time: 14 minutes
Servings: 4
Ingredients:
- 1 teaspoon kosher salt
- 1/3 teaspoon cayenne pepper
- 1½ pounds ground pork
- 1/3 cup tomato paste
- 3 cloves garlic, minced
- 1/2 medium-sized white onion, peeled and chopped
- 1/3 tablespoon fresh cilantro, chopped
- 1/2 tablespoon extra-virgin olive oil
- 1/3 teaspoon freshly cracked black pepper
- 1/2 teaspoon grated fresh ginger

Directions:
1. Begin by preheating your Air Fryer to 395 degrees F. Then, thoroughly combine all the ingredients until the mixture is uniform.
2. Transfer the meat mixture to the Air Fryer baking dish and air fry for about 14 minutes. Serve with zucchini noodles and enjoy.

Chapter 10. Lamb

347. Caraway, Sichuan 'n Cumin Lamb Kebabs
Preparation Time: 15 minutes
Cooking time: 1 hour
Servings: 3
Ingredients:
- 1 ½ pounds lamb shoulder, bones removed and cut into pieces
- 1 tablespoon Sichuan peppercorns
- 1 teaspoon sugar
- 2 tablespoons cumin seeds, toasted
- 2 teaspoons caraway seeds, toasted
- 2 teaspoons crushed red pepper flakes
- Salt and pepper to taste

Directions:
1. Place all fixing in a bowl and let the meat to marinate in the fridge for 2 hours. Preheat the air fryer to 390F. Place the grill pan accessory in the air fryer. Grill the meat for 15 minutes per batch. Flip the meat every 8 minutes for even grilling.

348. Garlic Lemon-Wine on Lamb Steak
Preparation Time: 20 minutes
Cooking time: 1 hour and 30 minutes
Servings: 4
Ingredients:
- ¼ cup extra virgin olive oil
- ½ cup dry white wine
- 1 tablespoon brown sugar
- 2 pounds lamb steak, pounded
- 2 tablespoons lemon juice
- 3 tablespoons ancho chili powder
- 8 cloves of garlic, minced
- Salt and pepper to taste

Directions:
1. Place all fixing in a bowl and allow the meat to marinate in the fridge for at least 2 hours. Preheat the air fryer to 390 F. Place the grill pans in the air fryer.
2. Grill the meat for 20 minutes per batch. Meanwhile, pour the marinade into a saucepan and allow simmering for 10 minutes until the sauce thickens.

349. Garlic-Rosemary Lamb BBQ
Preparation Time: 5 minutes
Cooking time: 12 minutes
Servings: 2
Ingredients:
- 1-lb cubed lamb leg
- Juice of 1 lemon
- Fresh rosemary
- 3 smashed garlic cloves
- Salt and pepper
- 1/2 cup olive oil

Directions:
1. In a shallow dish, mix well all ingredients and marinate for 3 hours. Thread lamb pieces in skewers. Place on skewer rack in the air fryer.
2. For 12 minutes, grill on 390 F. Halfway through cooking time, turnover skewers. If needed, cook in batches. Serve and enjoy.

350. Maras Pepper Lamb Kebab Recipe from Turkey
Preparation Time: 5 minutes
Cooking time: 15 minutes
Servings: 2
Ingredients:
- 1-lb lamb meat, cut into 2-inch cubes
- Kosher salt
- Freshly cracked black pepper
- 2 tablespoons Maras pepper, or 2 teaspoons other dried chili powder mixed with 1 tablespoon paprika
- 1 teaspoon minced garlic
- 2 tablespoons roughly chopped fresh mint
- 1/2 cup extra-virgin olive oil, divided
- 1/2 cup dried apricots, cut into medium dice

Directions:
1. In a bowl, mix pepper, salt, and half of the olive oil. Add lamb and toss well to coat. Thread lamb into 4 skewers. Grill in the air fryer for 5 minutes at 390 F or to the desired doneness.

2. In a large bowl, mix well the remaining oil, mint, garlic, Maras pepper, and apricots. Add cooked lamb. Season with salt and pepper. Toss well to coat. Serve and enjoy.

351. Saffron Spiced Rack of Lamb
Preparation Time: 20 minutes
Cooking time: 1 hour and 10 minutes
Servings: 4
Ingredients:
- ½ teaspoon crumbled saffron threads
- 1 cup plain Greek yogurt
- 1 teaspoon lemon zest
- 2 cloves of garlic, minced
- 2 racks of lamb, rib bones frenched
- 2 tablespoons olive oil
- Salt and pepper to taste

Directions:
1. Preheat the air fryer to 3900F. Place the grill pan accessory in the air fryer. Flavor the lamb meat with salt and pepper to taste. Set aside.
2. In a bowl, combine the rest of the ingredients. Brush the mixture onto the lamb. Place on the grill pan and cook for 1 hour and 10 minutes. Serve.

352. Simple Lamb BBQ with Herbed Salt
Preparation Time: 20 minutes
Cooking time: 1 hour 20 minutes
Servings: 8
Ingredients:
- 2 ½ tablespoons herb salt
- 2 tablespoons olive oil
- 4 pounds boneless lamb legs, cut into 2-inch chunks

Directions:
1. Preheat the air fryer to 390F. Season the meat with the herb salt and brush with olive oil. Grill the meat for 20 minutes per batch. Make sure to flip the meat every 10 minutes for even cooking. Serve.

353. Greek Lamb Meatballs
Preparation Time: 12 minutes
Cooking time: 12 minutes
Servings: 12
Ingredients:
- 1-pound ground lamb
- ½ cup breadcrumbs
- ¼ cup milk
- 2 egg yolks
- 1 teaspoon ground coriander
- 1 teaspoon ground cumin
- 3 garlic cloves, minced
- 1 teaspoon dried oregano
- ½ teaspoon salt
- ½ teaspoon black pepper
- 1 lemon, juiced and zested
- ¼ cup fresh parsley, chopped
- ½ cup crumbled feta cheese
- Olive oil, for shaping
- Tzatziki, for dipping

Directions:
1. Combine all fixing except olive oil in a large mixing bowl and mix until fully incorporated. Form 12 meatballs, about 2 ounces each. Use olive oil on your hands, so they don't stick to the meatballs. Set aside.
2. Preheat your air fryer, place the meatballs on the food tray, then insert the tray at the top position in the preheated air fryer. Broil on your air fryer for to 12 minutes. Take out the meatballs when done and serve with a side of tzatziki.

354. Glazed Lamb Chops
Preparation Time: 10 minutes
Cooking time: 15 minutes
Servings: 4
Ingredients:
- 1 tablespoon Dijon mustard
- ½ tablespoon fresh lime juice
- 1 teaspoon honey
- ½ teaspoon olive oil
- Salt and ground black pepper, as required
- 4 (4-ounce) lamb loin chops

Directions:
1. In a black pepper large bowl, mix the mustard, lemon juice, oil, honey, salt, and black pepper. Add the chops and coat with the mixture generously. Place the chops onto the greased sheet pan.
2. Set the air fryer at 390 degrees F. Bake for 15 minutes. Flip the chops once halfway through. Serve hot.

355. Lamb Burgers
Preparation Time: 10 minutes
Cooking time: 8 minutes
Servings: 6
Ingredients:
- 2 pounds ground lamb
- ½ tablespoon onion powder
- ½ tablespoon garlic powder
- ¼ teaspoon ground cumin
- Salt and ground black pepper, as required

Directions:
1. Mix all the fixing in a bowl. Make 6 equal-sized patties from the mixture. Arrange the patties onto the greased sheet pan in a single layer.
2. Set the air fryer the temperature at 360 degrees F. Air fry for 8 minutes, flip the burgers once halfway through. Serve hot.

356. Oregano Lamb Chops
Preparation Time: 10 minutes
Cooking time: 30 minutes
Servings: 4
Ingredients:
- 4 lamb chops
- 1 garlic clove, peeled
- 1 tbsp. plus
- 2 tsp. olive oil
- ½ tbsp. oregano
- ½ tbsp. thyme

- Salt and black pepper to taste

Directions:
1. Preheat the Air Fryer to 390 F. Coat the garlic clove with 1 tsp. of olive oil and place it in the air fryer for 10 minutes. Meanwhile, mix the herbs and seasonings with the remaining olive oil.
2. Using a towel or a mitten, squeeze the hot roasted garlic clove into the herb mixture and stir to combine. Coat the lamb chops with the mixture well and place it in the fryer. Air fry for 8 to 12 minutes. Serve hot.

357. Lamb Steaks with Fresh Mint and Potatoes

Preparation Time: 10 minutes
Cooking time: 25 minutes
Servings: 2
Ingredients:
- 2 lamb steaks
- 2 tbsp. olive oil
- 2 garlic cloves, crushed
- Salt and pepper, to taste
- A handful of fresh thyme, chopped
- 4 red potatoes, cubed

Directions:
1. Rub the steaks with oil, garlic, salt, and black pepper. Put thyme in the fryer and place the steaks on top. Oil the potato chunks and sprinkle with salt and pepper.
2. Arrange the potatoes next to the steaks, and air fry on 360 F for 14 minutes, turning once halfway through cooking.

358. Crunchy Cashew Lamb Rack

Preparation Time: 10 minutes
Cooking time: 30 minutes
Servings: 4
Ingredients:
- 3 oz. chopped cashews
- 1 tbsp. chopped rosemary
- 1 ½ lb. rack of lamb
- 1 garlic clove, minced
- 1 tbsp. breadcrumbs
- 1 egg, beaten
- 1 tbsp. olive oil
- Salt and pepper to taste

Directions:
1. Preheat air fryer to 210 F. Combine olive oil with the garlic and brush this mixture onto lamb. Combine rosemary, cashews, and crumbs in a bowl.
2. Brush egg over the lambs, and coat it with the cashew mixture. Place the lamb into the air fryer's basket, air fry for 25 minutes.
3. Increase the temperature to 390 F, and air fry for 5 more minutes. Cover with a foil and let sit for a couple of minutes before serving.

359. Lamb Meatballs

Preparation Time: 10 minutes
Cooking time: 40 minutes
Servings: 12
Ingredients:
- 1 ½ lb. ground lamb
- ½ cup minced onion
- 2 tbsp. chopped mint leaves
- 3 garlic cloves, minced
- 2 tsp. paprika
- 2 tsp. coriander seeds
- ½ tsp. cayenne pepper
- 1 tsp. salt
- 1 tbsp. chopped parsley
- 2 tsp. cumin
- ½ tsp. ground ginger

Directions:
1. Soak 24 skewers in water until ready to use. Preheat the air fryer to 330 F. Combine all ingredients in a large bowl. Mix well with your hands until the herbs and spices are evenly distributed, and the mixture is well incorporated.
2. Shape the lamb mixture into 12 sausage shapes around 2 skewers. Air fry for 12 to 15 minutes, or until it reaches the preferred doneness. Served with tzatziki sauce and enjoy.

360. Herbed Lamb Loin Chops

Preparation Time: 15 minutes
Cooking Time: 12 minutes
Servings: 2
Ingredients:
- 4 (4-ounce) (½-inch thick) lamb loin chops
- 1 teaspoon fresh thyme, minced
- 1 teaspoon fresh rosemary, minced
- 1 teaspoon fresh oregano, minced
- 2 garlic cloves, crushed
- Salt and ground black pepper, as required

Directions:
1. In a large bowl, place all ingredients and mix well. Refrigerate to marinate overnight. Arrange the chops onto the greased steak tray.
2. Bake in your air fryer at a temperature of 400 degrees F for 12 minutes. Flip the chops once halfway through. Remove the chops and serve hot.

361. Mustard Lamb Chops

Preparation Time: 15 minutes
Cooking Time: 15 minutes
Servings: 2
Ingredients:
- 1 tablespoon Dijon mustard
- ½ tablespoon white wine vinegar
- 1 teaspoon olive oil
- ½ teaspoon dried tarragon
- Salt and ground black pepper, as required
- 4 (4-ounce) lamb loin chops

Directions:
1. Mix the mustard, vinegar, oil, tarragon, salt, and black pepper in a large bowl. Add the chops and coat with the mixture generously. Arrange the chops onto the greased steak tray.

2. Bake at a temperature of 390 degrees F for 15 minutes. Flip the chops once halfway through. Remove and serve hot.

362. Herbed Leg of Lamb

Preparation Time: 15 minutes
Cooking Time: 1¼ hours
Servings: 8
Ingredients:
- 1 (2¼-pound) boneless leg of lamb
- 3 tablespoons olive oil
- Salt and ground black pepper, as required
- 2 fresh rosemary sprigs
- 2 fresh thyme sprigs

Directions:
1. Rub the leg of lamb with oil and sprinkle with salt and black pepper. Wrap the leg of lamb with herb sprigs. Arrange the leg of lamb into the greased air frying basket.
2. Air fry to preheated air fryer 300 degrees F for 75 minutes. Remove the leg of lamb and place it onto a cutting board for about 10 minutes before slicing. Slice the leg of lamb into desired sized pieces and serve.

363. Cheesy Lamb Burgers

Preparation Time: 15 minutes
Cooking Time: 18 minutes
Servings: 4
Ingredients:
For Burgers:
- 1-pound ground lamb
- ½ cup simple breadcrumbs
- ¼ cup red onion, chopped finely
- 3 tablespoons brown mustard
- 3 teaspoons low-sodium soy sauce
- 2 teaspoons fresh parsley, chopped finely
- Salt, to taste

For Topping:
- 2 tablespoons mustard
- 1 tablespoon brown sugar
- 1 teaspoon low-sodium soy sauce
- 4 Swiss cheese slices

Directions:
1. For burgers, in a large bowl, add all the ingredients and mix until well combined. Make 4 equal-sized patties from the mixture.
2. Arrange the patties onto the greased steak tray in a single layer. Preheat your air fryer at 370 degrees F. Air fry for 15 minutes. Flip the burgers once halfway through.
3. Meanwhile, in a small bowl, add the mustard, brown sugar, soy sauce, and mix well. Remove the tray and coat the burgers with mustard mixture.
4. Arrange 1 cheese slice over each burger. Return the tray to the air fryer. Broil for 3 minutes, remove the burgers, and serve hot.

364. Spicy Lamb Burgers

Preparation Time: 15 minutes
Cooking Time: 10 minutes
Servings: 6
Ingredients:
- 2 pounds ground lamb
- ½ tablespoon garlic powder
- ¼ teaspoon ground cumin
- ¼ teaspoon cayenne pepper
- Salt and ground black pepper, as required

Directions:
1. In a bowl, add all the fixing and mix well. Make 6 equal-sized patties from the mixture. Arrange the patties onto the greased steak tray in a single layer.
2. Preheat your air fryer to 360 degrees F. Air fry for 10 minutes. Flip the burgers once halfway through. Serve.

Chapter 11. Fish and Seafood

365. Bacon-Wrapped Shrimp
Preparation time: 20 minutes
Cooking time: 7 minutes
Servings: 4
Ingredients:
- 1¼ pound tiger shrimp, peeled and deveined
- 1-pound bacon

Directions:
1. Wrap the shrimp using a slice of bacon. Refrigerate for about 20 minutes. Warm air fryer to 390 degrees F. Arranges the shrimp in the rack/basket. Air fry for about 5-7 minutes. Serve.

366. Crispy Paprika Fish Fillets
Preparation time: 5 minutes
Cooking time: 15 minutes
Servings: 4
Ingredients:
- 1/2 cup seasoned breadcrumbs
- 1 tablespoon balsamic vinegar
- 1/2 teaspoon seasoned salt
- 1 teaspoon paprika
- 1/2 teaspoon ground black pepper
- 1 teaspoon celery seed
- 2 fish fillets, halved
- 1 egg, beaten

Directions:
1. Process the breadcrumbs, vinegar, salt, paprika, ground black pepper, plus celery seeds to your food processor for 30 seconds.
2. Cover the fish fillets with the beaten egg; then, coat them with the breadcrumb's mixture. Air fry at 350 degrees F for about 15 minutes.

367. Air Fryer Salmon
Preparation time: 5 minutes
Cooking time: 10 minutes
Servings: 2
Ingredients:
- ½ tsp. salt
- ½ tsp. garlic powder
- ½ tsp. smoked paprika
- Salmon

Directions:
1. Mix spices and sprinkle onto salmon. Place seasoned salmon into the air fryer. Set temperature to 400°F and air fry to 10 minutes.

368. Quick Paella
Preparation time: 15 minutes
Cooking time: 17 minutes
Servings: 4
Ingredients:
- 1 (10-ounce) package frozen cooked rice, thawed
- 1 (6-ounce) jar artichoke hearts, drained and chopped
- ¼ cup vegetable broth
- ½ teaspoon turmeric
- ½ teaspoon dried thyme
- 1 cup frozen cooked small shrimp
- ½ cup frozen baby peas
- 1 tomato, diced

Directions:
1. In a 6-by-6-by-2-inch pan, combine the rice, artichoke hearts, vegetable broth, turmeric, and thyme, and stir gently.
2. Place in the air fryer and bake for 8 to 9 minutes or until the rice is hot. Remove from the air fryer and gently stir in the shrimp, peas, and tomato. Cook for 5 to 8 minutes or until the shrimp and peas are hot, and the paella is boiling.

369. Coconut Shrimp
Preparation time: 15 minutes
Cooking time: 7 minutes
Servings: 4
Ingredients:
- 1 (8-ounce) can crush pineapple, juice reserve
- ½ cup sour cream
- ¼ cup pineapple preserves
- 2 egg whites
- 2/3 cup cornstarch

- 2/3 cup sweetened coconut
- 1 cup panko bread crumbs
- 1-pound uncooked large shrimp, thawed if frozen, deveined and shelled
- Olive oil for misting

Directions:
1. Mix the pineapple, sour cream, and preserves in a small bowl. Set aside.
2. Mix the egg whites plus 2 tablespoons of the reserved pineapple liquid in a shallow bowl. Place the cornstarch on a plate. Combine the coconut and bread crumbs on another plate.
3. Dip the shrimp into the cornstarch, shake it off, then dip into the egg white mixture and finally into the coconut mixture.
4. Place the shrimp in the air fryer rack/basket and mist with oil. Air fry for 5 to 7 minutes or until the shrimp is crisp and golden brown.

370. Cilantro-Lime Fried Shrimp

Preparation time: 30 minutes
Cooking time: 10 minutes
Servings: 4
Ingredients:
- 1-pound raw shrimp, peeled and deveined with tails on or off
- ½ cup chopped fresh cilantro
- Juice of 1 lime
- 1 egg
- ½ cup all-purpose flour
- ¾ cup bread crumbs
- Salt
- Pepper
- Cooking oil
- ½ cup cocktail sauce (optional)

Directions:
1. Place the shrimp in a plastic bag and add the cilantro and lime juice. Seal the bag. Shake to combine. Marinate in the refrigerator for 30 minutes.
2. In a small bowl, beat the egg. In another small bowl, place the flour. Place the bread crumbs in a third small bowl, and season with salt and pepper to taste.
3. Spray the air fryer rack/basket with cooking oil. Remove the shrimp from the plastic bag. Dip each in the flour, then the egg, and then the bread crumbs.
4. Place the shrimp in the air fryer. It is okay to stack them. Spray the shrimp with cooking oil. Air fry for 4 minutes.
5. Open the air fryer and flip the shrimp. Air fry again for 4 minutes, or until crisp. Cool before serving. Serve with cocktail sauce if desired.

371. Lemony Tuna

Preparation time: 2 hours
Cooking time: 12 minutes
Servings: 4
Ingredients:
- 2 (6-ounce) cans water-packed plain tuna
- 2 teaspoons Dijon mustard
- ½ cup breadcrumbs
- 1 tablespoon fresh lime juice
- 2 tablespoons fresh parsley, chopped
- 1 egg
- Chef man of hot sauce
- 3 tablespoons canola oil
- Salt
- Ground black pepper

Directions:
1. Strain most of the liquid from the canned tuna. In a bowl, add the fish, mustard, crumbs, citrus juice, parsley, and hot sauce and mix till well combined. Add a little canola oil if it seems too dry. Add egg, salt, and stir to combine.
2. Make the patties from tuna mixture. Refrigerate the tuna patties for about 2 hours. Warm air fryer to 355 degrees F. Air fry for about 10-12 minutes.

372. Grilled Soy Salmon Fillets

Preparation time: 5 minutes
Cooking time: 9 minutes
Servings: 4
Ingredients:
- 4 salmon fillets
- 1/4 teaspoon ground black pepper
- 1/2 teaspoon cayenne pepper
- 1/2 teaspoon salt
- 1 teaspoon onion powder
- 1 tablespoon fresh lemon juice
- 1/2 cup soy sauce
- 1/2 cup water
- 1 tablespoon honey
- 2 tablespoons extra-virgin olive oil

Directions:
1. Pat dries the salmon fillets using kitchen towels. Season the salmon with black pepper, cayenne pepper, salt, and onion powder.
2. For the marinade, combine the lemon juice, soy sauce, water, honey, and olive oil. Marinate the salmon for at least 2 hours in your refrigerator.
3. Arrange the fish fillets on a grill basket in your air fryer. Bake at 330 degrees for 8 to 9 minutes, or until salmon fillets is easily flaked with a fork. Work with batches and serve warm.

373. Old Bay Crab Cake

Preparation time: 15 minutes
Cooking time: 20 minutes
Servings: 4
Ingredients:
- 2 slices dried bread, crusts removed
- A small amount of milk
- 1 tablespoon mayonnaise
- 1 tablespoon Worcestershire sauce
- 1 tablespoon baking powder
- 1 tablespoon parsley flakes
- 1 teaspoon Old Bay Seasoning
- 1/4 teaspoon salt

- 1 egg
- 1-pound lump crabmeat

Directions:
1. Crush your bread over a large bowl until it is broken down into small pieces. Add milk and stir until bread crumbs are moistened. Mix in mayo and Worcestershire sauce.
2. Add remaining ingredients and mix well. Shape into 4 patties. Air fry at 360 degrees for 20 minutes, flipping halfway through.

374. Scallops and Spring Veggies

Preparation time: 15 minutes
Cooking time: 10 minutes
Servings: 4
Ingredients:
- ½ pound asparagus ends trimmed, cut into 2-inch pieces
- 1 cup sugar snap peas
- 1-pound sea scallops
- 1 tablespoon lemon juice
- 2 teaspoons olive oil
- ½ teaspoon dried thyme
- Pinch salt
- Freshly ground black pepper

Directions:
1. Put the asparagus plus sugar snap peas in the rack/basket. Put the rack in the air fryer. Air fry for 2 to 3 minutes or until the vegetables are just starting to get tender.
2. Meanwhile, check the scallops for a small muscle attached to the side, and pull it off and discard it. Toss the scallops with lemon juice, olive oil, thyme, salt, and pepper in a medium bowl. Place into the rack/basket on top of the vegetables.
3. Put the rack in the air fryer. Air fry for 5 to 7 minutes. Until the scallops are just firm, and the vegetables are tender. Serve immediately.

375. Fried Calamari

Preparation time: 15 minutes
Cooking time: 15 minutes
Servings: 8
Ingredients:
- ½ tsp. salt
- ½ tsp. Old Bay seasoning
- 1/3 cup plain cornmeal
- ½ cup semolina flour
- ½ cup almond flour
- 5-6 cup olive oil
- 1 ½ pounds baby squid

Directions:
1. Rinse squid in cold water and slice tentacles, keeping just ¼-inch of the hood in one piece. Combine 1-2 pinches of pepper, salt, Old Bay seasoning, cornmeal, and both flours.
2. Dredge squid pieces into the flour mixture and place it into the air fryer. Spray liberally with olive oil. Air fry for 15 minutes at 345 degrees till coating turns a golden brown.

376. Soy and Ginger Shrimp

Preparation time: 15 minutes
Cooking time: 10 minutes
Servings: 4
Ingredients:
- 2 tablespoons olive oil
- 2 tablespoons scallions, finely chopped
- 2 cloves garlic, chopped
- 1 teaspoon fresh ginger, grated
- 1 tablespoon dry white wine
- 1 tablespoon balsamic vinegar
- 1/4 cup soy sauce
- 1 tablespoon sugar
- 1-pound shrimp
- Salt and ground black pepper, to taste

Directions:
1. For the marinade, warm the oil in a saucepan; cook all ingredients, except the shrimp, salt, and black pepper. Now, let it cool. Marinate the shrimp, covered, at least an hour, in the refrigerator.
2. After that, bake the shrimp in the air fryer at 350 degrees F for 8 to 10 minutes (depending on the size), turning once or twice. Season prepared shrimp with salt and black pepper and serve right away.

377. Crispy Cheesy Fish Fingers

Preparation time: 15 minutes
Cooking time: 20 minutes
Servings: 4
Ingredients:
- Large codfish filet, approximately 6-8 ounces, fresh or frozen and thawed, cut into 1 ½-inch strip
- 2 raw eggs
- ½ cup of breadcrumbs
- 2 tablespoons of shredded or powdered parmesan cheese
- 1 tablespoon of shredded cheddar cheese
- Pinch of salt and pepper

Directions:
1. Wrap the basket of the air fryer using a lining of tin foil. Preheat the air fryer to 350 degrees.
2. In a large mixing bowl, beat the eggs until fluffy until the yolks and whites are thoroughly combined. Dunk all the fish strips in the beaten eggs, fully submerging.
3. Mix the bread crumbs with the parmesan, cheddar, salt, and pepper in a separate mixing bowl.
4. One by one, coat the egg-covered fish strips in the mixed dry ingredients so that they're fully covered, and place on the foil-lined rack. Put the rack on the middle shelf of the air fryer.
5. Air fry for 20 minutes. Shake the handle of the air-fryer halfway through the cooking time so that the breaded fish jostles inside and fry-coverage is even. Using tongs, remove from the air fryer and set on a serving dish to cool.

378. Panko-Crusted Tilapia

Preparation time: 15 minutes
Cooking time: 11 minutes
Servings: 3
Ingredients:
- 2 tsp. Italian seasoning
- 2 tsp. lemon pepper
- 1/3 cup panko breadcrumbs
- 1/3 cup egg whites
- 1/3 cup almond flour
- 3 tilapia fillets
- Olive oil

Directions:
1. Place panko, egg whites, and flour into separate bowls. Mix lemon pepper and Italian seasoning in with breadcrumbs. Pat tilapia fillets dry. Dredge in flour, egg, then breadcrumb mixture.
2. Add to the rack/basket and spray lightly with olive oil. Put the rack on the middle shelf of the air fryer. Air fry for 10-11 minutes at 400 degrees, making sure to flip halfway through cooking.

379. Firecracker Shrimp

Preparation time: 15 minutes
Cooking time: 8 minutes
Servings: 4
Ingredients:
For the shrimp:
- 1-pound raw shrimp, peeled and deveined
- Salt
- Pepper
- 1 egg
- ½ cup all-purpose flour
- ¾ cup panko bread crumbs
- Cooking oil

For the firecracker sauce:
- 1/3 cup sour cream
- 2 tablespoons Sriracha
- ¼ cup sweet chili sauce

Directions:
1. Flavor the shrimp with salt and pepper to taste. In a small bowl, beat the egg. In another small bowl, place the flour. In the last small bowl, add the panko bread crumbs.
2. Spray the rack/basket with cooking oil. Dip the shrimp in the flour, then the egg, and then the bread crumbs. Place the shrimp in the rack/basket.
3. Spray the shrimp with cooking oil. Put the rack in the air fryer. Air fry for 4 minutes. Open the air fryer and flip the shrimp. Air fry for an additional 4 minutes or until crisp.
4. For the firecracker sauce, mix the sour cream, Sriracha, and sweet chili sauce in a small bowl, then serve with the shrimp.

380. Lemon Pepper Shrimp

Preparation Time: 10 minutes
Cooking Time: 10 minutes
Servings: 2
Ingredients:
- 1 tablespoon lemon juice
- 1 tablespoon olive oil
- 1 teaspoon lemon pepper
- ¼ teaspoon garlic powder
- ¼ teaspoon paprika
- 12 oz. shrimp, peeled and deveined

Directions:
1. Warm your air fryer to 400 degrees F. Mix lemon juice, olive oil, lemon pepper, garlic powder, and paprika in a bowl. Stir in shrimp and coat evenly with the mixture. Add to the air fryer. Air fry for 8 minutes.

381. Crumbed Fish

Preparation Time: 10 minutes
Cooking Time: 15 minutes
Servings: 4
Ingredients:
- ¼ cup olive oil
- 1 cup dry breadcrumbs
- 4 white fish fillets
- Pepper to taste

Directions:
1. Warm your air fryer to 350 degrees F. Sprinkle both sides of fish with pepper. Combine oil and breadcrumbs in a bowl.
2. Dip the fish into the mixture. Press breadcrumbs to adhere to. Place fish in the air fryer. Air fry for 15 minutes.

382. Cajun Salmon

Preparation Time: 10 minutes
Cooking Time: 10 minutes
Servings: 2
Ingredients:
- 2 salmon fillets
- Cooking spray
- 1 tablespoon Cajun seasoning
- 1 tablespoon honey

Directions:
1. Warm your air fryer to 390 degrees F. Spray both sides of fish with oil. Sprinkle with Cajun seasoning. Spray air fryer basket with oil. Add salmon to the air fryer basket. Air fry for 10 minutes.

383. Lime & Chili Salmon

Preparation Time: 10 minutes
Cooking Time: 8 minutes
Servings: 2
Ingredients:
- 1 lb. salmon
- 1 tablespoon lime juice
- ½ teaspoon pepper
- ½ teaspoon chili powder
- 4 lime slices

Directions:
1. Drizzle salmon with lime juice. Sprinkle both sides with pepper and chili powder. Add salmon to the air

fryer. Place lime slices on top of salmon. Air fry at 375 degrees F for 8 minutes. Serve.

384. Fish Patties

Preparation Time: 5 minutes
Cooking Time: 7 minutes
Servings: 2
Ingredients:
- 8 oz. white fish fillet, flaked
- Garlic powder to taste
- 1 teaspoon lemon juice

Directions:
1. Warm your air fryer to 390 degrees F. Combine all the ingredients. Form patties from the mixture. Place fish patties in the air fryer. Air fry for 7 minutes. Serve.

385. Crispy Shrimp

Preparation Time: 15 minutes
Cooking Time: 3 minutes
Servings: 4
Ingredients:
- 1 lb. shrimp, peeled and deveined
- ½ cup fish breading mix
- Cooking spray

Directions:
1. Warm your air fryer to 390 degrees F. Spray shrimp with oil. Coat with the breading mix. Spray air fryer basket with oil. Add shrimp to the air fryer basket. Air fry for 3 minutes. Serve.

386. Coconut Crusted Fish Strips

Preparation Time: 2 hours and 20 minutes
Cooking Time: 12 minutes
Servings: 4
Ingredients:
Marinade:
- 1 tablespoon soy sauce
- 1 teaspoon ground ginger
- ½ cup of coconut milk
- 2 tablespoons maple syrup
- ½ cup pineapple juice
- 2 teaspoons hot sauce

Fish:
- 1 lb. fish fillet, sliced into strips
- Pepper to taste
- 1 cup breadcrumbs
- 1 cup coconut flakes (unsweetened)
- Cooking spray

Directions:
1. Mix marinade ingredients in a bowl. Stir in fish strips. Cover and refrigerate for 2 hours. Warm your air fryer to 375 degrees F.
2. In a bowl, mix pepper, breadcrumbs, and coconut flakes. Dip fish strips in the breadcrumb mixture. Spray your air fryer basket with oil. Add fish strips to the air fryer basket. Air fry for 6 minutes per side. Serve.

387. Fish Tacos

Preparation Time: 15 minutes
Cooking Time: 20 minutes
Servings: 4
Ingredients:
- Cooking spray
- 1 tablespoon olive oil
- 4 cups cabbage slaw
- 1 tablespoon apple cider vinegar
- 1 tablespoon lime juice
- Pinch cayenne pepper
- Pepper to taste
- 2 tablespoons taco seasoning mix
- ¼ cup all-purpose flour
- 1 lb. cod fillet, sliced into cubes
- 4 corn tortillas

Directions:
1. Warm your air fryer to 400 degrees F. Spray your air fryer basket with oil. In a bowl, mix the olive oil, cabbage slaw, vinegar, lime juice, cayenne pepper, and pepper.
2. In another bowl, mix the taco seasoning and flour. Coat the fish cubes with the taco seasoning mixture. Add these to the air fryer basket.
3. Air fry for 10 minutes, shaking halfway through. Top the corn tortillas with the fish and cabbage slaw mixture and roll them up. Serve.

388. Popcorn Shrimp

Preparation Time: 15 minutes
Cooking Time: 10 minutes
Servings: 4
Ingredients:
- ½ teaspoon onion powder
- ½ teaspoon garlic powder
- ½ teaspoon paprika
- ¼ teaspoon ground mustard
- 1/8 teaspoon dried sage
- 1/8 teaspoon ground thyme
- 1/8 teaspoon dried oregano
- 1/8 teaspoon dried basil
- Pepper to taste
- 3 tablespoons cornstarch
- 1 lb. shrimp, peeled and deveined
- Cooking spray

Directions:
1. Combine all fixing except shrimp in a bowl. Coat shrimp with the mixture. Spray air fryer basket with oil. Warm your air fryer to 390 degrees F. Add shrimp inside. Air fry for 4 minutes. Shake the basket. Air fry for another 5 minutes.

389. Shrimp Bang-Bang

Preparation Time: 15 minutes
Cooking Time: 25 minutes
Servings: 4
Ingredients:
- 1 tablespoon hot sauce
- ¼ cup sweet chili sauce
- ½ cup light mayonnaise

- ¼ cup all-purpose flour
- 1 cup breadcrumbs
- 1 lb. shrimp, peeled and deveined

Directions:
1. Warm air fryer to 400 degrees F. In a bowl, mix the hot sauce, chili sauce, and mayo. Divide mixture into 2 bowls. Reserve 1 bowl for dipping.
2. Coat the shrimp with flour. Dip in mayo mixture. Dredge with breadcrumbs. Air fry for 12 minutes, shaking once halfway through. Serve.

390. Mexican Fish

Preparation Time: 20 minutes
Cooking Time: 10 minutes
Servings: 2
Ingredients:
- 4 fish fillets
- 2 teaspoons Mexican oregano
- 4 teaspoons cumin
- 4 teaspoons chili powder
- Pepper to taste
- Cooking spray

Directions:
1. Warm your air fryer to 400 degrees F. Spray fish with oil. Season both sides of fish with spices and pepper. Place fish in the air fryer basket. Air fry for 5 minutes. Flip and air fry for another 5 minutes. Serve.

391. Crispy Garlic Shrimp

Preparation Time: 10 minutes
Cooking Time: 10 minutes
Servings: 4
Ingredients:
- 1 lb. shrimp, peeled and deveined
- 2 teaspoons garlic powder
- Pepper to taste
- ¼ cup flour
- Cooking spray

Directions:
1. Season shrimp with garlic powder and pepper. Coat with flour. Spray your air fryer basket with oil. Add shrimp to the air fryer basket. Air fry at 400 degrees F for 10 minutes, shaking once halfway through. Serve.

392. Crispy Halibut Strips

Preparation time: 20 minutes
Cooking time: 14 minutes
Servings: 2
Ingredients:
- 4 tablespoons taco seasoning mix
- 2 eggs
- 1 tablespoon water
- ¾ cup plain panko breadcrumbs
- ¾ pound skinless halibut fillets, cut into 1-inch strips

Directions:
1. In a shallow bowl, add the taco seasoning mix. In a second bowl, beat eggs and water. In a third bowl, place the breadcrumbs.
2. Coat fish with the taco seasoning mix, then dip into the egg mixture, and finally, coat with the breadcrumb.
3. Warm air fryer to 350 degrees F. Line the air fryer basket with lightly greased parchment paper.
4. Arrange halibut strips into the prepared air fryer basket in a single layer. Air fry for about 12-14 minutes, flipping once halfway through. Remove from the air fryer and transfer the halibut strips onto serving plates. Serve warm.

393. Pesto Haddock

Preparation time: 15 minutes
Cooking time: 8 minutes
Servings: 2
Ingredients:
- 2 (6-ounces) haddock fillets
- 1 tablespoon olive oil
- Salt and ground black pepper, as required
- 2 tablespoons pine nuts
- 3 tablespoons fresh basil, chopped
- 1 tablespoon Parmesan cheese, grated
- 1/3 cup extra-virgin olive oil

Directions:
1. Warm air fryer to 355 degrees F. Grease an air fryer basket. Coat the fish fillets evenly with oil and then sprinkle with salt and black pepper.
2. Arrange fish fillets into the air fryer basket in a single layer. Air fry for about 8 minutes. Meanwhile, for the pesto: add the remaining ingredients in a food processor and pulse until smooth.
3. Remove from the air fryer and transfer the flounder fillets onto serving plates. Top with the pesto and serve.

394. Breaded Flounder

Preparation time: 15 minutes
Cooking time: 12 minutes
Servings: 3
Ingredients:
- 1 egg
- 1 cup dry breadcrumbs
- ¼ cup of vegetable oil
- 3 (6-ounces) flounder fillets
- 1 lemon, sliced

Directions:
1. In a shallow bowl, beat the egg. Mix the breadcrumbs and oil in another bowl. Mix until a crumbly mixture is formed.
2. Dip flounder fillets into the beaten egg and then coat with the breadcrumb mixture. Set the temperature of the air fryer to 356 degrees F. Grease an air fryer basket.
3. Arrange flounder fillets into the prepared air fryer basket in a single layer. Air fry for 12 minutes. Remove from the air fryer and transfer the flounder fillets onto serving plates. Serve with the lemon slices.

395. 3-Ingredients Catfish
Preparation time: 10 minutes
Cooking time: 23 minutes
Servings: 4
Ingredients:
- 4 (6-ounces) catfish fillets
- ¼ cup seasoned fish fry
- 1 tablespoon olive oil

Directions:
1. Warm your air fryer to 400 degrees F. Grease an air fryer basket. In a bowl, add the catfish fillets and seasoned fish fry. Toss to coat well.
2. Then, drizzle each fillet evenly with oil. Arrange catfish fillets into your air fryer basket in a single layer. Air fry for about 10 minutes.
3. Flip the side and spray with the cooking spray. Air fry for another 10 minutes. Flip one last time and air fry for about 2-3 more minutes. Remove from air fryer and transfer the catfish fillets onto serving plates. Serve hot.

396. Cajun Coated Catfish
Preparation time: 15 minutes
Cooking time: 14 minutes
Servings: 4
Ingredients:
- 2 tablespoons cornmeal polenta
- 2 teaspoons Cajun seasoning
- ½ teaspoon paprika
- ½ teaspoon garlic powder
- Salt, as required
- 2 (6-ounces) catfish fillets
- 1 tablespoon olive oil

Directions:
1. Mix the cornmeal, Cajun seasoning, paprika, garlic powder, and salt in a bowl. Add the catfish fillets and coat evenly with the mixture.
2. Now, coat each fillet with oil. Warm air fryer at 400 degrees F, then grease and air fryer basket. Arrange catfish fillets into the prepared air fryer basket in a single layer.
3. Air fry for about 13-14 minutes, flipping once halfway through. Remove from air fryer and transfer the catfish fillets onto serving plates. Serve hot.

397. Southern Style Catfish
Preparation time: 15 minutes
Cooking time: 15 minutes
Servings: 5
Ingredients:
- 5 (6-ounces) catfish fillets
- 1 cup milk
- 2 teaspoons fresh lemon juice
- ½ cup yellow mustard
- ½ cup cornmeal
- ¼ cup all-purpose flour
- 2 tablespoons dried parsley flakes
- ¼ teaspoon red chili powder
- ¼ teaspoon cayenne pepper
- ¼ teaspoon onion powder
- ¼ teaspoon garlic powder
- Salt and ground black pepper, as required
- Olive oil cooking spray

Directions:
1. Place the catfish, milk, plus lemon juice in a large bowl, then refrigerate for about 15 minutes. In a shallow bowl, add the mustard.
2. In another bowl, mix the cornmeal, flour, parsley flakes, and spices. Remove the catfish fillets from the milk batter, pat dry with paper towels.
3. Coat each fish fillet with mustard and then roll evenly into the cornmeal mixture. Warm air fryer to 400 degrees F. Grease an air fryer basket.
4. Arrange catfish fillets into the prepared air fryer basket in a single layer and spray with the cooking spray. Air fry for about 10 minutes.
5. Flip the side and spray with the cooking spray. Air fry for about 3-5 minutes. Remove and transfer the catfish fillets onto serving plates. Serve hot.

398. Sesame Seeds Coated Haddock
Preparation time: 15 minutes
Cooking time: 14 minutes
Servings: 4
Ingredients:
- 4 tablespoons plain flour
- 2 eggs
- ½ cup sesame seeds, toasted
- ½ cup breadcrumbs
- 1/8 teaspoon dried rosemary, crushed
- Salt and ground black pepper, as required
- 3 tablespoons olive oil
- 4 (6-ounces) frozen haddock fillets

Directions:
1. In a shallow bowl, place the flour. In a second bowl, whisk the eggs. Mix the sesame seeds, breadcrumbs, rosemary, salt, black pepper, and oil in a third bowl until a crumbly mixture form.
2. Cover each fillet with flour, then dip into beaten egg, and finally, coat with the breadcrumb's mixture. Warm air fryer to 390 degrees F. Line an air fryer basket with a lightly greased piece of foil.
3. Arrange haddock fillets into the air fryer basket in a single layer. Air fry for about 14 minutes, flipping once halfway through. Remove from air fryer and transfer the haddock fillets onto serving plates. Serve hot.

399. Breaded Hake
Preparation time: 15 minutes
Cooking time: 12 minutes
Servings: 2
Ingredients:
- 1 egg
- 4 ounces breadcrumbs
- 2 tablespoons vegetable oil
- 4 (6-ounces) hake fillets
- 1 lemon, slice into wedges

Directions:
1. Beat the egg in a shallow bowl. Mix the breadcrumbs and oil in another bowl until a crumbly mixture form.
2. Dip fish fillets into the egg and then coat with the breadcrumb's mixture. Set your air fryer to 350 degrees F. Grease an air fryer basket.
3. Arrange haddock fillets into the air fryer basket in a single layer. Air fry for 12 minutes. Remove from air fryer and transfer the hake fillets onto serving plates. Garnish with lemon wedges and serve hot.

400. Ranch Tilapia
Preparation time: 15 minutes
Cooking time: 13 minutes
Servings: 4
Ingredients:
- ¾ cup cornflakes, crushed
- 1 (1-ounce) packet dry ranch-style dressing mix
- 2½ tablespoons vegetable oil
- 2 eggs
- 4 (6-ounces) tilapia fillets

Directions:
1. In a shallow bowl, beat the eggs. In another bowl, add the cornflakes, ranch dressing, and oil and mix until a crumbly mixture form.
2. Dip the fish fillets into the egg and then coat with the breadcrumb's batter. Warm air fryer to 356 degrees F, then grease the air fryer basket.
3. Arrange tilapia fillets into your air fryer basket in a single layer. Air fry for 12-13 minutes. Remove from the air fryer and transfer the tilapia fillets onto serving plates. Serve hot.

401. Tuna & Potato Cakes
Preparation time: 20 minutes
Cooking time: 12 minutes
Servings: 4
Ingredients:
- ½ tablespoon olive oil
- 1 onion, chopped
- 1 tablespoon fresh ginger, grated
- 1 green chili, seeded and finely chopped
- 2 (6-ounces) cans tuna, drained
- 1 medium boiled potato, mashed
- 2 tablespoons celery, finely chopped
- Salt, as required
- 1 cup breadcrumbs
- 1 egg

Directions:
1. Warm-up olive oil in a frying pan, then sauté onions, ginger, and green chili for about 30 seconds. Add the tuna and stir fry for about 2-3 minutes or until all the liquid is absorbed.
2. Remove from heat and transfer the tuna mixture onto a large bowl. Set aside to cool. In the bowl of tuna mixture, mix well the mashed potato, celery, and salt.
3. Make 4 equal-sized patties from the mixture. In a shallow bowl, place the breadcrumbs. In another bowl, beat the egg.
4. Coat each patty with breadcrumbs, dip into egg, and finally coat with the breadcrumbs. Warm air fryer to 390 F. Grease an air fryer basket.
5. Arrange tuna cakes into the prepared air fryer basket in a single layer. Air fry for about 2-3 minutes.
6. Flip the side and air fry for about 4-5 minutes. Remove from air fryer and transfer the tuna cakes onto serving plates. Serve warm.

402. Spicy Shrimp
Preparation time: 13 minutes
Cooking time: 5 minutes
Servings: 2
Ingredients:
- ¾ pound tiger shrimp, peeled and deveined
- 1½ tablespoons olive oil
- ½ teaspoon old bay seasoning
- ¼ teaspoon smoked paprika
- ¼ teaspoon cayenne pepper
- Salt, as required

Directions:
1. Warm air fryer to 390 degrees F. Grease an air fryer basket. In a large bowl, mix well shrimp, oil, and spices.
2. Arrange shrimp into the prepared air fryer basket in a single layer. Air fry for about 5 minutes. Remove, then transfer the shrimp onto plates. Serve hot.

403. Lemon Garlic Shrimp
Preparation time: 15 minutes
Cooking time: 8 minutes
Servings: 2
Ingredients:
- 1½ tablespoons fresh lemon juice
- 1 tablespoon olive oil
- 1 teaspoon lemon pepper
- ¼ teaspoon paprika
- ¼ teaspoon garlic powder
- ¾ pound medium shrimp, peeled and deveined

Directions:
1. In a large bowl, mix well lemon juice, oil, and spices. Add the shrimp and toss to combine. Warm air fryer to 400 F. Grease an air fryer basket.
2. Arrange shrimp into the air fryer basket in a single layer. Air fry for about 6-8 minutes. Remove from the air fryer and transfer the shrimp onto serving plates. Serve hot.

404. Cheesy Shrimp
Preparation time: 20 minutes
Cooking time: 20 minutes
Servings: 4
Ingredients:
- 2/3 cup Parmesan cheese, grated
- 4 garlic cloves, minced
- 2 tablespoons olive oil
- 1 teaspoon dried basil

- ½ teaspoon dried oregano
- 1 teaspoon onion powder
- ½ teaspoon red pepper flakes, crushed
- Ground black pepper, as required
- 2 pounds shrimp, peeled and deveined
- 1-2 tablespoons fresh lemon juice

Directions:
1. In a large bowl, mix Parmesan cheese, garlic, oil, herbs, and spices. Add the shrimp and toss to combine.
2. Set the temperature of the air fryer to 350 degrees F. Grease an air fryer basket. Arrange shrimp into the air fryer basket in 2 batches in a single layer.
3. Air fry for about 8-10 minutes. Remove from the air fryer and transfer the shrimp onto serving plates. Drizzle with lemon juice and serve immediately.

405. Rice Flour Coated Shrimp

Preparation time: 20 minutes
Cooking time: 20 minutes
Servings: 3
Ingredients:
- 3 tablespoons rice flour
- 2 tablespoons olive oil
- 1 teaspoon powdered sugar
- Salt and ground black pepper, as required
- 1-pound shrimp, peeled and deveined

Directions:
1. In a bowl, mix flour, oil, sugar, salt, and black pepper. Add the shrimp and toss to coat well. Set the temperature of the air fryer to 325 degrees F. Grease an air fryer basket.
2. Arrange shrimp into the prepared air fryer basket in 2 batches in a single layer. Air fry for about 8-10 minutes, tossing once halfway through. Remove from the air fryer and transfer the shrimp onto serving plates. Serve hot.

406. Shrimp Kebabs

Preparation time: 15 minutes
Cooking time: 8 minutes
Servings: 2
Ingredients:
- ¾ pound shrimp, peeled and deveined
- 2 tablespoons fresh lemon juice
- 1 teaspoon garlic, minced
- ½ teaspoon paprika
- ½ teaspoon ground cumin
- Salt and ground black pepper, as required
- 1 tablespoon fresh cilantro, chopped

Directions:
1. Warm air fryer to 350 degrees F. Grease an air fryer basket. In a bowl, mix the lemon juice, garlic, and spices. Add the shrimp and mix well.
2. Thread the shrimp onto presoaked wooden skewers. Arrange shrimp skewers into the prepared air fryer basket. Air fry for about 5-8 minutes, flipping once halfway through.
3. Remove from the air fryer and transfer the shrimp kebabs onto serving plates. Garnish with fresh cilantro and serve immediately.

407. Fried Masala Fish

Preparation Time: 15 minutes.
Cooking Time: 10 minutes.
Servings: 4
Ingredients:
- 2 pounds fish fillets
- 4 tablespoons olive oil
- 3/4 teaspoon turmeric
- 1 teaspoon cayenne pepper
- 1 teaspoon salt
- 1 tablespoon fenugreek leaves
- 1 ½ teaspoon freshly ground cumin
- 2 teaspoons amchur powder
- 2 tablespoons ground almonds

To finish:
- Extra lemon juice
- Chopped coriander leaves
- Sliced almonds

Directions:
1. Mix turmeric with fenugreek leaves, almond ground, amchur powder, cumin, salt, and cayenne pepper in a small bow. Place the prepared fish fillets in a tray and rub it with the spice mixture.
2. Marinate for 15 minutes., then place the fish in the Air Fryer basket. Air Fry at 450 degrees F for 10 minutes. Garnish with lemon juice, cilantro, and almond slices. Serve.

408. Scallops with Herb Sauce

Preparation time: 15 minutes
Cooking time: 6 minutes
Servings: 2
Ingredients:
- 8 large sea scallops, cleaned
- ¼ teaspoon ground black pepper
- 1/8 teaspoon salt
- Cooking spray
- ¼ cup olive oil
- 2 tablespoons parsley, chopped
- 2 teaspoons capers, chopped
- 1 teaspoon lemon zest, grated
- ½ teaspoon garlic, chopped
- Lemon wedges

Directions:
1. Season cleaned scallops with salt and black pepper. Place the prepared scallops in the Air Fryer basket and spray them with cooking oil. Air fry at 400 degrees F for 6 minutes.
2. Meanwhile, mix capers, parsley, oil, garlic, and lemon zest in a small bowl. Serve the scallops with capers mixture. Enjoy.

409. Breaded Scallops

Preparation time: 10 minutes
Cooking time: 5 minutes
Servings: 4
Ingredients:
- ½ cup buttery crackers, crushed
- ½ teaspoon garlic powder
- ½ teaspoon seafood seasoning
- 2 tablespoons butter, melted
- 1-pound sea scallops
- Cooking spray

Directions:
1. At 390 degrees F, preheat your Air Fryer. Mix seafood seasoning, garlic powder, and cracker crumbs in a bowl. Add melted butter to a bowl and keep it aside.
2. Dip the scallops in the melted butter and then coat with the breading. Spread the scallops in the Air Fryer basket and spray with cooking spray.
3. Air fry for 4 minutes. Flip the scallops once cooked halfway through and resume cooking. Serve.

410. White Fish with Garlic

Preparation time: 10 minutes
Cooking time: 12 minutes
Servings: 2
Ingredients:
- 2 -6 ounces tilapia filets
- 1/2 teaspoon garlic powder
- 1/2 teaspoon lemon pepper seasoning
- 1/2 teaspoon onion powder
- Sea salt, to taste
- Black pepper, to taste
- Fresh chopped parsley
- Lemon wedges

Directions:
1. At 360 degrees F, preheat your Air Fryer. Coat the fish fillets with olive oil, lemon pepper, garlic powder, black pepper, salt, and onion powder.
2. Place the fish in the Air Fryer basket and top it with lemon wedges. Air fry at 360 degrees F for 12 minutes. Garnish with parsley and lemon wedges. Serve warm.

411. Lobster Tails with Garlic Butter

Preparation time: 15 minutes
Cooking time: 8 minutes
Servings: 2
Ingredients:
- 2 (4 ounces) lobster tails
- 4 tablespoons butter
- 1 teaspoon lemon zest
- 1 garlic clove, grated
- Salt and black pepper, to taste
- 1 teaspoon fresh parsley, chopped
- 2 wedges lemon

Directions:
1. Spread the lobster tails into a butterfly by cutting the shell lengthwise. Place the butterflied lobster tails in the Air Fryer basket.
2. Sauté garlic and lemon zest with butter in a saucepan for 30 seconds. Brush the butter over the lobster tail and drizzle black pepper and salt on top.
3. Place the buttered lobster tail in the Air Fryer basket. Air fry at 380 degrees F for 7 minutes. Garnish with remaining butter, parsley, and lemon wedges. Serve warm.

412. Lobster Stuffed Mushrooms

Preparation time: 20 minutes
Cooking time: 15 minutes
Servings: 5
Ingredients:
- 1 garlic clove, minced
- 1 celery stalk, chopped
- 1/2 red pepper, chopped
- 1 teaspoon Old Bay seasonings
- 1 egg
- 10 mushrooms caps
- 1 tablespoon olive oil
- 1/2 cup lobster meat, chopped
- 10 saltine crackers, crumbled
- 1 cup Mozzarella cheese, shredded

Directions:
1. Sauté celery, garlic, and pepper with olive oil in a pan for 5 minutes. Stir in onion, garlic, seasoning, crushed cracker, and crab meat. Add one egg, then mix well.
2. Divide the mixture into the mushroom caps. Place the mushroom caps in the Air Fryer basket and drizzle cheese on top. Air fry for 10 minutes at 350 degrees F. Serve warm.

413. Beer Battered Cod

Preparation time: 15 minutes
Cooking time: 12 minutes
Servings: 4
Ingredients:
- 1 ¾ cup all-purpose flour
- 2 tablespoons cornstarch
- ½ teaspoon baking soda
- 6 ounces beer
- 1 egg beaten
- ½ teaspoon paprika
- 1 teaspoon salt
- ¼ teaspoon black pepper
- Pinch cayenne pepper
- 1½ pounds cod, cut into 4 pieces
- Vegetable oil

Directions:
1. Mix baking soda, cornstarch, and 1 cup flour in a large bowl. Stir in egg and beer, then mix well until smooth. Cover the batter with a plastic sheet and refrigerate for 20 minutes.

2. Mix ¾ cup flour with cayenne pepper, black pepper, salt, and paprika in another bowl. Coat the fish with the flour mixture, then dip it in the flour batter.
3. Place the fish in the Air Fryer basket and spray them with cooking oil. Air fry at 390 degrees F for 12 minutes. Serve warm.

414. Calamari with Tomato Sauce

Preparation time: 15 minutes
Cooking time: 8 minutes
Servings: 4
Ingredients:
- 3 lbs. calamari
- 1/3 cup olive oil
- 1 tablespoon fresh oregano
- 1 teaspoon lemon juice
- 1 tablespoon garlic, minced
- ¼ teaspoon chopped fresh lemon peel
- ¼ teaspoon crushed red pepper
- ¼ cup vinegar

Sauce:
- 1 lb. fresh whole tomatoes
- 3 cloves garlic, minced
- 1 stalk of celery, chopped
- 1 tablespoon olive oil
- ½ green bell pepper
- Salt and pepper to taste
- ½ cup onion, chopped

Directions:
1. For the sauce, mix all the sauce fixing and add to blender. Blend until the mixture is smooth. Clean the calamari and slice it into ½-inch rings. Season calamari with vinegar, red pepper, lemon peel, garlic, lemon juice, and oregano.
2. Add oil to the air fryer. Add calamari with its juice. Air fry for about 6-minutes. Stir once and air fry for another 2-minutes. Serve with hot with sauce.

415. Salmon & Eggs

Preparation time: 15 minutes
Cooking time: 10 minutes
Servings: 2
Ingredients:
- 2 eggs
- 1 lb. salmon, seasoned and cooked
- 1 cup celery, chopped
- 1 onion, chopped
- 1 tablespoon olive oil
- Salt and pepper to taste

Directions:
1. Whisk the eggs in a bowl. Add celery, onion, salt, and pepper. Add the oil to a round baking tray and pour in the egg mixture. Place in air fryer on 300 Fahrenheit. Let it air fry for 10-minutes. When done, serve with cooked salmon.

416. Tilapia with Egg

Preparation time: 15 minutes
Cooking time: 15 minutes
Servings: 3
Ingredients:
- 2 egg yolks
- 4 wheat buns
- 1 lb. tilapia fillets, sliced
- 1 tablespoon nectar
- 1 tablespoon hot sauce
- 3 teaspoons of sweet pickle relish
- 2 tablespoons mayonnaise
- 1 tablespoon fish sauce

Directions:
1. Mix the fish sauce and egg yolks in a bowl. Add mayonnaise, sweet pickle relish, hot sauce, and nectar. Pour mixture into the round baking tray. Place the tray inside the air fryer with tilapia fillets inside. Air fry for 15 minutes at 300 Fahrenheit.

417. Seafood Super Veggie Fritters

Preparation time: 15 minutes
Cooking time: 30 minutes
Servings: 4
Ingredients:
- 2 cups clam meat
- 2 tablespoons olive oil
- ¾ cup of water
- 1 cup chickpea flour
- ¼ teaspoon black pepper
- ½ cup shredded zucchini
- 1 cup shredded carrot

Directions:
1. Preheat your air fryer to 390 Fahrenheit. Mix clam meat, olive oil, shredded carrot, and zucchini along with black pepper in a bowl.
2. Form small balls using your hands. Mix chickpea flour plus water to form a batter. Coat balls with batter. Place in the air fryer and air fry for 30-minutes.

418. Breaded Fish

Preparation time: 15 minutes
Cooking time: 12 minutes
Servings: 4
Ingredients:
- 4 fish fillets
- 1 egg
- 5-ounces breadcrumbs
- 4 tablespoons olive oil

Directions:
1. Preheat your air fryer to 350 Fahrenheit. In a bowl, mix oil and breadcrumbs. Whisk egg. Gently dip the fish into the egg and then into the crumb mixture. Put into the air fryer and air fry for 12-minutes.

419. Tuna with Roast Potatoes

Preparation time: 30 minutes
Cooking time: 30 minutes
Servings: 2
Ingredients:
- 4 medium potatoes

- 1 teaspoon olive oil
- ½ tablespoon capers
- Salt and pepper to taste
- 1 green onion, sliced
- 1 tablespoon Greek yogurt
- ½ teaspoon chili powder
- ½ can of tuna in oil, drained
- 2 boiled eggs, sliced

Directions:
1. Soak the potatoes in water for 30-minutes. Pat dry with a kitchen towel. Brush the potatoes with olive oil. Place potatoes in the air fryer and air fry for 30-minutes at 355 Fahrenheit.
2. Put tuna in a bowl with yogurt and chili powder, mix well. Add half of the green onion plus salt and pepper. Slit potatoes lengthwise. Stuff tuna mixture in the middle of potatoes and place them on a serving plate.
3. Sprinkle with chili powder and remaining green onions over potatoes. Serve with capers and a salad of your choice and topped with boiled egg slices.

420. Glazed Halibut Steak
Preparation time: 30 minutes
Cooking time: 12 minutes
Servings: 3
Ingredients:
- 1 lb. halibut steak
- 2/3 cup soy sauce
- ¼ teaspoon ginger, ground
- 1 garlic clove, minced
- ¼ cup of orange juice
- ¼ teaspoon crushed red pepper flakes
- 2 tablespoon lime juice
- 1 teaspoon liquid stevia
- ½ cup mirin

Directions:
1. Prepare teriyaki glaze by combining all ingredients except halibut steak in a saucepan. Bring mixture to a boil and then reduce heat by half. Set aside and allow to cool.
2. Pour half of the glaze into a re-sealable bag with halibut and place it in the fridge for 30 minutes. Preheat your air fryer to 390 Fahrenheit.
3. Place marinated halibut in the air fryer and air fry for 12-minutes. When finished, brush some of the remaining glazes over halibut steak.

421. Nacho-Crusted Shrimp
Preparation time: 15 minutes
Cooking time: 8 minutes
Servings: 8
Ingredients:
- 18 jumbo shrimps, peeled and deveined
- 1 egg, beaten
- 8-9-ounce nacho-flavored chips, crushed
- Salt and pepper to taste

Directions:
1. Prepare 2 shallow dishes, one with egg and one with crushed chips. Flavor with a pinch of salt plus pepper. Dip shrimp in the egg and then coat in nacho crumbs.
2. Preheat your air fryer to 350 Fahrenheit. Arrange the shrimp in an air fryer and ai fry for 8-minutes.

422. Sriracha and Honey Tossed Calamari
Preparation time: 15 minutes
Cooking time: 13 minutes
Servings: 2
Ingredients:
- ½ lb. calamari tubes, about ¼ inch wide, rinsed, and patted dry
- 1 cup club soda
- ½ cup honey
- Red pepper flakes to taste
- 1 cup almond flour
- Salt and black pepper to taste
- 2 tablespoons sriracha

Directions:
1. Cover calamari rings with club soda in a bowl. Set aside for 10-minutes. Mix flour, salt, and black pepper in another bowl. In a third bowl, combine honey, sriracha, and red pepper flakes.
2. Drain the calamari, pat dry, and cover with flour mixture. Grease your air fryer basket with cooking spray. Add calamari in one layer, leaving little space in between.
3. Set temperature to 380 Fahrenheit and air fry for 11-minutes. Shake basket a couple of times during the process.
4. Remove the calamari from the air fryer and cover with half of the honey sauce, and place inside the air fryer. Air fry for an additional 2-minutes. When ready to serve, cover with remaining sauce.

423. Kataifi-Wrapped Shrimp with Lemon-Garlic Butter
Preparation time: 15 minutes
Cooking time: 20 minutes
Servings: 5
Ingredients:
- 20 large green shrimps, peeled and deveined
- 7 tablespoons unsalted butter
- 12-ounces of kataifi pastry
- Wedges of lemon or lime
- Salt and pepper to taste
- 5 cloves of garlic, crushed
- 2 lemons, zested and juiced

Directions:
1. Dissolve the butter in a pan over low heat. Add the garlic and lemon zest, and sauté for about 2-minutes. Season with salt, pepper, and lemon juice.
2. Cover the shrimp with half of garlic butter sauce and set aside the remaining half of the sauce. Preheat your air fryer to 360 Fahrenheit and cover the tray with a sheet of foil. Remove the pastry from the bag and tease out strands.

3. On the countertop lay 6-inch strands. Roll shrimp and butter into the pastry. Shrimp tail should be exposed. Repeat process for all shrimp. Place the shrimp into an air fryer to air fry for 10-minutes.
4. Flip shrimp over and air fry for another 10-minutes. Serve with a salad and lime or lemon wedges. Dip the shrimp into the remaining garlic butter sauce.

424. Grilled Barramundi with Lemon Butter
Preparation time: 15 minutes
Cooking time: 40 minutes
Servings: 2
Ingredients:
- 1 lb. small potatoes
- 7-ounces barramundi fillets
- 1 teaspoon olive oil
- ¼ bunch of fresh thyme, chopped
- Green beans, cooked, optional

Lemon Butter Sauce:
- 1 scallion, chopped
- ½ cup thickened cream
- ½ cup white wine
- 1 bay leaf
- 10 black peppercorns
- 1 clove garlic, chopped
- 8-ounces unsalted butter
- 1 lemon, juiced
- Salt and pepper to taste

Directions:
1. Preheat your air fryer to 390 Fahrenheit for 5-minutes. In a bowl, add potatoes, salt, thyme, and olive oil. Mix ingredients well.
2. Put potatoes into air fryer basket and air fry for 20-minutes. Layer the fish fillets in a basket on top of potatoes. Air fry for another 20-minutes. Prepare the sauce on top of the stove.
3. Heat scallion and garlic over medium-high heat and add the peppercorns and bay leaf. Pour in the wine and reduce heat to low.
4. Add the thickened cream and stir to blend. Add the butter and whisk over low heat. When the butter has melted, add salt, pepper, and lemon juice.
5. Strain the sauce to remove peppercorns and bay leaves. Place the fish and potatoes on a serving plate and add sauce and serve with green beans.

425. Cranberry Cod
Preparation time: 15 minutes
Cooking time: 20 minutes
Servings: 2
Ingredients:
- 3 fillets cod
- 1 tablespoon olive oil
- 3 tablespoons cranberry jam

Directions:
1. Preheat your air fryer to 390 Fahrenheit. Brush the cod fillets with olive oil. Spoon a tablespoon of cranberry jam on each filet. Air fry for 20-minutes.

426. Cod Fish Teriyaki with Oysters, Mushrooms & Veggies
Preparation time: 15 minutes
Cooking time: 10 minutes
Servings: 2

Ingredients:
- 1 tablespoon olive oil
- 6 pieces mini king oyster
- Mushrooms, thinly sliced
- 2 slices (1-inch) codfish
- 1 Napa cabbage leaf, sliced
- 1 clove garlic, chopped
- Salt to taste
- 1 green onion, minced
- Veggies, steamed of your choice

Teriyaki Sauce:
- 1 teaspoon liquid stevia
- 2 tablespoons mirin
- 2 tablespoons soy sauce

Directions:
1. Prepare teriyaki sauce by mixing all the ingredients in a bowl, then set aside. Grease the air fryer basket with oil. Place the mushrooms, garlic, Napa cabbage leaf, and salt inside.
2. Layer the fish on top. Preheat your air fryer to 360 Fahrenheit for 3-minutes. Place the basket in an air fryer and air fry for 5-minutes. Stir.
3. Pour the teriyaki sauce over ingredients in the basket. Air fry for an additional 5-minutes. Serve with your choice of steamed veggies.

427. Salmon with Dill Sauce
Preparation time: 15 minutes
Cooking time: 23 minutes
Servings: 4
Ingredients:
- 1 ½ lb. of salmon
- 4 teaspoons olive oil
- Pinch of sea salt
- Dill Sauce:
- ½ cup non-fat Greek yogurt
- ½ cup light sour cream
- 2 tablespoons dill, finely chopped
- Pinch of sea salt

Directions:
1. Preheat your air fryer to 270 Fahrenheit. Cut salmon into four 6-ounce portions and drizzle 1 teaspoon of olive oil over each piece. Season with sea salt.
2. Place salmon into the cooking basket and air fry for 23-minutes. Make dill sauce. In a mixing bowl, mix sour cream, yogurt, chopped dill, and sea salt. Top cooked salmon with sauce and garnish with additional dill and serve.

428. Black Cod with Grapes, Pecans, Fennel & Kale

Preparation time: 15 minutes
Cooking time: 15 minutes
Servings: 2
Ingredients:
- 2 fillets black cod (8-ounces)
- 3 cups kale, minced
- 2 teaspoons white balsamic vinegar
- ½ cup pecans
- 1 cup grapes, halved
- 1 small bulb fennel, cut into inch-thick slices
- 4 tablespoons extra-virgin olive oil
- Salt and black pepper to taste

Directions:
1. Preheat your air fryer to 400 Fahrenheit. Use salt and pepper to season your fish fillets. Drizzle with 1 teaspoon of olive oil.
2. Place the fish inside of the air fryer with the skin side down and air fry for 10-minutes. Take the fish out and cover loosely with aluminum foil. Combine fennel, pecans, and grapes.
3. Pour 2 tablespoons of olive oil and season with salt and pepper. Add to the air fryer basket. Air fry for an additional 5-minutes. In a bowl, combine minced kale and cooked grapes, fennel, and pecans.
4. Cover ingredients with balsamic vinegar and the remaining 1 tablespoon of olive oil. Toss gently. Serve fish with sauce and enjoy!

429. Honey Glazed Salmon

Preparation Time: 10 minutes
Cooking Time: 8 minutes
Servings: 2
Ingredients:
- 2 (6-oz.) salmon fillets
- Salt, as required
- 2 tablespoons honey

Directions:
1. Sprinkle the salmon fillets with salt and then coat with honey. Preheat the air fryer at 355 degrees F. Arrange the salmon fillets in the oiled air fryer basket, then air fry for 8 minutes. Serve.

430. Sweet & Sour Glazed Salmon

Preparation Time: 12 minutes
Cooking Time: 20 minutes
Servings: 2
Ingredients:
- 1/3 cup soy sauce
- 1/3 cup honey
- 3 teaspoons rice wine vinegar
- 1 teaspoon water
- 4 (3½-oz.) salmon fillets

Directions
1. Mix the soy sauce, honey, vinegar, and water in a small bowl. In another small bowl, reserve about half of the mixture.
2. Add salmon fillets in the remaining mixture and coat well. Cover the bowl and refrigerate to marinate for about 2 hours. Preheat the air fryer at 355 degrees F.
3. Arrange the salmon fillets in a greased air fryer basket, the air fry to 12 minutes. Flip the salmon fillets once halfway through and coat with the reserved marinade after every 3 minutes. Serve hot.

431. Salmon Parcel

Preparation Time: 15 minutes
Cooking Time: 23 minutes
Servings: 2
Ingredients:
- 2 (4-oz.) salmon fillets
- 6 asparagus stalks
- ¼ cup white sauce
- 1 teaspoon oil
- ¼ cup champagne
- Salt and ground black pepper, as required

Directions:
1. In a bowl, mix all the ingredients. Divide the salmon mixture over 2 pieces of foil evenly. Seal the foil around the salmon mixture to form the packet.
2. Preheat the air fryer at 355 degrees F. Arrange the salmon parcels in the air fryer basket, then air fry for 13 minutes. Serve hot.

432. Salmon with Broccoli

Preparation Time: 15 minutes
Cooking Time: 12 minutes
Servings: 2
Ingredients:
- 1½ cups small broccoli florets
- 2 tablespoons vegetable oil, divided
- Salt and ground black pepper, as required
- 1 (½-inch) piece fresh ginger, grated
- 1 tablespoon soy sauce
- 1 teaspoon rice vinegar
- 1 teaspoon light brown sugar
- ¼ teaspoon cornstarch
- 2 (6-oz.) skin-on salmon fillets
- 1 scallion, thinly sliced

Directions:
1. In a bowl, mix the broccoli, 1 tablespoon of oil, salt, and black pepper. In another bowl, mix well the ginger, soy sauce, vinegar, sugar, and cornstarch.
2. Coat the salmon fillets with remaining oil and then with the ginger mixture. Preheat the air fryer at 375 degrees F.
3. Arrange the broccoli florets in a greased air fryer basket and top with the salmon fillets. Air fry for 12 minutes. Serve hot.

433. Salmon with Prawns & Pasta

Preparation Time: 20 minutes
Cooking Time: 18 minutes
Servings: 4
Ingredients:
- 14 oz. pasta (of your choice)
- 4 tablespoons pesto, divided

- 4 (4-oz.) salmon steaks
- 2 tablespoons olive oil
- ½ lb. cherry tomatoes, chopped
- 8 large prawns, peeled and deveined
- 2 tablespoons fresh lemon juice
- 2 tablespoons fresh thyme, chopped

Directions
1. Cook the pasta for 8-10 minutes or until the desired doneness in a large pan of salted boiling water.
2. Meanwhile, at the bottom of a baking pan, spread 1 tablespoon of pesto. Place salmon steaks and tomatoes over pesto in a single layer and drizzle with the oil.
3. Arrange the prawns on top in a single layer. Drizzle with lemon juice and sprinkle with thyme. Preheat your air fryer temperature at 390 degrees F. Arrange the baking pan in the air fryer basket.
4. Air fry for 8 minutes. Strain the pasta and transfer it into a large bowl. Add the remaining pesto and toss to coat well. Divide the pasta onto a serving plate and top with salmon mixture. Serve immediately.

434. Salmon Burgers

Preparation Time: 20 minutes
Cooking Time: 22 minutes
Servings: 6
Ingredients:
- 3 large russet potatoes, peeled and cubed
- 1 (6-oz.) cooked salmon fillet
- 1 egg
- ¾ cup frozen vegetables (of your choice), parboiled and drained
- 2 tablespoons fresh parsley, chopped
- 1 teaspoon fresh dill, chopped
- Salt and ground black pepper, as required
- 1 cup breadcrumbs
- ¼ cup olive oil

Directions:
1. In a pan of boiling water, cook the potatoes for about 10 minutes. Drain the potatoes well. Put the potatoes into a bowl and mash with a potato masher. Set aside to cool completely.
2. In another bowl, add the salmon and flake with a fork. Add the cooked potatoes, egg, parboiled vegetables, parsley, dill, salt, and black pepper and mix until well combined.
3. Make 6 equal-sized patties from the mixture. Coat patties with breadcrumb evenly and then drizzle with the oil evenly. Preheat the air fryer at 355 degrees F.
4. Arrange the patties in a greased air fryer basket. Air fry for 12 minutes. Flip the patties once halfway through. Serve hot.

435. Chinese Cod

Preparation Time: 15 minutes
Cooking Time: 15 minutes
Servings: 2
Ingredients:
- 2 (7-oz.) cod fillets
- Salt and ground black pepper, as required
- ¼ teaspoon sesame oil
- 1 cup of water
- 5 little squares of rock sugar
- 5 tablespoons light soy sauce
- 1 teaspoon dark soy sauce
- 2 scallions (green part), sliced
- ¼ cup fresh cilantro, chopped
- 3 tablespoons olive oil
- 5 ginger slices

Directions:
1. Season each cod fillet evenly with salt and black pepper and drizzle with sesame oil. Set aside at room temperature for about 15-20 minutes.
2. Dip the fish fillets into the egg and then coat with the breadcrumb's mixture. Preheat your air fryer at 355 degrees F. Arrange the cod fillets in a greased air fryer basket, then Air fry for 12 minutes.
3. Meanwhile, in a small pan, add the water and bring it to a boil. Add the rock sugar and both soy sauces and cook until sugar is dissolved, stirring continuously. Remove from the heat and set aside.
4. Remove the cod fillets from the air fryer and transfer onto serving plates. Top each fillet with scallion and cilantro.
5. In a small frying pan, heat the olive oil over medium heat and sauté the ginger slices for about 2-3 minutes. Remove the frying pan from heat and discard the ginger slices. Carefully pour the hot oil evenly over cod fillets. Top with the sauce mixture and serve.

436. Cod Parcel

Preparation Time: 20 minutes
Cooking Time: 15 minutes
Servings: 2
Ingredients:
- 2 tablespoons butter, melted
- 1 tablespoon fresh lemon juice
- ½ teaspoon dried tarragon
- Salt and ground black pepper, as required
- ½ cup red bell peppers, thinly sliced
- ½ cup carrots, peeled and julienned
- ½ cup fennel bulbs, julienned
- 2 (5-oz.) frozen cod fillets, thawed
- 1 tablespoon olive oil

Directions:
1. Mix the butter, lemon juice, tarragon, salt, and black pepper in a large bowl. Add the bell pepper, carrot, and fennel bulb and generously coat with the mixture.
2. Arrange 2 large parchment squares onto a smooth surface. Coat the cod fillets with oil and then sprinkle evenly with salt and black pepper.
3. Arrange 1 cod fillet onto each parchment square and top each evenly with the vegetables. Top with any remaining sauce from the bowl.
4. Fold the parchment paper and crimp the sides to secure fish and vegetables. Preheat your air fryer at

350 degrees F. Arrange the cod parcels in the air fryer basket, then air fry for 15 minutes. Serve hot.

437. Cod Burgers

Preparation Time: 15 minutes
Cooking Time: 7 minutes
Servings: 6
Ingredients:
- ½ lb. cod fillets
- ½ teaspoon fresh lime zest, grated finely
- ½ egg
- ½ teaspoon red chili paste
- Salt, to taste
- ½ tablespoon fresh lime juice
- 3 tablespoons coconut, grated and divided
- 1 small scallion, chopped finely
- 1 tablespoon fresh parsley, chopped

Directions:
1. In a food processor, add cod filets, lime zest, egg, chili paste, salt, and lime juice and pulse until smooth. Transfer the cod mixture into a bowl.
2. Add 1½ tablespoons coconut, scallion, and parsley and mix until well combined. Make 6 equal-sized patties from the mixture.
3. In a shallow dish, place the remaining coconut. Coat the patties in coconut evenly. Preheat the air fryer at 375 degrees F. Arrange the patties in a greased air fryer basket, then air fry for 7 minutes. Serve hot.

438. Spicy Catfish

Preparation Time: 15 minutes
Cooking Time: 13 minutes
Servings: 2
Ingredients:
- 2 tablespoons almond flour
- 1 teaspoon red chili powder
- ½ teaspoon paprika
- ½ teaspoon garlic powder
- Salt, as required
- 2 (6-oz.) catfish fillets
- 1 tablespoon olive oil

Directions"
1. In a bowl, mix the flour, paprika, garlic powder, and salt. Add the catfish fillets and coat with the mixture evenly. Now, coat each fillet with oil.
2. Preheat the air fryer at 400 degrees F. Arrange the fish fillets in a greased air fryer basket, then air fry for 13 minutes. Flip the fish fillets once halfway through. Serve hot.

439. Seasoned Catfish

Preparation Time: 15 minutes
Cooking Time: 23 minutes
Servings: 4
Ingredients:
- 4 (4-oz.) catfish fillets
- 2 tablespoons Italian seasoning
- Salt and ground black pepper, as required
- 1 tablespoon olive oil
- 1 tablespoon fresh parsley, chopped

Directions:
1. Rub the fish fillets with seasoning, salt, and black pepper generously and then coat with oil. Preheat the air fryer at 400 degrees F.
2. Arrange the fish fillets in a greased air fryer basket. Flip the fish fillets once halfway through. Serve hot with the garnishing of parsley.

440. Crispy Catfish

Preparation Time: 15 minutes
Cooking Time: 15 minutes
Servings: 5
Ingredients:
- 5 (6-oz.) catfish fillets
- 1 cup milk
- 2 teaspoons fresh lemon juice
- ½ cup yellow mustard
- ½ cup cornmeal
- ¼ cup all-purpose flour
- 2 tablespoons dried parsley flakes
- ¼ teaspoon red chili powder
- ¼ teaspoon cayenne pepper
- ¼ teaspoon onion powder
- ¼ teaspoon garlic powder
- Salt and ground black pepper, as required
- Olive oil cooking spray

Directions:
1. Mix the catfish, milk, plus lemon juice in a large bowl and refrigerate for about 15 minutes. In a shallow bowl, add the mustard. In another bowl, mix the cornmeal, flour, parsley flakes, and spices.
2. Remove the catfish fillets from the milk mixture, and with paper towels, pat them dry. Coat each fish fillet with mustard and then roll into cornmeal mixture. Then, spray each fillet with the cooking spray.
3. Preheat your air fryer at 400 F. Put the catfish fillets in the oiled air fryer basket, then air fry for 15 minutes. After 10 minutes of cooking, flip the fillets, then spray using a cooking spray. Serve hot.

441. Cornmeal Coated Catfish

Preparation Time: 15 minutes
Cooking Time: 14 minutes
Servings: 4
Ingredients:
- 2 tablespoons cornmeal
- ½ teaspoon paprika
- ½ teaspoon garlic powder
- Salt, as required
- Pepper seasoning
- 2 (6-oz.) catfish fillets
- 1 tablespoon olive oil

Directions:
1. In a bowl, mix the cornmeal, pepper seasoning, paprika, garlic powder, and salt. Add the catfish fillets and coat with the mixture. Now, coat each fillet with oil.

2. Preheat the air fryer at 400 degrees F. Arrange the catfish fillets in a greased air fryer basket, then air fry for 14 minutes. After 10 minutes of cooking, flip the fillets and spray with the cooking spray. Serve hot

442. Glazed Haddock

Preparation Time: 15 minutes
Cooking Time: 15 minutes
Servings: 4
Ingredients:

- 1 garlic clove, minced
- ¼ teaspoon fresh ginger, grated finely
- ½ cup low-sodium soy sauce
- ¼ cup fresh orange juice
- 2 tablespoons fresh lime juice
- ½ cup cooking wine
- ¼ cup of sugar
- ¼ teaspoon red pepper flakes, crushed
- 1 lb. haddock steaks

Directions:
1. In a pan, add all the fixing except haddock steaks and bring to a boil. Cook for about 3-4 minutes, stirring continuously. Remove from the heat and set aside to cool.
2. In a resealable bag, add half of marinade and haddock steaks. Seal the bag and shake to coat well. Refrigerate for about 30 minutes. Remove the fish steaks from the bag, reserving the remaining marinade.
3. Warm air fryer at 390 degrees F. Arrange the haddock steaks in the greased air fryer basket, then air fry for 11 minutes.
4. Transfer the haddock steak onto a serving platter and immediately coat with the remaining glaze. Serve immediately.

443. Simple Haddock

Preparation Time: 15 minutes
Cooking Time: 8 minutes
Servings: 2
Ingredients:

- 2 (6-oz.) haddock fillets
- 1 tablespoon olive oil
- Salt and ground black pepper, as required

Directions:
1. Coat the fish fillets with oil and then sprinkle with salt and black pepper. Preheat your air fryer at 355 degrees F. Arrange the haddock fillets in a greased air fryer basket, then air fry for 8 minutes. Serve hot.

Chapter 12. Healthy Vegetable Recipes

444. Air Fryer Asparagus

Preparation time: 15 minutes
Cooking time: 8 minutes
Servings: 2
Ingredients:
- Nutritional yeast
- Olive oil non-stick spray
- 1 bunch of asparagus

Directions:
- Wash asparagus and then trim off thick, woody ends. Oiled asparagus using a olive oil spray and sprinkle with yeast.
- In your Air fryer, lay asparagus in a singular layer. Set your air fryer at 360°F and air fry for 8 minutes. Serve.

445. Roasted Garlic Asparagus

Preparation time: 15 minutes
Cooking time: 10 minutes
Servings: 4
Ingredients:
- 1-pound asparagus
- 2 tablespoons olive oil
- 1 tablespoon balsamic vinegar
- 2 teaspoons minced garlic
- Salt
- Freshly ground black pepper

Directions:
1. Cut or snap off the white end of the asparagus. In a large bowl, combine the asparagus, olive oil, vinegar, garlic, salt, and pepper.
2. Using your hands, gently mix all the ingredients, making sure that the asparagus is thoroughly coated. Put the asparagus in the air fryer basket or on an air fryer–sized baking sheet set in the basket.
3. Set the temperature of your AF to 400°F. Set the timer and roast for 5 minutes. Using tongs, flip the asparagus. Reset the timer and roast for 5 minutes more.

446. Almond Flour Battered and Crisped Onion Rings

Preparation time: 15 minutes
Cooking time: 15 minutes
Servings: 3
Ingredients:
- ½ cup almond flour
- ¾ cup of coconut milk
- 1 big white onion, sliced into rings
- 1 egg, beaten
- 1 tablespoon baking powder
- 1 tablespoon smoked paprika
- Salt and pepper to taste

Directions:
1. Preheat the air fryer for 5 minutes. Mix the almond flour, baking powder, smoked paprika, salt, and pepper in a mixing bowl.
2. In another bowl, combine the eggs and coconut milk. Soak the onion slices into the egg mixture. Dredge the onion slices in the almond flour mixture.
3. Place in the air fryer basket. Air fry for 15 minutes at 325 °F. Halfway through the cooking time, shake the fryer basket for even cooking.

447. Crispy Nacho Avocado Fries

Preparation time: 15 minutes
Cooking time: 15 minutes
Servings: 6
Ingredients:
- 3 firm, barely ripe avocados, halved, peeled, and pitted
- 2 cups of pork dust
- 2 teaspoons fine sea salt
- 2 teaspoons ground black pepper
- 2 teaspoons ground cumin
- 1 teaspoon chili powder
- 1 teaspoon paprika
- ½ teaspoon garlic powder
- ½ teaspoon onion powder
- 2 large eggs
- Salsa, for serving (optional)
- Freshly chopped cilantro leaves, for garnish (optional)

Directions:

1. Oiled air fryer basket with avocado oil. Preheat the air fryer to 400°F.
2. Slice the avocados into thick-cut French fry shapes. In a bowl, mix the pork dust, salt, pepper, and seasonings. In a separate shallow bowl, beat the eggs.
3. Dip the avocado fries into the beaten eggs, shake off any excess, and then dip them into the pork dust mixture. Press the breading into each fry using your hands.
4. Spray the fries with avocado oil and place them in the air fryer basket in a single layer, leaving space between them. If there are too many fries to fit in a single layer, work in batches.
5. Air fry for 13 to 15 minutes, until golden brown, flipping after 5 minutes. Serve with salsa, then garnish with fresh chopped cilantro, if desired.

448. Chermoula-Roasted Beets

Preparation time: 15 minutes
Cooking time: 25 minutes
Servings: 4
Ingredients:
For the Chermoula:
- 1 cup packed fresh cilantro leaves
- ½ cup packed fresh parsley leaves
- 6 cloves garlic, peeled
- 2 teaspoons smoked paprika
- 2 teaspoons ground cumin
- 1 teaspoon ground coriander
- ½ to 1 teaspoon cayenne pepper
- Pinch crushed saffron (optional)
- ½ cup extra-virgin olive oil
- Kosher salt

For the Beets:
- 3 medium beets, trimmed, peeled, and cut into 1-inch chunks
- 2 tablespoons chopped fresh cilantro
- 2 tablespoons chopped fresh parsley

Directions:
1. For the chermoula, pulse the cilantro, parsley, garlic, paprika, cumin, coriander, and cayenne in a food processor until coarsely chopped. Add the saffron, if using, and process until combined.
2. Slowly put the olive oil in a steady stream; process until the sauce is uniform. Season to taste with salt.
3. For the beets, in a large bowl, drizzle the beets with ½ cup of the chermoula, or enough to coat.
4. Arrange the beets in the air fryer basket. Roast to 375°F for 25 to minutes, or until the beets are tender. Transfer the beets to a serving platter. Sprinkle with chopped cilantro and parsley and serve.

449. Fried Plantains

Preparation time: 15 minutes
Cooking time: 8 minutes
Servings: 2
Ingredients:
- 2 ripe plantains, peeled and cut at a diagonal into ½-inch-thick pieces
- 3 tablespoons ghee, melted
- ¼ teaspoon kosher salt

Directions:
1. Mix the plantains with the ghee and salt in a medium bowl. Arrange the plantain pieces in the air fryer basket.
2. Set the air fryer to 400°F for air fry for 8 minutes. The plantains are done when they are soft and tender on the inside and have plenty of crisp, sweet, brown spots on the outside.

450. Parmesan Breaded Zucchini Chips

Preparation time: 15 minutes
Cooking time: 20 minutes
Servings: 5
Ingredients:
For the zucchini chips:
- 2 medium zucchinis
- 2 eggs
- 1/3 cup bread crumbs
- 1/3 cup grated Parmesan cheese
- Salt
- Pepper
- Cooking oil

For the lemon aioli:
- ½ cup mayonnaise
- ½ tablespoon olive oil
- Juice of ½ lemon
- 1 teaspoon minced garlic
- Salt
- Pepper

Directions:
1. For the zucchini chips, slice the zucchini into thin chips (about 1/8-inch-thick) using a knife or mandoline.
2. In a small bowl, beat the eggs. Mix the bread crumbs, Parmesan cheese, and salt and pepper in another small bowl.
3. Oiled air fryer basket with cooking oil. Soak the zucchini slices one at a time in the eggs and then the bread crumb mixture.
4. You can also sprinkle the bread crumbs onto the zucchini slices with a spoon. Put the zucchini chips in the Air fryer basket, but do not stack.
5. Cook in batches. Spray the chips with cooking oil from a distance (otherwise, the breading may fly off). Air fry for 10 minutes. Remove the cooked zucchini chips from the air fryer, then repeat the process with the remaining zucchini.
6. For the lemon aioli, combine the mayonnaise, olive oil, lemon juice, and garlic in a small bowl, adding salt and pepper to taste. Mix well until fully combined. Cool the zucchini and serve alongside the aioli.

451. Bell Pepper-Corn Wrapped in Tortilla

Preparation time: 15 minutes
Cooking time: 15 minutes
Servings: 4
Ingredients:

- 1 small red bell pepper, chopped
- 1 small yellow onion, diced
- 1 tablespoon water
- 2 cobs grilled corn kernels
- 4 large tortillas
- 4 pieces commercial vegan nuggets, chopped
- Mixed greens for garnish

Directions:
1. Preheat the air fryer to 400°F. Sautés the vegan nuggets with the onions, bell peppers, and corn kernels in a skillet heated over medium heat with water. Set aside.
2. Place filling inside the corn tortillas. Fold the tortillas and place inside the air fryer and air fry for 15 minutes until the tortilla wraps are crispy. Serve with mixed greens on top.

452. Blooming Onion

Preparation time: 15 minutes
Cooking time: 35 minutes
Servings: 8
Ingredients:
- 1 extra-large onion
- 2 large eggs
- 1 tablespoon water
- ½ cup powdered Parmesan cheese
- 2 teaspoons paprika
- 1 teaspoon garlic powder
- ¼ teaspoon cayenne pepper
- ¼ teaspoon fine sea salt
- ¼ teaspoon ground black pepper

For garnish (optional):
- Fresh parsley leaves
- Powdered Parmesan cheese
- For serving (optional):
- Prepared yellow mustard
- Ranch Dressing
- Reduced-sugar or sugar-free ketchup

Directions:
1. Oiled the air fryer basket with avocado oil. Preheat the air fryer to 350°F.
2. Using a sharp knife, cut the top ½ inch off the onion and peel off the outer layer. Cut the onion into 8 equal parts, stopping 1 inch from the bottom—you want the onion to stay at the base. Gently spread the onion petals apart.
3. Whisk the eggs into a large bowl, then put the water. Place the onion in the dish and coat it well in the egg. Use a spoon to coat the inside of the onion and all the petals.
4. In a small bowl, combine the Parmesan, seasonings, salt, and pepper. Place the onion in a 6-inch pie pan or casserole dish.
5. Sprinkle the seasoning mixture all over the onion and use your fingers to press it into the petals. Spray the onion with avocado oil. Loosely cover the onion with parchment paper and then foil.
6. Place the dish in the air fryer. Air fry for 30 minutes, remove it from the air fryer and increase the air fryer temperature to 400°F.
7. Remove the foil and parchment and spray the onion with avocado oil again. Transfer the onion to the air fryer basket. Air fry for an additional 3 to 5 minutes, until light brown and crispy.
8. Garnish with fresh parsley and powdered Parmesan, if desired. Serve with mustard, ranch dressing, and ketchup, if desired.

453. Mexican Corn in A Cup

Preparation time: 15 minutes
Cooking time: 10 minutes
Servings: 4
Ingredients:
- 4 cups (32-ounce bag) frozen corn kernels (do not thaw)
- Vegetable oil spray
- 2 tablespoons butter
- ¼ cup sour cream
- ¼ cup mayonnaise
- ¼ cup grated Parmesan cheese (or feta, cotija, or queso fresco)
- 2 tablespoons fresh lemon or lime juice
- 1 teaspoon chili powder
- Chopped fresh green onion (optional)
- Chopped fresh cilantro (optional)

Directions:
1. Place the corn in the bottom of the air fryer basket and spray with vegetable oil spray. Set the air fryer to 350°F to air fry for 10 minutes.
2. Transfer the corn to a serving bowl. Add the butter and stir until melted. Add the sour cream, mayonnaise, cheese, lemon juice, and chili powder; stir until well combined. Serve immediately with green onion and cilantro (if using).

454. Honey Roasted Carrots

Preparation time: 15 minutes
Cooking time: 12 minutes
Servings: 4
Ingredients:
- 3 cups baby carrots
- 1 tablespoon extra-virgin olive oil
- 1 tablespoon honey
- Salt
- Freshly ground black pepper
- Fresh dill (optional)

Directions:
1. Mix the carrots, olive oil, honey, salt, and pepper in a large bowl. Make sure that the carrots are thoroughly coated with oil. Place the carrots in the air fryer basket.
2. Set the temperature of your air fryer to 390°F. Set the timer and roast for 12 minutes, or until fork-tender.
3. Remove the air fryer drawer and release the air fryer basket. Pour the carrots into a bowl, sprinkle with dill, if desired, and serve.

455. Crispy Sesame-Ginger Broccoli

Preparation time: 15 minutes
Cooking time: 15 minutes
Servings: 4
Ingredients:
- 3 tablespoons toasted sesame oil
- 2 teaspoons sesame seeds
- 1 tablespoon chili-garlic sauce
- 2 teaspoons minced fresh ginger
- ½ teaspoon kosher salt
- ½ teaspoon black pepper
- 1 (16-ounce) package frozen broccoli florets (do not thaw)

Directions:
1. In a large bowl, combine the sesame oil, sesame seeds, chili-garlic sauce, ginger, salt, and pepper. Stir until well combined. Add the broccoli and toss until well coated.
2. Arrange the broccoli in the air fryer basket. Set the air fryer to 325°F to air fry for 15 minutes, or until the broccoli is crisp, tender, and the edges are lightly browned, gently tossing halfway through the cooking time. Serve.

456. Tomatoes Provençal

Preparation time: 15 minutes
Cooking time: 15 minutes
Servings: 4
Ingredients:
- 4 small ripe tomatoes connected on the vine
- ¼ teaspoon fine sea salt
- ¼ teaspoon ground black pepper
- ½ cup powdered Parmesan cheese (about 1½ ounces)
- 2 tablespoons chopped fresh parsley
- ¼ cup minced onions
- 2 cloves garlic, minced
- ½ teaspoon chopped fresh thyme leaves

For garnish:
- Fresh parsley leaves
- Ground black pepper
- A sprig of fresh basil

Directions:
1. Oiled the air fryer basket with avocado oil. Preheat the air fryer to 350°F. Slice the tops of the tomatoes without removing them from the vine. Do not discard the tops.
2. Use a large spoon to scoop the seeds out of the tomatoes. Sprinkle the insides of the tomatoes with salt and pepper.
3. In a medium-sized bowl, combine the cheese, parsley, onions, garlic, and thyme. Stir to mix well. Divide the mixture evenly among the tomatoes. Spray avocado oil on the tomatoes and place them in the air fryer basket.
4. Place the tomato tops in the air fryer basket next to, not on top of, the filled tomatoes. Bake for 15 minutes, or until the filling is golden and the tomatoes are soft yet still holding their shape.
5. Garnish with fresh parsley, ground black pepper, and a sprig of basil. Serve warm, with the tomato tops on the vine.

457. Roasted Cabbage

Preparation time: 15 minutes
Cooking time: 7 minutes
Servings: 4
Ingredients:
- 1 head cabbage, sliced in 1-inch-thick ribbons
- 1 tablespoon olive oil
- 1 teaspoon salt
- 1 teaspoon freshly ground black pepper
- 1 teaspoon garlic powder
- 1 teaspoon red pepper flakes

Directions:
1. Mix the cabbage, olive oil, salt, pepper, garlic powder, and red pepper flakes in a large bowl. Make sure that the cabbage is thoroughly coated with oil. Place the cabbage in the air fryer basket.
2. Set the temperature of your air fryer to 350°F. Set the timer and roast for 4 minutes. Using tongs, flip the cabbage. Reset the timer and roast for 3 minutes more. Serve.

458. Crispy Brussels Sprouts

Preparation time: 15 minutes
Cooking time: 8 minutes
Servings: 4
Ingredients:
- 3 tablespoons ghee or coconut oil, melted
- 1 teaspoon fine sea salt or smoked salt
- Dash of lime or lemon juice
- Thinly sliced Parmesan cheese, for serving (optional; omit for dairy-free)
- Lemon slices, for serving (optional)

Directions:
1. Oiled the air fryer basket with avocado oil. Preheat the air fryer to 400°F. In a large bowl, toss the Brussels sprouts, ghee, and salt. Add the lime or lemon juice.
2. Place the Brussels sprouts in the air fryer basket and air fry for 8 minutes, or until crispy, shaking the basket after 5 minutes. Serve with thinly sliced Parmesan and lemon slices, if desired.

459. Caramelized Baby Carrots

Preparation time: 10 minutes
Cooking time: 15 minutes
Servings: 4
Ingredients:
- 1/2 cup butter, melted
- 1/2 cup brown sugar
- 1 lb. bag baby carrots

Directions:
1. Warm your air fryer at 400 degrees F. In a bowl, mix the butter, brown sugar, and carrots. Arrange the

carrots in a greased Air Fry Basket. Air fry to 15 minutes. Serve warm.

460. Carrot with Zucchini

Preparation time: 15 minutes
Cooking time: 35 minutes
Servings: 4
Ingredients:
- 4 teaspoons butter, melted and divided
- 1/4 lb. carrots, peeled and sliced
- 1 lb. zucchinis, sliced
- 1 tablespoon fresh basil, chopped
- Salt and ground black pepper

Directions:
1. In a bowl, mix 2 teaspoons of the butter and carrots. Warm your air fryer at 400 degrees F. Arrange the carrots in a greased Air Fry Basket, then air fry for 35 minutes.
2. Meanwhile, in a large bowl, mix remaining butter, zucchini, basil, salt, and black pepper. After 5 minutes of cooking, place the zucchini mixture into the basket with carrots. Toss the vegetable mixture 2-3 times during the cooking. Serve hot.

461. Broccoli with Olives

Preparation time: 15 minutes
Cooking time: 15 minutes
Servings: 6
Ingredients:
- 1-1/2 lbs. broccoli head, stemmed and cut into 1-inch florets
- 2 tablespoons olive oil
- Salt and ground black pepper
- 1/3 cup Kalamata olives, halved and pitted
- 2 teaspoons fresh lemon zest, grated
- 1/4 cup Parmesan cheese, grated

Directions:
1. Cook the broccoli for 3-4 minutes in a pan of boiling water. Drain the broccoli well. Place the broccoli, oil, salt, and black pepper in a bowl and toss to coat well.
2. Set your air fryer set at 355 degrees F to preheat. Arrange the broccoli in a greased Air Fry Basket. Air fry for 15 minutes.
3. For the 8 minutes of cooking, toss the broccoli florets. Transfer the broccoli into a large bowl and immediately stir in the olives, lemon zest, and cheese. Serve immediately.

462. Basil Tomatoes

Preparation time: 5 minutes
Cooking time: 10 minutes
Servings: 2
Ingredients:
- 3 tomatoes, halved
- Olive oil cooking spray
- Salt and ground black pepper
- 1 tablespoon fresh basil, chopped

Directions:
1. Drizzle cut sides of the tomato halves with cooking spray evenly. Sprinkle with salt, black pepper, and basil. Arrange the tomatoes in Air Fry Basket. Set the air fryer at 320 F to preheat. Air fry for 10 minutes. Serve warm.

463. Stuffed Tomatoes

Preparation time: 15 minutes
Cooking time: 15 minutes
Servings: 2
Ingredients:
- 2 large tomatoes
- 1/2 cup broccoli, chopped finely
- 1/2 cup Cheddar cheese, shredded
- Salt and ground black pepper
- 1 tablespoon unsalted butter, melted
- 1/2 teaspoon dried thyme, crushed

Directions:
1. Carefully cut the top of each tomato and scoop out pulp and seeds. In a bowl, mix chopped broccoli, cheese, salt, and black pepper. Stuff each tomato with broccoli mixture evenly.
2. Arrange the tomatoes in a greased Air Fry Basket. Set your air fryer to preheat at 355 degrees F. Air fry for 15 minutes. Serve warm with the garnishing of thyme.

464. Parmesan Asparagus

Preparation time: 10 minutes
Cooking time: 10 minutes
Servings: 3
Ingredients:
- 1 lb. fresh asparagus, trimmed
- 1 tablespoon Parmesan cheese, grated
- 1 tablespoon butter, melted
- 1 teaspoon garlic powder
- Salt and ground black pepper

Directions:
1. In a bowl, mix the asparagus, cheese, butter, garlic powder, salt, and black pepper. Set your air fryer to preheat 400 degrees F. Arrange the veggie batter in a greased Air Fry Basket, then air fry for 10 minutes. Serve hot.

465. Almond Asparagus

Preparation time: 5 minutes
Cooking time: 6 minutes
Servings: 3
Ingredients:
- 1 lb. asparagus
- 2 tablespoons olive oil
- 2 tablespoons balsamic vinegar
- Salt and ground black pepper
- 1/3 cup almonds, sliced

Directions:
1. In a bowl, mix the asparagus, oil, vinegar, salt, and black pepper. Set your air fryer to preheat at 400 degrees F. Put the veggie mixture in a greased Air Fry Basket, then air fry for 6 minutes. Serve hot.

466. Spicy Butternut Squash
Preparation time: 15 minutes
Cooking time: 20 minutes
Servings: 4
Ingredients:
- 1 medium butternut squash, cut into chunk
- 2 teaspoons cumin seeds
- 1/8 teaspoon garlic powder
- 1/8 teaspoon chili flakes, crushed
- Salt and ground black pepper
- 1 tablespoon olive oil
- 2 tablespoons pine nuts
- 2 tablespoons fresh cilantro, chopped

Directions:
1. Mix the squash, spices, and oil in a bowl. Preheat your air fryer at 375 F. Put the squash chunks in a oiled Air Fry Basket, then air fry for 20 minutes. Serve hot with the garnishing of pine nuts and cilantro.

467. Sweet & Spicy Parsnips
Preparation time: 15 minutes
Cooking time: 44 minutes
Servings: 5
Ingredients:
- 1-1/2 lbs. parsnip, peeled and cut into 1-inch chunks
- 1 tablespoon butter, melted
- 2 tablespoons honey
- 1 tablespoon dried parsley flakes, crushed
- 1/4 teaspoon red pepper flakes, crushed
- Salt and ground black pepper

Directions:
1. Mix the parsnips and butter in a large bowl. Preheat your air fryer at 355 F. Arrange the squash chunks in a greased Air Fry Basket, then air fry for 44 minutes.
2. Meanwhile, in another large bowl, mix the remaining ingredients. After 40 minutes of cooking, transfer the parsnips chunks into the honey mixture bowl and toss to coat well. Again, arrange the parsnip chunks in Air Fry Basket and finish the remaining 4 minutes to air fry. Serve hot.

468. Pesto Tomatoes
Preparation time: 15 minutes
Cooking time: 14 minutes
Servings: 4
Ingredients:
- 3 large heirloom tomatoes, cut into ½ inch thick slices.
- 1 cup pesto
- 8 oz. feta cheese, cut into ½ inch thick slices.
- 1/2 cup red onions, sliced thinly
- 1 tablespoon olive oil

Directions:
1. Spread some pesto on each slice of tomato. Top each tomato slice with a feta slice and onion and drizzle with oil. Warm your air fryer at 390 F. Arrange the tomatoes in a greased Air Fry Basket, air fry for 14 minutes. Serve warm.

469. Rosemary-Roasted Red Potatoes
Preparation time: 5 minutes
Cooking time: 20 minutes
Servings: 6
Ingredients:
- 1-pound red potatoes, quartered
- ¼ cup olive oil
- ½ teaspoon kosher salt
- ¼ teaspoon black pepper
- 1 garlic clove, minced
- 4 rosemary sprigs

Directions:
1. Preheat the air fryer to 360°F. Mix the potatoes, olive oil, salt, pepper, and garlic until well-coated in a large bowl.
2. Put the potatoes into the air fryer basket and top with the sprigs of rosemary. Roast for 10 minutes, then stir or toss the potatoes and roast for 10 minutes more.
3. Remove the rosemary sprigs and serve the potatoes. Flavor with additional salt plus pepper, if needed. Serve.

470. Roasted Radishes with Sea Salt
Preparation time: 5 minutes
Cooking time: 18 minutes
Servings: 4
Ingredients:
- 1-pound radishes end trimmed if needed
- 2 tablespoons olive oil
- ½ teaspoon of sea salt

Directions:
1. Preheat the air fryer to 360°F. Mix the radishes with olive oil and sea salt in a large bowl. Pour the radishes into the air fryer and roast for 10 minutes. Stir or turn the radishes over and roast for 8 minutes more, then serve.

471. Garlic Zucchini and Red Peppers
Preparation time: 5 minutes
Cooking time: 15 minutes
Servings: 6
Ingredients:
- 2 medium zucchinis, cubed
- 1 red bell pepper, diced
- 2 garlic cloves, sliced
- 2 tablespoons olive oil
- ½ teaspoon salt

Directions:
1. Preheat the air fryer to 380°F. Mix the zucchini, bell pepper, and garlic with the olive oil and salt in a large bowl.
2. Pour the mixture into the air fryer basket, and roast for 7 minutes. Shake or stir, then roast for 7 to 8 minutes more.

472. Parmesan and Herb Sweet Potatoes
Preparation time: 10 minutes
Cooking time: 18 minutes
Servings: 4

Ingredients:
- 2 large sweet potatoes, peeled and cubed
- ¼ cup olive oil
- 1 teaspoon dried rosemary
- ½ teaspoon salt
- 2 tablespoons shredded Parmesan

Directions:
1. Preheat the air fryer to 360°F. Toss the sweet potatoes, olive oil, rosemary, and salt in a large bowl. Put the potatoes into the air fryer basket and roast for 10 minutes, then stir the potatoes and sprinkle the Parmesan over the top. Continue roasting for 8 minutes more. Serve hot and enjoy.

473. Roasted Brussels Sprouts with Orange and Garlic

Preparation time: 5 minutes
Cooking time: 10 minutes
Servings: 4
Ingredients:
- 1-pound Brussels sprouts, quartered
- 2 garlic cloves, minced
- 2 tablespoons olive oil
- ½ teaspoon salt
- 1 orange, cut into rings

Directions:
1. Preheat the air fryer to 360°F. Mix the quartered brussels sprouts with the garlic, olive oil, and salt in a large bowl until well coated.
2. Put the brussels sprouts into the air fryer, lay the orange slices on top of them, and roast for 10 minutes. Remove from the air fryer and set the orange slices aside. Toss the Brussels sprouts before serving.

474. Crispy Lemon Artichoke Hearts

Preparation time: 10 minutes
Cooking time: 15 minutes
Servings: 2
Ingredients:
- 1 can of artichoke hearts, drained
- 1 egg
- 1 tablespoon water
- ¼ cup whole wheat bread crumbs
- ¼ teaspoon salt
- ¼ teaspoon paprika
- ½ lemon

Directions:
1. Preheat the air fryer to 380°F. Beat the egg plus water until frothy in a medium shallow bowl. In a separate medium shallow bowl, mix the bread crumbs, salt, and paprika.
2. Dip each artichoke heart into the egg mixture, then into the bread crumb mixture, coating the outside with the crumbs. Place the artichokes hearts in a single layer of the air fryer basket.
3. Air Fry the artichoke hearts for 15 minutes. Remove the artichokes from the air fryer and squeeze fresh lemon juice over the top before serving.

475. Spiced Honey-Walnut Carrots

Preparation time: 5 minutes
Cooking time: 12 minutes
Servings: 6
Ingredients:
- 1-pound baby carrots
- 2 tablespoons olive oil
- ¼ cup raw honey
- ¼ teaspoon ground cinnamon
- ¼ cup black walnuts, chopped

Directions:
1. Preheat the air fryer to 360°F. Toss the baby carrots with olive oil, honey, and cinnamon in a large bowl until well coated.
2. Pour into the air fryer and roast for 6 minutes. Shake the basket, sprinkle the walnuts on top, and roast for 6 minutes more. Remove the carrots from the air fryer and serve.

476. Roasted Grape Tomatoes and Asparagus

Preparation time: 5 minutes
Cooking time: 12 minutes
Servings: 6
Ingredients:
- 2 cups grape tomatoes
- 1 bunch asparagus, trimmed
- 2 tablespoons olive oil
- 3 garlic cloves, minced
- ½ teaspoon kosher salt

Directions:
1. Preheat the air fryer to 380°F. Mix all the fixings in a large bowl, tossing until the vegetables are well coated with oil.
2. Pour the vegetable mixture into the air fryer basket and spread into a single layer, then roast for 12 minutes. Serve.

477. Stuffed Red Peppers with Herbed Ricotta and Tomatoes

Preparation time: 10 minutes
Cooking time: 20 minutes
Servings: 4
Ingredients:
- 2 red bell peppers
- 1 cup cooked brown rice
- 2 Roma tomatoes, diced
- 1 garlic clove, minced
- ¼ teaspoon salt
- ¼ teaspoon black pepper
- 4 ounces ricotta
- 3 tablespoons fresh basil, chopped
- 3 tablespoons fresh oregano, chopped
- ¼ cup shredded Parmesan, for topping

Directions:
1. Preheat the air fryer to 360°F. Slice the bell peppers in half and discard the seeds and stem. In a medium bowl, combine the brown rice, tomatoes, garlic, salt, and pepper.

2. Distribute the rice filling evenly among the four bell pepper halves. In a small bowl, combine the ricotta, basil, and oregano. Put the herbed cheese over the top of the rice mixture in each bell pepper.
3. Place the bell peppers into the air fryer and roast for 20 minutes. Remove and serve with shredded Parmesan on top.

478. Ratatouille

Preparation time: 15 minutes
Cooking time: 40 minutes
Servings: 6
Ingredients:
- 2 russet potatoes, cubed
- ½ cup Roma tomatoes, cubed
- 1 eggplant, cubed
- 1 zucchini, cubed
- 1 red onion, chopped
- 1 red bell pepper, chopped
- 2 garlic cloves, minced
- 1 teaspoon dried mint
- 1 teaspoon dried parsley
- 1 teaspoon dried oregano
- ½ teaspoon salt
- ½ teaspoon black pepper
- ¼ teaspoon red pepper flakes
- 1/3 cup olive oil
- 1 (8-ounce) can tomato paste
- ¼ cup vegetable broth
- ¼ cup of water

Directions:
1. Preheat the air fryer to 320°F. Mix the potatoes, tomatoes, eggplant, zucchini, onion, bell pepper, garlic, mint, parsley, oregano, salt, black pepper, and red pepper flakes in a large bowl.
2. Mix the olive oil, tomato paste, broth, and water in a small bowl. Pour the oil-and-tomato-paste mixture over the vegetables and toss until everything is coated.
3. Pour the coated vegetables into the air fryer basket in an even layer and roast for 20 minutes. After 20 minutes, stir well and spread out again. Roast for an additional 10 minutes, then repeat the process and cook for another 10 minutes.

479. Parmesan-Thyme Butternut Squash

Preparation time: 15 minutes
Cooking time: 20 minutes
Servings: 4
Ingredients:
- 2 ½ cups butternut squash, 1-inch pieces (approximately 1 medium)
- 2 tablespoons olive oil
- ¼ teaspoon salt
- ¼ teaspoon garlic powder
- ¼ teaspoon black pepper
- 1 tablespoon fresh thyme
- ¼ cup grated Parmesan

Directions:
1. Preheat the air fryer to 360°F. Mix the cubed squash with the olive oil, salt, garlic powder, pepper, and thyme in a large bowl until the squash is well coated.
2. Pour this mixture into the air fryer basket, and roast for 10 minutes. Stir and roast another 8 to 10 minutes more. Remove the squash from the air fryer and toss with freshly grated Parmesan before serving.

480. Crispy Garlic Sliced Eggplant

Preparation time: 5 minutes
Cooking time: 25 minutes
Servings: 4
Ingredients:
- 1 egg
- 1 tablespoon water
- ½ cup whole wheat bread crumbs
- 1 teaspoon garlic powder
- ½ teaspoon dried oregano
- ½ teaspoon salt
- ½ teaspoon paprika
- 1 medium eggplant, sliced into ¼-inch-thick rounds
- 1 tablespoon olive oil

Directions:
1. Preheat the air fryer to 360°F. Whisk the egg and water in a medium shallow bowl. In a separate medium, shallow bowl, mix bread crumbs, garlic powder, oregano, salt, and paprika.
2. Dip each eggplant slice into the egg mixture, then into the bread crumb mixture, coating the outside with crumbs. Place the slices in a single layer in the bottom of the air fryer basket.
3. Drizzle the tops of the eggplant slices with the olive oil, then air fry for 15 minutes. Turn each slice and air fry for an additional 10 minutes.

481. Dill-and-Garlic Beets

Preparation time: 10 minutes
Cooking time: 30 minutes
Servings: 4
Ingredients:
- 4 beets, cleaned, peeled, and sliced
- 1 garlic clove, minced
- 2 tablespoons chopped fresh dill
- ¼ teaspoon salt
- ¼ teaspoon black pepper
- 3 tablespoons olive oil

Directions:
1. Preheat the air fryer to 380°F. Mix all the fixings in a large bowl so the beets are well coated with the oil. Pour the beet mixture into the air fryer basket, and roast for 15 minutes before stirring, then continue roasting for 15 minutes more. Serve.

482. Citrus-Roasted Broccoli Florets

Preparation time: 5 minutes
Cooking time: 12 minutes
Servings: 6
Ingredients:
- 4 cups broccoli florets (approximately 1 large head)

- 2 tablespoons olive oil
- ½ teaspoon salt
- ½ cup of orange juice
- 1 tablespoon raw honey
- Orange wedges, for serving (optional)

Directions:
1. Preheat the air fryer to 360°F. Mix the broccoli, olive oil, salt, orange juice, and honey in a large bowl. Toss the broccoli in the liquid until well coated.
2. Pour the broccoli mixture into the air fryer basket and cook for 6 minutes. Stir and cook for 6 minutes more. Serve alone or with orange wedges for additional citrus flavor, if desired.

483. Tasty Hasselback Potatoes

Preparation Time: 10 minutes
Cooking Time: 45 minutes
Servings: 4
Ingredients:
- 4 potatoes, wash and dry
- 1 tbsp. dried thyme
- 1 tbsp. dried rosemary
- 1 tbsp. dried parsley
- ½ cup butter, melted
- Pepper
- Salt

Directions:
1. Place potato in Hasselback slicer and slice potato using a sharp knife. Mix melted butter, thyme, rosemary, parsley, pepper, and salt in a small bowl.
2. Rub melted butter mixture over potatoes and arrange potatoes on air fryer tray. Bake potatoes at 350 F for 25 minutes. Serve and enjoy.

484. Honey Sriracha Brussels Sprouts

Preparation Time: 10 minutes
Cooking Time: 15 minutes
Servings: 4
Ingredients:
- ½ lb. Brussels sprouts, cut stems then cut each in half
- 1 tbsp. olive oil
- ½ tsp. salt

For sauce:
- 1 tbsp. sriracha sauce
- 1 tbsp. vinegar
- 1 tbsp. lemon juice
- 2 tsp. sugar
- 1 tbsp. honey
- 1 tsp. garlic, minced
- ½ tsp. olive oil

Directions:
1. Add all sauce ingredients into the small saucepan and heat over low heat for 2-3 minutes or until thickened. Remove saucepan from heat and set aside. Add Brussels sprouts, oil, and salt in a zip-lock bag and shake well.
2. Transfer Brussels sprouts on air fryer tray and air fry at 390 F for 15 minutes. Shake halfway through. Transfer Brussels sprouts to the mixing bowl. Drizzle with prepared sauce and toss until well coated. Serve and enjoy.

485. Roasted Carrots

Preparation Time: 10 minutes
Cooking Time: 20 minutes
Servings: 6
Ingredients:
- 2 lbs. carrots, peeled, slice in half again slice half
- 2 ½ tbsp. dried parsley
- 1 tsp. dried oregano
- 1 tsp. dried thyme
- 3 tbsp. olive oil
- Pepper
- Salt

Directions:
1. Add carrots to a mixing bowl. Add remaining ingredients on top of carrots and toss well. Arrange carrots on an air fryer pan and roast at 400 F for 10 minutes. After 10 minutes, turn carrots slice to the other side and roast for 10 minutes more. Serve and enjoy.

486. Roasted Parmesan Broccoli

Preparation Time: 10 minutes
Cooking Time: 5 minutes
Servings: 4
Ingredients:
- 1 lb. broccoli florets
- ¼ cup parmesan cheese, grated
- 1 tbsp. garlic, minced
- 2 tbsp. olive oil
- Pepper
- Salt

Directions:
1. Add broccoli florets into the mixing bowl. Add cheese, garlic, oil, pepper, and salt on top of broccoli florets and toss well.
2. Arrange broccoli florets on an air fryer pan and bake at 350 F for 4 minutes. Turn broccoli florets to the other side and cook for 2 minutes more. Serve and enjoy.

487. Simple Baked Potatoes

Preparation Time: 10 minutes
Cooking Time: 40 minutes
Servings: 4
Ingredients:
- 4 potatoes, scrubbed and washed
- ¾ tsp. garlic powder
- ½ tsp. Italian seasoning
- ½ tbsp. butter, melted
- ½ tsp. sea salt

Directions:
1. Prick potatoes using a fork. Rub potatoes with melted butter and sprinkle with garlic powder, Italian seasoning, and sea salt. Arrange potatoes on air fryer drip pan and bake at 400 F for 40 minutes. Serve and enjoy.

488. Parmesan Green Bean

Preparation Time: 10 minutes
Cooking Time: 5 minutes
Servings: 6
Ingredients:
- 1 lb. fresh green beans
- ½ cup flour
- 2 eggs, lightly beaten
- ¾ tbsp. garlic powder
- ½ cup parmesan cheese, grated
- 1 cup breadcrumbs

Directions:
1. In a shallow dish, add flour. In a second shallow dish, add eggs. In a third shallow dish, mix breadcrumbs, garlic powder, and cheese.
2. Coat beans with flour, then coat with eggs, and finally coat with breadcrumbs. Arrange coated beans on air fryer pan and air fry at 390 F for 5 minutes. Serve and enjoy.

489. Roasted Asparagus

Preparation Time: 10 minutes
Cooking Time: 9 minutes
Servings: 4
Ingredients:
- 1 lb. asparagus, cut the ends
- 1 tsp. olive oil
- Pepper
- Salt

Directions:
1. Arrange asparagus on air fryer pan. Put with olive oil and season with pepper and salt. Place pan in the air fryer and bake asparagus at 370 F for 7-9 minutes. Turn asparagus halfway through. Serve and enjoy.

490. Healthy Air fryer Veggies

Preparation Time: 10 minutes
Cooking Time: 18 minutes
Servings: 4
Ingredients:
- 1 cup carrots, sliced
- 1 cup cauliflower, cut into florets
- 1 cup broccoli florets
- 1 tbsp. olive oil
- Pepper
- Salt

Directions:
1. Add all vegetables to a mixing bowl. Put olive oil and season with pepper and salt. Toss well. Add vegetables to the rotisserie basket and air fry at 380 F for 18 minutes. Serve and enjoy.

491. Baked Sweet Potatoes

Preparation Time: 10 minutes
Cooking Time: 40 minutes
Servings: 4
Ingredients:
- 4 sweet potatoes, scrubbed and washed
- ½ tbsp. butter, melted
- ½ tsp. sea salt

Directions:
1. Prick sweet potatoes using a fork. Rub sweet potatoes with melted butter and season with salt. Arrange sweet potatoes on an air fryer drip pan and bake at 400 F for 40 minutes. Serve and enjoy.

Chapter 13. Dehydrated Recipes

492. Squash Chips
Preparation Time: 5 minutes
Cooking Time: 12 hours
Servings: 8
Ingredients:
- 2 cups yellow squash, sliced 1/8-inch thick
- 2 tbsp. apple cider vinegar
- 2 tsp. olive oil
- Salt

Directions:
1. In a mixing bowl, mix squash slices, vinegar, oil, and salt. Arrange squash slices on cooking pan in a single layer. Place cooking pan in the air fryer. Dehydrate at 110 F for 12 hours. Serve and enjoy.

493. Kiwi Chips
Preparation Time: 5 minutes
Cooking Time: 10 hours
Servings: 4
Ingredients:
- 6 kiwis, wash and pat dry well

Directions:
1. Peel kiwis and cut into 1/4-inch thick slices. Arrange kiwi slices on the air fryer basket in a single layer. Dehydrate in your air fryer at 135F for 10 hours. Serve and enjoy.

494. Cinnamon Apples Slices
Preparation Time: 5 minutes
Cooking Time: 12 hours
Servings: 4
Ingredients:
- 2 apples, core, and sliced 1/4-inch thick
- 1/2 tsp. vanilla
- 1/4 tsp. ground nutmeg
- 1 tsp. ground cinnamon
- 1/2 lemon juice

Directions:
1. Add apple slices, vanilla, nutmeg, cinnamon, and lemon juice into the zip-lock bag. Seal bag shakes well, and let's sit for 10 minutes.
2. Arrange marinated apple slices on a cooking pan in the air fryer. Dehydrate at 135 F for 12 hours. Serve.

495. Smoky Eggplant Bacon
Preparation Time: 10 minutes
Cooking Time: 4 hours
Servings: 4
Ingredients:
- 1 medium eggplant
- 1/4 tsp. onion powder
- 1/4 tsp. garlic powder
- 1 1/2 tsp. smoked paprika

Directions:
1. Cut eggplant into 1/4-inch thick slices. Toss eggplant slices with onion powder, garlic powder, and paprika in a mixing bowl. Arrange eggplant slices on a cooking pan in the air fryer, then dehydrate at 145 F for 4 hours. Serve and enjoy.

496. Pineapple Chunks
Preparation Time: 10 minutes
Cooking Time: 12 hours
Servings: 4
Ingredients:
- 1 ripe pineapple, peel and cut in half

Directions:
1. Cut pineapple into the 1/4-inch to 1/2-inch thick chunks. Arrange pineapple chunks on a cooking pan in the air fryer. Dehydrate at 135 F for 12 hours. Serve and enjoy.

497. Spicy Kale Chips
Preparation Time: 10 minutes
Cooking Time: 11 hours
Servings: 4
Ingredients:
- 5 oz. fresh kale leaves

For sauce:
- 1 chipotle pepper
- 2 tbsp. lemon juice
- 1 cup of water
- 1/2 cup sunflower seeds

- 1 cup cashews
- 1/4 tsp. salt

Directions:
1. Add all sauce ingredients into the blender and blend until smooth. Add kale leaves into the mixing bowl. Pour sauce over kale leaves mix until kale leaves are well coated with sauce.
2. Line cooking pan with parchment paper. Arrange kale leaves on the cooking pan in the air fryer. Dehydrate at 155 F for 1 hour. Serve and enjoy.

498. Asian Turkey Jerky

Preparation Time: overnight & 10 minutes
Cooking Time: 5 hours
Servings: 4
Ingredients:
- 1 lb. turkey meat, cut into thin slices
- 1 1/2 tsp. brown sugar
- 1/3 cup Worcestershire sauce
- 1/4 tsp. Tabasco sauce
- 1 1/2 tbsp. soy sauce
- 1 tbsp. liquid smoke
- 1 1/2 tsp. garlic powder
- 1/2 tbsp. onion powder
- 1 tsp. salt

Directions:
1. Add all ingredients except turkey slices in the ziplock bag and mix well. Add turkey slices to the bag. Seal bag and shake well and place it in the refrigerator overnight. Arrange marinated turkey slices on a cooking pan in the air fryer. Dehydrate at 160 F for 5 hours. Serve.

499. Chicken Jerky

Preparation Time: 10 minutes
Cooking Time: 7 hours
Servings: 4
Ingredients:
- 1 lb. chicken tenders, boneless, skinless, and cut into 1/4-inch slices
- 1/2 tsp. garlic powder
- 1 tsp. lemon juice
- 1/2 cup soy sauce
- 1/4 tsp. ground ginger
- 1/4 tsp. black pepper

Directions:
1. Mix all ingredients except chicken slices into the ziplock bag. Add chicken and seal bag and mix well. Put the bag in the refrigerator for 30 minutes. Arrange chicken slices on a cooking pan in the air fryer. Dehydrate at 145 F for 7 hours. Serve.

500. Dehydrated Bell Peppers

Preparation Time: 10 minutes
Cooking Time: 24 hours
Servings: 4
Ingredients:
- 4 bell peppers, cut in half and remove seeds

Directions:
1. Cut bell peppers into strips, then cut each strip into 1/2-inch pieces. Arrange bell pepper strips on the cooking pan in a single layer. Dehydrate in your air fryer at 135 F for 24 hours. Serve.

501. Cinnamon Sweet Potato Chips

Preparation Time: 10 minutes
Cooking Time: 12 hours
Servings: 2
Ingredients:
- 2 sweet potatoes, peel and sliced thinly
- 1 tsp. coconut oil, melted
- 1/8 tsp. ground cinnamon
- Salt

Directions:
1. Add sweet potato slices in a mixing bowl. Add cinnamon, coconut oil, and salt and toss well. Arrange sweet potato slices on the cooking pan in a single layer. Dehydrate in your air fryer at 125 F for 12 hours. Serve.

502. Shredded Carrots

Preparation Time: 10 minutes
Cooking Time: 10 hours
Servings: 4
Ingredients:
- 10 oz. shredded carrots
- 2 tbsp. coconut oil, melted
- 1/2 tsp. ground cinnamon
- 1 tbsp. sugar
- 1/2 tsp. sea salt

Directions:
1. Add melted coconut oil in a large mixing bowl. Add sugar, cinnamon, and salt to the bowl and stir well. Add shredded carrots to the bowl and mix well to coat. Arrange shredded carrots on a cooking pan in your air fryer, dehydrate at 125 F for 10 hours. Serve.

503. Flavorful Almonds

Preparation Time: 10 minutes
Cooking Time: 24 hours
Servings: 6
Ingredients:
- 2 cups almonds, soak in water overnight
- 1 tbsp. fresh rosemary, chopped
- 1 tsp. chili powder
- 1 tbsp. olive oil
- 3/4 tsp. kosher salt

Directions:
- Add all fixing listed into the mixing bowl and mix well. Arrange almonds on cooking pan. Dehydrate in your air fryer at 125 F for 24 hours. Serve.

504. Strawberry Slices

Preparation Time: 10 minutes
Cooking Time: 12 hours
Servings: 4
Ingredients:
- 2 cups strawberries, cut into 1/4-inch thick slices

Directions:

1. Arrange strawberry slices on a cooking pan in a single layer, then dehydrate in your air fryer at 135 F for 12 hours. Serve.

505. Banana Slices
Preparation Time: 10 minutes
Cooking Time: 8 hours
Servings: 4
Ingredients:
- 2 bananas, cut into 1/8-inch thick slices
- 1/2 cup fresh lemon juice

Directions:
1. Add sliced bananas and lemon juice in a mixing bowl and mix well. Arrange sliced bananas on the cooking pan in a single layer. Dehydrate in the air fryer at 135 F for 8 hours. Serve.

506. Avocado Slices
Preparation Time: 10 minutes
Cooking Time: 10 hours
Servings: 4
Ingredients:
- 4 avocados, halved and pitted
- 1/4 tsp. cayenne pepper
- 2 tbsp. fresh cilantro, chopped
- 1/2 lemon juice
- 1/4 tsp. sea salt

Directions:
1. Cut avocado into the slices. Drizzle lemon juice over avocado slices. Arrange avocado slices on a cooking pan in your air fryer, then dehydrate at 160 F for 10 hours. Serve.

507. Dried Raspberries
Preparation Time: 10 minutes
Cooking Time: 18 hours
Servings: 4
Ingredients:
- 4 cups raspberries, wash and dry
- 1/4 cup lemon juice

Directions:
1. Add raspberries and lemon juice in a bowl and toss well. Arrange raspberries in an air fryer basket. Place the dehydrating tray and arrange the remaining raspberries on the dehydrating tray. Place basket into the air fryer. Dehydrate at 135 F for 15-18 hours. Store in an air-tight container.

508. Green Apple Chips
Preparation Time: 10 minutes
Cooking Time: 8 hours
Servings: 4
Ingredients:
- 4 green apples, cored and sliced 1/8-inch thick
- 1/2 lime juice

Directions:
1. Add apple slices and lime juice in a bowl and toss well and set aside for 5 minutes. Arrange apple slices in an air fryer basket.
2. Place the dehydrating tray in the air fryer basket and arrange the remaining apple slices on it. Dehydrate at 145 F for 8 hours. Store in an air-tight container.

509. Peach Wedges
Preparation Time: 10 minutes
Cooking Time: 8 hours
Servings: 4
Ingredients:
- 3 peaches, cut and remove pits and sliced
- 1/2 cup lemon juice

Directions:
1. Add lemon juice and peach slices into the bowl and toss well. Arrange peach slices in an air fryer basket.
2. Place the dehydrating tray in the air fryer basket and arrange the remaining peach slices on the dehydrating tray. Dehydrate at 135 F for 8 hours. Store in an air-tight container.

510. Dried Mango Slices
Preparation Time: 10 minutes
Cooking Time: 12 hours
Servings: 6
Ingredients:
- 4 mangoes, peel & cut into 1/4-inch thick slices
- 1/4 cup lemon juice
- 1 tbsp. honey

Directions:
1. Mix lemon juice plus honey in a bowl and set aside. Add mango slices in lemon-honey mixture and coat well. Arrange mango slices in the air fryer basket.
2. Place the dehydrating tray in the air fryer basket and arrange remaining mango slices on the dehydrating tray. Dehydrate at 135 F for 12 hours.

511. Asian Tofu Jerky
Preparation Time: 10 minutes
Cooking Time: 4 hours
Servings: 4
Ingredients:
- 1 block tofu, pressed, cut tofu in half then cut into the slices
- 2 tbsp. Worcestershire sauce
- 2 tbsp. sriracha
- 4 drops liquid smoke

Directions:
1. In a bowl, mix liquid smoke, Worcestershire sauce, and sriracha. Add tofu slices in a bowl and mix until well coated. Cover and place in the refrigerator overnight.
2. Place marinated tofu slices in the air fryer basket. Arrange remaining tofu slices on the dehydrating tray. Dehydrate at 145 F for 4 hours.

512. Sun-Dried Tomatoes
Preparation Time: 10 minutes
Cooking Time: 12 hours
Servings: 4
Ingredients:
- 2 lbs. fresh tomatoes, cut into 1/4-inch slices

Directions:

1. Arrange tomato slices in a multi-level air fryer basket. Place the dehydrating tray in the air fryer basket and arrange the remaining tomato slices on the dehydrating tray. Dehydrate at 145 F for 6-12 hours.

513. Dried Green Bean
Preparation Time: 10 minutes
Cooking Time: 12 hours
Servings: 4
Ingredients:
- 2 lbs. frozen green beans, thawed
- 2 tbsp. coconut oil, melted
- 2 tbsp. nutritional yeast
- 1 1/2 tsp. salt

Directions:
1. Toss green beans with oil, nutritional yeast, and salt. Arrange green beans in the air fryer basket. Arrange the remaining green beans on the dehydrating tray. Dehydrate at 125 F for 12 hours.

514. Cucumber Chips
Preparation Time: 10 minutes
Cooking Time: 12 hours
Servings: 6
Ingredients:
- 2 medium cucumbers, thinly sliced
- 1 tbsp. olive oil
- 2 tsp. vinegar
- 1/2 tsp. sea salt

Directions:
1. Toss cucumber slices with vinegar, oil, and salt. Arrange cucumber slices in the air fryer basket. Arrange remaining cucumber slices on the dehydrating tray. Dehydrate at 125 F for 12 hours.

515. Dried Beet Chips
Preparation Time: 10 minutes
Cooking Time: 8 hours
Servings: 4
Ingredients:
- 3 medium beets, peel & thinly sliced
- 1 tsp. olive oil
- Pepper
- Salt

Directions:
1. Toss beet slices with olive oil, pepper, and salt. Arrange beet slices in the air fryer basket. Place the dehydrating tray in the air fryer basket and arrange remaining beet slices on the dehydrating tray. Dehydrate at 130 F for 8 hours.

516. Snap Pea Chips
Preparation Time: 10 minutes
Cooking Time: 8 hours
Servings: 6
Ingredients:
- 3 cups snap peas
- 2 tbsp. nutritional yeast
- 2 tbsp. olive oil
- 1/2 tsp. garlic powder
- 1/2 tsp. sea salt

Directions:
1. Toss snap peas with oil, garlic powder, nutritional yeast, and salt. Arrange snap peas in the air fryer basket. Dehydrate at 135 F for 8 hours.

517. Dried Okra
Preparation Time: 10 minutes
Cooking Time: 24 hours
Servings: 4
Ingredients:
- 10 pods okra, slice into rounds

Directions:
1. Place the cooking tray in the air fryer basket, then arrange okra slices on it. Dehydrate mode at 130 F for 24 hours.

518. Lemon Slices
Preparation Time: 10 minutes
Cooking Time: 5 hours
Servings: 6
Ingredients:
- 4 lemons, cut into 1/4-inch thick slices

Directions:
1. Arrange lemon slices in the air fryer basket. Dehydrate at 165 F for 5 hours. Store in an air-tight container.

519. Dried Pear Chips
Preparation Time: 10 minutes
Cooking Time: 8 hours
Servings: 4
Ingredients:
- 3 pears, cut into slices

Directions:
1. Arrange pear slices in the air fryer basket. Dehydrate at 130 F for 8 hours. Store in an air-tight container.

520. Dehydrated Almonds
Preparation Time: 10 minutes
Cooking Time: 18 hours
Servings: 4
Ingredients:
- 1 cup almonds
- 2 cups of water
- 1 tbsp. salt

Directions:
1. Add almonds, water, and salt into the bowl. Cover and soak for 24 hours. Drain well. Arrange almonds in the air fryer basket. Dehydrate at 115 F for 18 hours.

521. Orange Slices
Preparation Time: 10 minutes
Cooking Time: 7 hours
Servings: 2
Ingredients:
- 2 oranges, cut into 1/4-inch thick slices

Directions:
1. Arrange orange slices in the air fryer basket. Dehydrate at 135 F for 7 hours. Store in an air-tight container.

Chapter 14. Sweet and Desserts

522. Fried Peaches
Preparation time: 2 hours
Cooking time: 14 minutes
Servings: 4
Ingredients:
- 4 ripe peaches (1/2 a peach = 1 serving)
- 1 1/2 cups flour
- Salt
- 2 egg yolks
- 3/4 cups cold water
- 1 1/2 tablespoons olive oil
- 2 tablespoons brandy
- 4 egg whites
- Cinnamon/sugar mix

Directions:
1. Mix flour, egg yolks, and salt in a mixing bowl. Slowly mix in water, then add brandy. Set the mixture aside for 2 hours.
2. Boil a large pot of water and cut an X at the bottom of each peach. While the water boils, fill another large bowl with water and ice.
3. Boil each peach for a minute, then plunge it in the ice bath. Now the peels should fall off the peach. Beat the egg whites and mix into the batter. Dip each peach in the mix to coat.
4. Air fry at 360 degrees for 10 Minutes. Prepare a plate with cinnamon/sugar mix, roll peaches in the mix, and serve.

523. Apple Dumplings
Preparation time: 15 minutes
Cooking time: 25 minutes
Servings: 4
Ingredients:
- 2 tbsp. melted coconut oil
- 2 puff pastry sheets
- 1 tbsp. brown sugar
- 2 tbsp. raisins
- 2 small apples of choice

Directions:
1. Ensure your air fryer is preheated to 356 F. Core and peel apples and mix with raisins and sugar. Place a bit of apple mixture into puff pastry sheets and brush sides with melted coconut oil. Place into the air fryer. Air fry for 25 minutes, turning halfway through. Serve.

524. Raspberry Cream Roll-Ups
Preparation time: 15 minutes
Cooking time: 10 minutes
Servings: 4
Ingredients:
- 1 cup of fresh raspberries rinsed and patted dry
- ½ cup of cream cheese softened to room temperature
- ¼ cup of brown sugar
- ¼ cup of sweetened condensed milk
- 1 egg
- 1 teaspoon of corn starch
- 6 spring roll wrappers
- ¼ cup of water

Directions:
1. Cover the basket of your air fryer with a lining of tin foil, leaving the edges uncovered. Preheat the air fryer to 350 F.
2. In a mixing bowl, combine the cream cheese, brown sugar, condensed milk, cornstarch, and egg. Beat or whip thoroughly until all ingredients are completely mixed and fluffy, thick, and stiff.
3. Spoon even amounts of the creamy filling into each spring roll wrapper, then top each dollop of filling with several raspberries.
4. Roll up the wraps around the creamy raspberry filling and seal the seams with a few dabs of water. Place each roll on the foil-lined air fryer basket, seams facing down.
5. Set to air fry for 10 minutes. During cooking, shake the handle of the fryer basket to ensure a nice even surface crisp. Remove with tongs and serve hot or cold

525. Chocolate Cake

Preparation time: 15 minutes
Cooking time: 45 minutes
Servings: 10
Ingredients:
- ½ cup hot water
- 1 tsp. vanilla
- ¼ cup olive oil
- ½ cup almond milk
- 1 egg
- ½ tsp. salt
- ¾ tsp. baking soda
- ¾ tsp. baking powder
- ½ cup unsweetened cocoa powder
- 2 cup almond flour
- 1 cup brown sugar

Directions:
1. Preheat your air fryer to 356 F. Stir all dry ingredients together. Then stir in wet ingredients. Add hot water last.
2. Pour cake batter into a pan that fits into the fryer. Cover with foil and poke holes into the foil. Bake for 35 minutes. Discard foil and then bake another 10 minutes.

526. Chocolate Donuts

Preparation time: 15 minutes
Cooking time: 16 minutes
Servings: 10
Ingredients:
- 8-ounce jumbo biscuits
- Cooking oil
- Chocolate sauce, such as Hershey's

Directions:
1. Separate the biscuit dough into 8 biscuits and place them on a flat work surface. Cut a hole in the center of each biscuit using a small circle cookie cutter. You can also cut the holes using a knife.
2. Spray the air fryer basket with cooking oil. Place 4 donuts in the air fryer. Do not stack. Spray with cooking oil. Air fry for 4 minutes.
3. Flip the donuts, then air fry for an additional 4 minutes. Remove the cooked donuts from the air fryer, repeat steps 3 and 4 for the remaining 4 donuts. Drizzle chocolate sauce over the donuts and enjoy while warm.

527. Fried Bananas with Chocolate Sauce

Preparation time: 15 minutes
Cooking time: 11 minutes
Servings: 2
Ingredients:
- 1 large egg
- ¼ cup cornstarch
- ¼ cup plain bread crumbs
- 3 bananas, halved crosswise
- Cooking oil
- Chocolate sauce

Directions:
1. In a small bowl, beat the egg. In another bowl, place the cornstarch. Put the bread crumbs in your third bowl. Dip the bananas in the cornstarch, then the egg, and then the bread crumbs.
2. Spray the air fryer basket with cooking oil. Place the bananas in the basket and spray them with cooking oil.
3. Air fry for 5 minutes. Open the air fryer and flip the bananas. Cook for an additional 2 minutes. Transfer the bananas to plates. Put the chocolate sauce on the bananas and serve.

528. Apple Hand Pies

Preparation time: 15 minutes
Cooking time: 8 minutes
Servings: 6
Ingredients:
- 15-ounces no-sugar-added apple pie filling
- 1 store-bought crust

Directions:
1. Layout pie crust and slice into equal-sized squares. Place 2 tbsp. filling into each square and seal the crust with a fork. Place into the air fryer. Bake for 8 minutes at 390 F until golden in color.

529. Chocolaty Banana Muffins

Preparation time: 15 minutes
Cooking time: 25 minutes
Servings: 12
Ingredients:
- ¾ cup whole wheat flour
- ¾ cup plain flour
- ¼ cup of cocoa powder
- ¼ teaspoon baking powder
- 1 teaspoon baking soda
- ¼ teaspoon salt
- 2 large bananas, peeled and mashed
- 1 cup of sugar
- 1/3 cup canola oil
- 1 egg
- ½ teaspoon vanilla essence
- 1 cup mini chocolate chips

Directions:
1. Mix flour, cocoa powder, baking soda, baking powder, plus salt in a large bowl. In another bowl, add bananas, sugar, oil, egg, and vanilla extract and beat till well combined.
2. Put flour batter to the egg batter and mix till just combined. Fold in chocolate chips. Preheat the Air fryer to 345 degrees F. Grease 12 muffin molds.
3. Transfer the mixture into prepared muffin molds evenly and bake for about 20-25 minutes or till a toothpick inserted in the center comes out clean.
4. Remove the Air fryer's muffin molds and keep on a wire rack to cool for about 10 minutes. Carefully turn on a wire rack to cool completely before serving.

530. Blueberry Lemon Muffins

Preparation time: 15 minutes
Cooking time: 10 minutes
Servings: 12
Ingredients:
- 1 tsp. vanilla
- Juice and zest of 1 lemon
- 2 eggs
- 1 cup blueberries
- ½ cup cream
- ¼ cup avocado oil
- ½ cup monk fruit
- 2 ½ cups almond flour

Directions:
1. Mix monk fruit and flour. In another bowl, mix vanilla, egg, lemon juice, and cream. Add mixtures together and blend well. Spoon batter into cupcake holders.
2. Place in the air fryer. Bake for 10 minutes at 320 F, checking at 6 minutes to ensure you don't overbake them.

531. Sweet Cream Cheese Wontons

Preparation time: 15 minutes
Cooking time: 5 minutes
Servings: 16
Ingredients:
- 1 egg mixed with a bit of water
- Wonton wrappers
- ½ cup powdered sweetener
- 8 ounces softened cream cheese
- Olive oil

Directions:
1. Mix sweetener and cream cheese together. Layout 4 wontons at a time and cover with a dish towel to prevent drying out. Place ½ of a teaspoon of cream cheese mixture into each wrapper.
2. Dip finger into egg/water mixture and fold diagonally to form a triangle. Seal edges well. Repeat with the remaining ingredients.
3. Place filled wontons into the air fryer and air fry for 5 minutes at 400 degrees, shaking halfway through cooking.

532. Cinnamon Rolls

Preparation time: 15 minutes
Cooking time: 5 minutes
Servings: 8
Ingredients:
- 1 ½ tbsp. cinnamon
- ¾ cup brown sugar
- ¼ cup melted coconut oil
- 1-pound frozen bread dough, thawed

Glaze:
- ½ tsp. vanilla
- 1 ¼ cup powdered sweetener
- 2 tbsp. softened ghee
- 3 oz. softened cream cheese

Directions:
1. Layout bread dough and roll out into a rectangle. Brush melted ghee over the dough and leave a 1-inch border along the edges.
2. Mix cinnamon and sweetener and then sprinkle over the dough. Roll dough tightly and slice into 8 pieces. Let sit 1-2 hours to rise.
3. For the glaze, simply mix ingredients till smooth. Once rolls rise, place into the air fryer and bake for 5 minutes at 350 degrees. Serve rolls drizzled in cream cheese glaze. Enjoy!

533. Black and White Brownies

Preparation time: 15 minutes
Cooking time: 20 minutes
Servings: 8
Ingredients:
- 1 egg
- ¼ cup brown sugar
- 2 tablespoons white sugar
- 2 tablespoons safflower oil
- 1 teaspoon vanilla
- ¼ cup of cocoa powder
- 1/3 cup all-purpose flour
- ¼ cup white chocolate chips
- Nonstick baking spray with flour

Directions:
1. Beat the egg, brown sugar plus white sugar in a medium bowl. Beat in the oil and vanilla. Put the cocoa powder and flour, then stir. Fold in the white chocolate chips.
2. Spray a 6-by-6-by-2-inch baking pan with nonstick spray. Spoon the brownie batter into the pan.
3. Bake for 20 minutes in your air fryer or until the brownies are set when lightly touched with a finger. Let cool for 30 minutes before slicing to serve.

534. Baked Apple

Preparation time: 15 minutes
Cooking time: 20 minutes
Servings: 4
Ingredients:
- ¼ cup of water
- ¼ tsp. nutmeg
- ¼ tsp. cinnamon
- 1 ½ tsp. melted ghee
- 2 tbsp. raisins
- 2 tbsp. chopped walnuts
- 1 medium apple

Directions:
1. Preheat your air fryer to 350 degrees. Slice an apple in half and discard some of the flesh from the center. Place into a frying pan.
2. Mix remaining ingredients together except water. Spoon mixture to the middle of apple halves. Pour water overfilled apples. Place pan with apple halves into the air fryer, bake for 20 minutes.

535. Cinnamon Fried Bananas

Preparation time: 15 minutes

Cooking time: 10 minutes
Servings: 3
Ingredients:
- 1 cup panko breadcrumbs
- 3 tbsp. cinnamon
- ½ cup almond flour
- 3 egg whites
- 8 ripe bananas
- 3 tbsp. vegan coconut oil

Directions:
1. Heat coconut oil and add breadcrumbs. Mix around 2-3 minutes until golden. Pour into a bowl. Peel and cut bananas in half.
2. Roll the half of each banana into flour, eggs, and crumb mixture. Place into the air fryer. Air fry for 10 minutes at 280 F. Serve.

536. Banana Cake
Preparation Time: 10 minutes
Cooking time: 30 minutes
Servings: 4
Ingredients:
- 1 tbsp. butter, soft
- 1 egg
- 1/3 cup of brown sugar
- 2 tbsp. honey
- 1 banana, mashed
- 1 cup of white flour
- 1 tsp. baking powder
- ½ tsp. cinnamon powder
- Cooking spray

Directions:
1. Oiled a cake pan using a cooking spray and set aside. Mix butter, sugar, banana, honey, egg, cinnamon, baking powder, and flour in a bowl.
2. Put this batter into a cake pan greased with cooking spray, introduce in your air fryer, and bake at 350 °F for 30 minutes. Leave the cake to cool down, slice, and serve.

537. Cheesecake
Preparation Time: 10 minutes
Cooking time: 15 minutes
Servings: 15
Ingredients:
- 1-pound cream cheese
- ½ teaspoon vanilla extract
- 2 eggs
- 4 tablespoons sugar
- 1 cup graham crackers, crumbled
- 2 tablespoons butter

Directions:
1. In a bowl, mix crackers with butter. Press crackers mix on the bottom of a lined cake pan, introduce in your air fryer, and bake at 350 °F for 4 minutes.
2. Meanwhile, in a bowl, mix sugar with cream cheese, eggs, and vanilla and whisk well. Spread filling over crackers crust and bake your cheesecake in your air fryer at 310 °F for 15 minutes. Leave cake in the fridge for 3 hours, slice, and serve.

538. Bread Pudding
Preparation Time: 10 minutes
Cooking time: 1 hour
Servings: 4
Ingredients:
- 6 glazed doughnuts, crumbled
- 1 cup cherries
- 4 egg yolks
- 1 and ½ cups whipping cream
- ½ cup raisins
- ¼ cup sugar
- ½ cup chocolate chips.

Directions:
1. In a bowl, mix cherries with egg yolks and whipping cream and stir well. In another bowl, mix raisins with sugar, chocolate chips, and doughnuts and stir.
2. Combine the 2 mixtures, transfer everything to a greased pan that fits your air fryer and bake at 310 F for 1 hour. Chill pudding before cutting and serving it.

539. Bread Dough and Amaretto Dessert
Preparation Time: 10 minutes
Cooking time: 12 minutes
Servings: 12
Ingredients:
- 1-pound bread dough
- 1 cup of sugar
- ½ cup butter, melted
- 1 cup heavy cream
- 12 ounces of chocolate chips
- 2 tablespoons amaretto liqueur

Directions:
1. Roll dough, cut into 20 slices, and then cut each slice in halves. Brush dough pieces with butter, sprinkle sugar, place them in your air fryer's basket after you've brushed it some butter, air fry them at 350 °F for 5 minutes, flip them, air fry for 3 minutes more, and transfer to a platter.
2. Heat a pan with the heavy cream over medium heat, add chocolate chips and stir until they melt. Add liqueur, stir again, transfer to a bowl and serve bread dippers with this sauce.

540. Pumpkin Pie
Preparation Time: 10 minutes
Cooking time: 15 minutes
Servings: 9
Ingredients:
- 1 tablespoon sugar
- 2 tablespoons flour
- 1 tablespoon butter
- 2 tablespoons water

For the pumpkin pie filling:
- 5 ounces of pumpkin flesh, chopped
- 1 teaspoon mixed spice

- 1 teaspoon nutmeg
- 3 ounces of water
- 1 egg, whisked
- 1 tablespoon sugar

Directions:
1. Put 3 ounces water in a pot, bring to a boil over medium-high heat, add pumpkin, egg, 1 tablespoon sugar, spice, and nutmeg, stir, boil for 20 minutes, take off the heat and blend using an immersion blender.
2. In a bowl, mix flour with butter, 1 tablespoon sugar, and 2 tablespoons water and knead your dough well.
3. Grease a pie pan that fits your air fryer with butter, press dough into the pan, fill with pumpkin pie filling. Place in your air fryer's basket and bake at 360 °F for 15 minutes. Slice and serve warm.

541. Wrapped Pears

Preparation Time: 10 minutes
Cooking time: 15 minutes
Servings: 4
Ingredients:
- 4 puff pastry sheets
- 14 oz. vanilla custard
- 2 pears, halved
- 1 egg, whisked
- ½ tsp. cinnamon powder
- 2 tbsp. sugar

Directions:
1. Put puff pastry slices on your working surface, add a spoonful of vanilla custard in the middle of each, top with pear halves plus wrap.
2. Brush pears with egg, sprinkle sugar and cinnamon, place them in your air fryer's basket and bake at 320 °F for 15 minutes. Divide parcels between plates and serve.

542. Strawberry Donuts

Preparation Time: 10 minutes
Cooking time: 15 minutes
Servings: 4
Ingredients:
- 8 ounces flour
- 1 tablespoon brown sugar
- 1 tablespoon white sugar
- 1 egg
- 2 and ½ tablespoons butter
- 4 ounces whole milk
- 1 teaspoon baking powder

For the strawberry icing:
- 2 tablespoons butter
- 5 ounces icing sugar
- ½ teaspoon pink coloring
- ¼ cup strawberries, chopped
- 1 tablespoon whipped cream

Directions:
1. In a bowl, mix butter, 1 tablespoon brown sugar, 1 tablespoon white sugar, and flour and stir. Mix the egg, 1 and ½ tablespoons butter and milk in a second bowl.
2. Combine the 2 mixtures, stir, shape donuts from this mix, and place them in your air fryer's basket and air fry at 360 °F for 15 minutes.
3. Put 1 tablespoon butter, icing sugar, food coloring, whipped cream, and strawberry puree and whisk well. Arrange donuts on a platter and serve with strawberry icing on top.

543. Cocoa Cake

Preparation Time: 10 minutes
Cooking time: 17 minutes
Servings: 6
Ingredients:
- 5 ounces butter, melted
- 3 eggs
- 3 ounces sugar
- 1 teaspoon of cocoa powder
- 3 ounces flour
- ½ teaspoon lemon juice

Directions:
1. In a bowl, mix 1 tablespoon butter with cocoa powder and whisk. In another bowl, mix the rest of the butter with sugar, eggs, flour, and lemon juice, whisk well, and pour half into a cake pan that fits your air fryer.
2. Add half of the cocoa mix, spread, add the rest of the butter layer, and top with the rest of the cocoa. Introduce in your air fryer and bake at 360 °F for 17 minutes. Cool cake down before slicing and serving.

544. Apple Bread

Preparation Time: 10 minutes
Cooking time: 40 minutes
Servings: 6
Ingredients:
- 3 cups apples, cored and cubed
- 1 cup of sugar
- 1 tablespoon vanilla
- 2 eggs
- 1 tablespoon apple pie spice
- 2 cups white flour
- 1 tablespoon baking powder
- 1 stick butter
- 1 cup of water

Directions:
1. In a bowl, mix the egg with 1 butter stick, apple pie spice, and sugar and stir using your mixer. Add apples and stir again well.
2. In another bowl, mix baking powder with flour and stir. Combine the 2 mixtures, stir, and pour into a springform pan. Put springform pan in your air fryer and bake at 320 °F for 40 minutes. Slice and serve.

545. Mini Lava Cakes

Preparation Time: 10 minutes
Cooking time: 20 minutes
Servings: 3
Ingredients:

- 1 egg
- 4 tablespoons sugar
- 2 tablespoons olive oil
- 4 tablespoons milk
- 4 tablespoons flour
- 1 tablespoon cocoa powder
- ½ teaspoon baking powder
- ½ teaspoon orange zest

Directions:
1. In a bowl, mix the egg with sugar, oil, milk, flour, salt, cocoa powder, baking powder, and orange zest, stir very well and pour this into greased ramekins. Add ramekins to your air fryer and bake at 320 °F for 20 minutes. Serve lava cakes warm.

546. Carrot Cake
Preparation Time: 10 minutes
Cooking time: 45 minutes
Servings: 6
Ingredients:
- 5 ounces flour
- ¾ teaspoon baking powder
- ½ teaspoon baking soda
- ½ teaspoon cinnamon powder
- ¼ teaspoon nutmeg, ground
- ½ teaspoon allspice
- 1 egg
- 3 tablespoons yogurt
- ½ cup of sugar
- ¼ cup pineapple juice
- 4 tablespoons sunflower oil
- 1/3 cup carrots, grated
- 1/3 cup pecans, toasted and chopped
- 1/3 cup coconut flakes, shredded
- Cooking spray

Directions:
1. In a bowl, mix flour with baking soda and powder, salt, allspice, cinnamon, and nutmeg and stir. In another bowl, mix the egg with yogurt, sugar, pineapple juice, oil, carrots, pecans, and coconut flakes and stir well.
2. Combine the two mixtures and stir well; pour this into a springform pan that fits your air fryer, which you've greased with some cooking spray, transfer to your air fryer and bake at 320 °F for 45 minutes. Let it cool down, slice, and serve.

546. Ginger Cheesecake
Preparation Time: 2 hours and 10 minutes
Cooking time: 20 minutes
Servings: 6
Ingredients:
- 2 teaspoons butter, melted
- ½ cup ginger cookies, crumbled
- 16 ounces cream cheese, soft
- 2 eggs
- ½ cup of sugar

- 1 teaspoon rum
- ½ teaspoon vanilla extract
- ½ teaspoon nutmeg, ground

Directions:
1. Grease a pan with the butter and spread cookie crumbs on the bottom. In a bowl, beat cream cheese with nutmeg, vanilla, rum, and eggs, whisk well, and spread over the cookie crumbs.
2. Introduce in your air fryer and bake at 340 °F for 20 minutes. Leave the cheesecake to cool down and keep in the fridge for 2 hours before slicing and serving it.

548. Coffee Cheesecakes
Preparation Time: 10 minutes
Cooking time: 20 minutes
Servings: 6
Ingredients:
For the cheesecakes:
- 2 tablespoons butter
- 8 ounces cream cheese
- 3 tablespoons coffee
- 3 eggs
- 1/3 cup sugar
- 1 tablespoon caramel syrup

For the frosting:
- 3 tablespoons caramel syrup
- 3 tablespoons butter
- 8 ounces mascarpone cheese, soft
- 2 tablespoons sugar

Directions:
1. In your blender, mix cream cheese with eggs, 2 tablespoons butter, coffee, 1 tablespoon caramel syrup, and 1/3 cup sugar and pulse very well; spoon into a cupcake pan that fits your air fryer.
2. Introduce in the fryer and cook at 320 °F and bake for 20 minutes. Leave aside to cool down and then keep in the freezer for 3 hours.
3. Meanwhile, in a bowl, mix 3 tablespoons butter with 3 tablespoons caramel syrup, 2 tablespoons sugar, and mascarpone, blend well, spoon these over cheesecakes and serve them.

549. Cocoa Cookies
Preparation Time: 10 minutes
Cooking time: 14 minutes
Servings: 12
Ingredients:
- 6 ounces coconut oil, melted
- 6 eggs
- 3 ounces of cocoa powder
- 2 teaspoons vanilla
- ½ teaspoon baking powder
- 4 ounces cream cheese
- 5 tablespoons sugar

Directions:
1. In a blender, mix eggs with coconut oil, cocoa powder, baking powder, vanilla, cream cheese, and swerve and stir using a mixer.

2. Pour this into a lined baking dish that fits your air fryer, introduce in the fryer at 320 °F and bake for 14 minutes. Slice cookie sheet into rectangles and serve.

550. Special Brownies

Preparation Time: 10 minutes
Cooking time: 17 minutes
Servings: 4
Ingredients:
- 1 egg
- 1/3 cup cocoa powder
- 1/3 cup sugar
- 7 tablespoons butter
- ½ teaspoon vanilla extract
- ¼ cup white flour
- ¼ cup walnuts, chopped
- ½ teaspoon baking powder
- 1 tablespoon peanut butter

Directions:
1. Heat a pan with 6 tablespoons butter and the sugar over medium heat, stir, cook for 5 minutes, transfer this to a bowl, add salt, vanilla extract, cocoa powder, egg, baking powder, walnuts, and flour, stir the whole thing well and pour into a pan that fits your air fryer.
2. In a bowl, mix 1 tablespoon butter with peanut butter, heat up in your microwave for a few seconds, stir well and drizzle this over brownies mix. Introduce in your air fryer and bake at 320 °F and bake for 17 minutes. Leave brownies to cool down, cut, and serve.

551. Sponge Cake

Preparation time: 15 minutes
Cooking time: 28 minutes
Servings: 8
Ingredients:
- 6 egg yolks
- 2 cups powdered sugar
- 1 cupcake flour
- 1½ teaspoons baking powder
- 3 tablespoons milk
- 3 tablespoons vegetable oil
- 2 teaspoons vanilla extract
- 6 egg whites
- ¼ cup granulated sugar
- Powdered sugar, for sprinkling

Directions:
1. Mix egg yolks plus powdered sugar. Mix flour plus baking powder into the batter. Mix in milk, vegetable oil, plus vanilla extract. Mix egg whites in a separate bowl until frothy. Put granulated sugar, mix until stiff peaks.
2. Fold egg whites into your batter using a rubber spatula. Oiled the 10 x 3-inch cake tin using a vegetable oil, then put the batter.
3. Put cake tin into your preheated air fryer, then bake for 28 minutes. Remove sponge cake, then let it cool for 10 minutes. Dust powdered sugar on top, then serve.

552. Walnut Raisin Pumpkin Bread

Preparation time: 15 minutes
Cooking time: 1 hour & 10 minutes
Servings: 16
Ingredients:
- 1 2/3 cup all-purpose flour
- 1½ cup sugar
- 1 teaspoon baking soda
- 1 teaspoon ground cinnamon
- ½ teaspoon ground nutmeg
- ½ teaspoon salt
- ½ teaspoon baking powder
- 2 large eggs, room temperature
- 1 can pumpkin puree (15 ounces)
- ½ cup canola oil
- ½ cup of water
- ½ cup chopped walnuts
- ½ cup raisins
- ½ cup of chocolate chips

Directions:
1. Mix flour, sugar, baking soda, cinnamon, nutmeg, salt, plus baking powder in a bowl. Mix eggs, pumpkin puree, canola oil, plus water in a different bowl.
2. Mix the dry fixing with the wet fixing, then gently fold in walnuts, raisins, and chocolate chips.
3. Put the batter into a 9 x 4.5-inch loaf pan. Bake in your preheated air fryer for 1 hour and 10 minutes. Remove, then let it rest for 10 minutes before transferring to a wire rack to cool before serving.

553. Summer Strawberry Crumble

Preparation time: 15 minutes
Cooking time: 45 minutes
Servings: 8
Ingredients:
- 2 pounds strawberries, halved
- ½ lemon, juiced and zested
- 1 tablespoon orange zest
- 8 basil leaves, chopped
- A pinch of sea salt
- 2½ tablespoons cornstarch
- 1 cup of sugar
- ¾ cup unsalted butter, room temperature
- 1¼ cups rolled oats
- 1¼ cups almond flour
- 1 egg yolk

Directions:
1. Mix all fruit filling fixing, then let them sit for 5 minutes. Mix all fixing for the crumble in a different bowl.
2. Put the filling to the 8 x 8-inch baking dish, then layer the crumble on top of the strawberries.
3. Bake for 40 minutes in your preheated air fryer. Remove when done, then serve. Best complemented by ice cream.

554. Vegan Coconut Milk Cupcakes
Preparation time: 15 minutes
Cooking time: 23 minutes
Servings: 6
Ingredients:
- ¾ cup all-purpose flour sifted
- 2¼ tsp. baking powder
- ¼ tsp. salt
- 6 tbsp. granulated sugar
- 2 tbsp. coconut oil, melted
- ¾ cup of full-fat coconut milk, unsweetened
- 1 tbsp. water
- ¼ tsp. vanilla extract
- ½ tsp. coconut extract
- ½ tsp. white distilled vinegar
- Grated coconut, for sprinkling

Directions:
1. Mix flour, baking powder, salt, plus sugar in a mixing bowl. Mix in coconut oil, coconut milk, water, vanilla extract, coconut extract, plus vinegar until smooth.
2. Preheat your air fryer at 350 F. Pour batter into the muffin pan with cupcake liners, then place the pan on the wire rack in the preheated air fryer.
3. Bake for 23 minutes, then sprinkle grated coconut on top after 5 minutes of cooking. Remove, cool for 15 minutes, then serve.

555. Double Chocolate Walnut Cookies
Preparation time: overnight & 15 minutes
Cooking time: 15 minutes
Servings: 15
Ingredients:
- ¾ cup of butter, room temperature
- ¾ cup of brown sugar
- ¾ cup white sugar
- 2 eggs
- 1 teaspoon vanilla extract
- 2 cups all-purpose flour
- ¼ teaspoon baking powder
- ½ teaspoon baking soda
- ¼ teaspoon salt
- ½ cup milk chocolate chips
- ½ cup dark chocolate chips
- 1 cup chopped walnuts

Directions:
1. Mix butter, brown sugar, plus white sugar in a large bowl. Put eggs plus vanilla extract to the butter mixture.
2. Mix in flour, baking powder, baking soda, plus salt. Mix in chocolate chips plus walnuts. Roll dough into 2.5-ounce balls, then put the balls in a bowl. Wrap the bowl and chill 6 hours or overnight.
3. Line the food tray using parchment paper, then put the cookie dough balls on top. Put the food tray on top of the wire rack in the preheated air fryer, bake for 15 minutes. Remove, then let the cookies rest for 10 minutes, then serve.

556. Strawberry Toaster Pastries
Preparation time: 15 minutes
Cooking time: 18 minutes
Servings: 5
Ingredients:
- ¾ cup of strawberry jam
- 2 tbsp. strawberry jam
- 1 tbsp. cornstarch
- 3 tbsp. water, divided
- 2 pre-made pie crusts (9-inch diameter), thawed
- 1 egg, beaten
- 1 tbsp. heavy cream
- ¾ cup of powdered sugar Sprinkles

Directions:
1. Mix ¾ cup strawberry jam, cornstarch, plus 1 tablespoon water, then set aside. Cut pre-made pie crusts into 103 x 4-inch rectangles. Mix egg with the rest of the 2 tablespoons water, then set aside.
2. Put 1½–2 tablespoons of the jam batter in the middle of 5 rectangles, leave a ½-inch border. Brush the edges using the whisked egg, then put another rectangle on top.
3. Crimp the edges using your fork. Put the toaster pastries on top of the lined baking sheet with parchment paper. Bake for 18 minutes in your preheated air fryer. Remove the pastries, then allow them to cool.
4. Mix the remaining 2 tablespoons strawberry jam, heavy cream plus powdered sugar. Spread icing on the cooled toaster pastries plus top it with sprinkles.

557. Blueberry Muffins
Preparation time: 8 minutes
Cooking time: 12 minutes
Servings: 6
Ingredients:
- 1 tablespoon coconut oil
- 1 ripe banana, mashed
- 1¼ cups almond flour
- 2 tablespoons granulated sugar
- ½ teaspoon baking powder
- 1 egg, beaten
- 1/8 cup maple syrup
- 1 teaspoon apple cider vinegar
- 1 teaspoon vanilla extract
- 1 teaspoon lemon zest
- A pinch of cinnamon
- ½ cup fresh or frozen blueberries
- Cooking spray

Directions:
1. Microwave the coconut oil until dissolved. Mix all fixing except blueberries and mix until well incorporated. Fold in blueberries gently. Preheat your air fryer at 375 F.
2. Oiled muffins pan with cooking spray and pour the batter in until cups are ¾ full. Put the muffin pan on top of the wire rack in the preheated air fryer, then

bake for 12 minutes. Remove muffins, then let them cool for 10 minutes, then serve.

558. Buttermilk Biscuits

Preparation time: 15 minutes
Cooking time: 15 minutes
Servings: 6
Ingredients:
- 2 cups all-purpose flour
- 2 tsp. baking powder
- ¼ tsp. baking soda
- 1 tsp. kosher salt
- 10 tbsp. butter, chilled
- 1 cup buttermilk, divided

Directions:
1. Mix flour, baking powder, baking soda, plus kosher salt in a mixing bowl. Grate or shred chilled butter into the flour batter, mix using a stand mixer.
2. Put ¾ cup of buttermilk, mixing until dough forms. Shape dough into a rectangle on a floured surface.
3. Fold the dough 3 times and flatten into an 8 x 5-inch rectangle. Slice into 6 biscuits that are 2½ inches in diameter.
4. Line the food tray using parchment paper and place the biscuits on top. Brush the remaining buttermilk on each biscuit. Preheat your air fryer at 350 F.
5. Insert food tray at mid-position in the preheated air fryer. Bake for 15 minutes. Remove when done and serve immediately.

559. Double Chocolate Brownies

Preparation time: 10 minutes
Cooking time: 35 minutes
Servings: 8
Ingredients:
- ½ cup butter
- 2 tablespoons butter
- 1 cup of sugar
- 2 eggs
- 2 teaspoons vanilla extract
- ½ cup milk chocolate chips, melted
- ¾ cup all-purpose flour
- ¼ cup of cocoa powder
- ½ teaspoon of sea salt
- 1 cup dark chocolate chips

Directions:
1. Dissolve the butter in a large bowl, then put sugar, eggs, vanilla extract, and milk chocolate chips then mix.
2. Put flour, cocoa powder, plus sea salt, then stir. Fold in the dark chocolate chips. Put the wire rack at a low position in the air fryer. Preheat at 330 F.
3. Line the 9 x 9-inch square pan using parchment paper, then put the batter in. Place the pan in the air fryer. Bake for 35 minutes, remove the brownies when done, then let them cool for 30 minutes before serving or chilling.

560. Peach Cobbler

Preparation time: 10 minutes
Cooking time: 40 minutes
Servings: 6
Ingredients:
Filling:
- 3 fresh peaches, peeled and sliced
- 1 tablespoon white sugar
- 2 tablespoons light brown sugar
- A pinch of ground cinnamon
- A pinch of ground nutmeg
- ½ teaspoon cornstarch

Topping:
- ½ cup unsalted butter, melted
- ¾ cup of sugar
- 1 teaspoon vanilla extract
- 1 cup all-purpose flour
- 1 teaspoon baking powder
- A pinch of salt

Directions:
1. Combine all fixing for the filling and mix well. Put filling in a greased glass pie pan, then put aside. Mix all fixing for the topping, then set aside. Preheat your air fryer at 350 F.
2. Put the glass pie pan into the preheated air fryer. Bake for 40 minutes. Put on the topping after 10 minutes of cooking time. Remove, then allow it to cool for 10 minutes. Serve with vanilla ice cream.

561. Snickerdoodles

Preparation time: 10 minutes
Cooking time: 23 minutes
Servings: 20
Ingredients:
- ½ cup butter softened
- ¾ cup white sugar
- 1 egg
- 1 teaspoon vanilla extract
- 1 cup all-purpose flour sifted
- 6 tablespoons all-purpose flour sifted
- 1 teaspoon cream of tartar
- ½ teaspoon baking soda
- 1/8 teaspoon salt
- 1 tablespoon white sugar
- 1 teaspoon ground cinnamon

Directions:
1. Cream butter plus sugar in a stand mixer on medium-high speed until fluffy. Mix in the egg plus vanilla extract.
2. Put the flour, cream of tartar, baking soda, salt into the dough at low speed. Form 20 pcs 1-inch dough balls.
3. Mix white sugar plus ground cinnamon in a small bowl. Roll the cookies in the cinnamon-sugar batter, then put on a baking sheet lined with parchment paper. You will need to work in batches.

4. Bake in your air fryer for 23 minutes. Remove the snickerdoodles, then allow to cool, or eat fresh.

562. Chia Cookies
Preparation time: 1 hour & 5 minutes
Cooking time: 15 minutes
Servings: 12
Ingredients:
- 57 g cream cheese
- 28 g grated Mozzarella
- 2 egg whites
- 3 tbsp. butter
- 168 g sweetener
- 1/2 teaspoon salt
- 1 tbsp. vanilla extract
- 1 teaspoon baking powder
- 100 g almond flour
- 2 tbsp. chia seeds

Directions:
1. Dissolve the cream cheese plus Mozzarella in a pan over low heat, mix well. Put aside. In a large bowl, mix the butter, egg whites, vanilla, salt, and sweetener.
2. Add almond flour and baking powder until well mixed. Add the cheese mixture, then stir in the chia seeds. Put in the refrigerator for 1 hour.
3. Preheat your air fryer to 180 C. Shape the dough into 12 balls of the same size and place on a baking sheet lined with baking paper, about 5 cm apart. Flatten balls with the palm of your hand or the bottom of a glass.
4. Bake for 15 minutes or until the cookies turn golden brown around the edges. Take out of the heat. Let rest on the baking sheet for 5 minutes.

563. Cranberry and Almond Cookies
Preparation time: 1 hour & 5 minutes
Cooking time: 10 minutes
Servings: 12
Ingredients:
- 28 g dried cranberries
- 23 g almond slices
- 100 g almond flour
- 1 egg
- 1 tbsp. coconut oil
- 2 sachets of stevia or about 1 to 2 teaspoons, depending on your taste

Directions:
1. Put the almond flour, egg, coconut oil, and sweetener in a bowl and mix well. Add the almond slices and cranberries and mix them in.
2. Shape cookie dough into a roll, wrap in baking paper, and place in the refrigerator for at least 1 hour. Preheating to 180 C.
3. Divide the cookie roll into 12 pieces and lay them out on a baking sheet lined with baking paper. Bake for 8 to 10 minutes, until the edges start to turn brown. Let cool down for 5 minutes.

564. Caramel Brownie Bites
Preparation time: 15 minutes
Cooking time: 13 minutes
Servings: 6
Ingredients:
- 3/4 cup (99 g) almond flour
- 1/2 cup (120 ml) melted ghee
- 1/2 cup sweetener
- 3/4 cup (99 g) unsweetened cocoa powder
- 2 eggs, whisked
- 1 teaspoon vanilla extract
- 1 pinch of salt

Directions:
1. Preheat your air fryer to 175 ° C. Mix all ingredients and fill in muffin cases. Bake for at least 13 minutes. Serve.

565. Pumpkin Cookies
Preparation time: 15 minutes
Cooking time: 15 minutes
Servings: 4
Ingredients:
- 1 1/4 cups (306 g) pumpkin puree
- 2 teaspoons of coconut oil
- 2 eggs
- 1/2 teaspoon vanilla extract
- 1 tbsp. coconut flour
- 1 teaspoon ground cinnamon
- 1 cup (85 g) unsweetened desiccated coconut

Directions:
1. Warm your air fryer to 180 ° C. Mix the pumpkin, oil, eggs, and vanilla in a bowl. Add the cinnamon and coconut flour and stir until everything is thoroughly combined.
2. Add coconut and mix thoroughly. Pour the mixture onto the baking sheet in small piles the size of a spoon and flatten it slightly. Bake for 15 minutes, until the edges are brown.

566. Pumpkin Cheesecake Bars
Preparation time: 1 hour & 15 minutes
Cooking time: 40 minutes
Servings: 9
Ingredients:
- 230 g cream cheese
- 5 eggs
- 24 g sweetener
- 425 g pumpkin
- 1 teaspoon pumpkin pie spice
- 1 teaspoon cinnamon
- 1 teaspoon vanilla extract

Directions:
1. Preheat your air fryer to 180 ° C. Spray the baking pan with oil spray.
2. Beat the cream cheese with a hand mixer on high speed until the cheese is smooth. Add the remaining ingredients and keep mixing until the batter is smooth.

3. Put the dough in the prepared baking pan and bake for about 40 minutes. Let cool for 10 minutes. Put in the refrigerator for 1 hour. Serve cold.

567. Pecan Cookies
Preparation time: 15 minutes
Cooking time: 12 minutes
Servings: 10
Ingredients:
- 220 g pecans, ground
- 1 large egg
- 1 tbsp. salted butter
- 1/2 teaspoon baking powder
- 84 g sweetener
- 20 pecan halves

Directions:
1. Preheat your air fryer to 175 ° C. Mix the ground pecans well with all the other ingredients. Shape small balls by hand and press flat.
2. Place the cookies on a parchment-lined baking paper. Place a pecan half on each cookie to taste. Bake for about 9 to 12 minutes, until the edges turn lightly brown.

568. Ricotta Cheesecake
Preparation time: 15 minutes
Cooking time: 25 minutes
Servings: 4
Ingredients:
- 2 cups ricotta (low fat)
- 3 packets of Splenda (or alternative sweetener)
- 1 teaspoon vanilla extract
- 2 eggs

Directions:
1. Warm your air fryer to 180 ° C. Mix, the ricotta, sweetener, and vanilla extract. Gradually add eggs and keep beating until the batter is smooth. Pour the batter into a baking dish or several muffin cups. Bake for about 20 to 25 minutes.

569. Chocolate Chip Cookies
Preparation time: 15 minutes
Cooking time: 12 minutes
Servings: 16
Ingredients:
- 125 g almond flour
- 2 tbsp. coconut flour
- 12 g sweetener
- 1/2 teaspoon baking powder
- 1/4 teaspoon salt
- 4 tbsp. melted coconut oil
- 1 egg
- 1 1/2 teaspoons vanilla extract
- 56 g chocolate chips
- 31 g chopped walnuts

Directions:
1. Preheat your air fryer to 190 C. Add all dry ingredients, then stir in the wet ingredients. Stir until the batter is smooth and all of the ingredients have combined well.
2. Divide the dough into 16 balls and place on a baking sheet. Flatten each ball with a glass bottom. Bake for 9 to 12 minutes, until the cookies are a light golden-brown color.

570. Chocolate Froth Cookies
Preparation time: 15 minutes
Cooking time: 20 minutes
Servings: 6
Ingredients:
- 4 large egg whites
- 1/4 teaspoon tartar baking powder
- 3 tbsp. sweetener (granulated)
- 60 g sweetener (powdered)
- 22 g cocoa powder, unsweetened

Directions:
1. Preheat your air fryer to 100 ° C. Place egg whites in an empty bowl and beat until frothy with a hand mixer on medium to high speed.
2. Add tartar baking powder, turn the hand mixer on high, and beat the egg white until stiff. Gradually add granulated sweetener.
3. Mix the powdered sweetener with the cocoa powder in a separate bowl. Work in thirds at a time. Pour the cocoa mixture over the egg white and fold in carefully.
4. Use a spoon to place 12 cookie-sized piles on a baking sheet. Bake for 1 hour until the biscuits are firm and dry. Let rest on the baking sheet for 15 minutes. Let cool down further, then carefully remove from the baking paper.

571. Cinnamon Cookies
Preparation time: 15 minutes
Cooking time: 25 minutes
Servings: 4
Ingredients:
- 190 g almond bran or almond flour
- 96 g melted ghee
- 1 egg
- 1 teaspoon vanilla extract
- 1 teaspoon ground cinnamon
- 2 teaspoons of honey

Directions:
1. Preheat your air fryer to 150 ° C. Place all ingredients in a mixing bowl and stir well until everything has combined well.
2. Roll 1 teaspoon each of the mixture into balls and place on a greased baking sheet. Press flat with a fork. Bake for 25 minutes. Serve.

572. Sugar Cookies
Preparation time: 15 minutes
Cooking time: 10 minutes
Servings: 4
Ingredients:
- 1 cup (227 g) soft butter
- 2 1/4 cups (470 g) vanilla shake (low carb)

- 1/2 cup (170 g) sweetener
- 1/2 teaspoon vanilla extract
- 1 large egg

Directions:
1. Preheat your air fryer to 190 ° C. Spray parchment paper with oil spray.
2. Mix the butter, vanilla shake, half of the sweetener, and vanilla extract well. Add the egg and mix until the egg is completely incorporated, and the mixture has a soft batter.
3. Shape cookie dough into 2.5 cm balls and place on a baking sheet, about 5 cm apart.
4. Place the remaining sweetener in a low bowl. Grease the bottom of a glass, then squeeze into the sweetener. Press the cookies flat with the glass, cover with sugar or sweetener after each cookie.
5. Bake on a baking sheet for 8 to 10 minutes or until the cookies are cooked through.

573. Summer Citrus Sponge Cake

Preparation time: 15 minutes
Cooking time: 15 minutes
Servings: 4
Ingredients:
- 1 cup of sugar
- 1 cup self-rising flour
- 1 cup butter
- 3 eggs
- 1 tsp. baking powder
- 1 tsp. vanilla extract
- Zest of 1 orange

Frosting:
- 4 egg whites
- 1 orange, zested and juiced
- 1 tsp. orange food coloring
- 1 cup superfine sugar

Directions:
1. Warm air fryer to 350 F. Place all cake ingredients in a bowl and whisk with an electric mixer. Transfer half of the batter into a greased cake pan and bake for 15 minutes.
2. Meanwhile, prepare the frosting by beating all frosting ingredients together. Spread the frosting mixture on top of the cake. Serve sliced.

574. Vanilla Brownie Squares

Preparation time: 15 minutes
Cooking time: 20 minutes
Servings: 2
Ingredients:
- 1 whole egg, beaten
- ¼ cup of chocolate chips
- 2 tbsp. white sugar
- 1/3 cup flour
- 2 tbsp. safflower oil
- 1 tsp. vanilla
- ¼ cup of cocoa powder

Directions:
1. Warm air fryer to 360 F. In a bowl, mix the egg, sugar, olive oil, and vanilla. In another bowl, mix cocoa powder and flour. Add the flour mixture to the vanilla mixture and stir until fully incorporated.
2. Pour the mixture into a greased baking pan and sprinkle chocolate chips on top. Bake for 20 minutes. Chill and cut into squares to serve.

575. Apple Pie

Preparation time: 15 minutes
Cooking time: 20 minutes
Servings: 4
Ingredients:
- 4 apples, diced
- 2 oz. butter, melted
- 2 oz. sugar
- 1 oz. brown sugar
- 2 tsp. cinnamon
- 1 egg, beaten
- 3 large puff pastry sheets
- ¼ tsp. salt

Directions:
1. Whisk white sugar, brown sugar, cinnamon, salt, and butter together. Put the apples in a greased baking pan and coat them with the sugar mixture. Place the baking dish in your air fryer and bake for 10 minutes at 350 F.
2. Meanwhile, roll out the pastry on a floured flat surface, and cut each sheet into 6 equal pieces. Divide the apple filling between the pieces. Brush the edges of the pastry squares using the egg.
3. Fold them and seal the edges with a fork. Place on a lined baking sheet and bake in the fryer at 350 F for 8 minutes. Flip over, increase the temperature to 390 F, and bake for 2 more minutes. Serve.

576. Dark Chocolate Lava Cakes

Preparation time: 15 minutes
Cooking time: 10 minutes
Servings: 4
Ingredients:
- 3 ½ oz. butter, melted
- 3 ½ tbsp. sugar
- 1 ½ tbsp. self-rising flour
- 3 ½ oz. dark chocolate, melted
- 2 eggs

Directions:
1. Grease 4 ramekins with butter. Preheat the air fryer to 375 F. Beat the eggs and sugar until frothy. Stir in butter and chocolate; gently fold in the flour.
2. Divide the mixture between the ramekins and bake for 10 minutes. Let cool for 2 minutes before turning the cakes upside down onto serving plates.

577. Chocolate Soufflé

Preparation time: 15 minutes
Cooking time: 18 minutes
Servings: 2
Ingredients:
- 2 eggs, whites, and yolks separated

- ¼ cup butter, melted
- 2 tbsp. flour
- 3 tbsp. sugar
- 3 oz. chocolate, melted
- ½ tsp. vanilla extract

Directions:
1. Beat the yolks and the sugar and vanilla extract; stir in butter, chocolate, and flour. Preheat your air fryer to 330 F. Whisk the whites until a stiff peak form.
2. Working in batches, gently combine the egg whites with the chocolate mixture. Divide the batter between two greased ramekins. Bake for 14-18 minutes. Serve.

578. Glazed Lemon Cupcakes

Preparation time: 15 minutes
Cooking time: 16 minutes
Servings: 6
Ingredients:
- 1 cup flour
- ½ cup of sugar
- 1 small egg
- 1 tsp. lemon zest
- ¾ tsp. baking powder
- ¼ tsp. baking soda
- ½ tsp. salt
- 2 tbsp. vegetable oil
- ½ cup milk
- ½ tsp. vanilla extract

Glaze:
- ½ cup powdered sugar
- 2 tsp. lemon juice

Directions:
1. Warm air fryer to 350 F. In a bowl, combine dry ingredients. In another bowl, whisk the wet fixing. Gently combine the two mixtures.
2. Split the batter into 6 greased muffin tins. Place them in the baking tray and bake for 13-16 minutes. Meanwhile, whisk the powdered sugar with the lemon juice. Spread the glaze over the muffins.

579. Sesame Banana Dessert

Preparation time: 15 minutes
Cooking time: 10 minutes
Servings: 5
Ingredients:
- 1 ½ cups flour
- 5 bananas, sliced
- 1 tsp. salt
- 3 tbsp. sesame seeds
- 1 cup of water
- 2 eggs, beaten
- 1 tsp. baking powder
- ½ tbsp. sugar

Directions:
1. Preheat the air fryer to 340 F. In a bowl, mix salt, sesame seeds, flour, baking powder, eggs, sugar, and water.
2. Coat sliced bananas with the flour mixture. Place the prepared slices in the Air Fryer basket and fit in the baking tray; bake for 8-10 minutes. Serve chilled.

580. Triple Berry Lemon Crumble

Preparation time: 15 minutes
Cooking time: 20 minutes
Servings: 6
Ingredients:
- 12 oz. fresh strawberries
- 7 oz. fresh raspberries
- 5 oz. fresh blueberries
- 5 tbsp. cold butter
- 2 tbsp. lemon juice
- 1 cup flour
- ½ cup of sugar
- 1 tbsp. water
- A pinch of salt

Directions:
1. Gently mash the berries, but make sure there are chunks left. Mix with the lemon juice and 2 tbsp. of the sugar. Place the berry mixture at the bottom of a prepared round cake.
2. Combine the flour with the salt and sugar in a bowl. Add the water and rub the butter with your fingers until the mixture becomes crumbled. Pour the batter over the berries. Bake in your air fryer at 390 F for 20 minutes. Serve chilled.

581. Honey Hazelnut Apples

Preparation time: 15 minutes
Cooking time: 10 minutes
Servings: 4
Ingredients:
- 4 apples
- 1 oz. butter
- 2 oz. breadcrumbs
- Zest of 1 orange
- 2 tbsp. chopped hazelnuts
- 2 oz. mixed seeds
- 1 tsp. cinnamon
- 2 tbsp. honey

Directions:
1. Warm your air fryer to 350 F. Core the apples. Make sure also to score their skin to prevent splitting. Combine the remaining ingredients in a bowl; stuff the apples with the mixture and bake for 10 minutes. Serve topped with chopped hazelnuts.

582. French Apple Cake

Preparation time: 15 minutes
Cooking time: 20 minutes
Servings: 9
Ingredients:
- 2 ¾ oz. flour
- 5 tbsp. sugar
- 1 ¼ oz. butter
- 3 tbsp. cinnamon
- 2 whole apples, sliced

Directions:
1. Warm air fryer to 360 F. In a bowl, mix 3 tbsp. sugar, butter, and flour and form a pastry dough. Roll out your pastry on a floured clean surface and transfer it to the fryer's baking dish. Arrange the apple slices atop.
2. Cover the apples with sugar and cinnamon and bake for 20 minutes. Sprinkle with powdered sugar and mint and serve.

583. Raisin Apple Treat
Preparation time: 15 minutes
Cooking time: 10 minutes
Servings: 4
Ingredients:
- 4 apples, cored
- 1 ½ oz. almonds
- ¾ oz. raisins
- 2 tbsp. sugar

Directions:
1. Warm your air fryer to 360 F. In a bowl, mix sugar, almonds, and raisins. Blend the mixture using a hand mixer.
2. Fill cored apples with the almond mixture. Put the apples in a baking tray and bake for 10 minutes. Serve with a sprinkle of powdered sugar.

584. Blackberries & Apricots Crumble
Preparation time: 15 minutes
Cooking time: 20 minutes
Servings: 4
Ingredients:
- 2 ½ cups fresh apricots, cubed
- 1 cup fresh blackberries
- ½ cup of sugar
- 2 tbsp. lemon Juice
- 1 cup flour
- 5 tbsp. butter

Directions:
1. Warm air fryer to 390 F. Add apricots to a bowl and mix with lemon juice, 2 tbsp. sugar, and blackberries. Spread the mixture onto the greased Air Fryer baking pan.
2. In another bowl, mix flour and remaining sugar. Add 1 tbsp. of cold water and butter and keep mixing until you have a crumbly mixture; top with crumb mixture. Bake for 20 minutes.

585. Coffee Cake
Preparation time: 15 minutes
Cooking time: 15 minutes
Servings: 2
Ingredients:
- ¼ cup butter
- ½ tsp. instant coffee
- 1 tbsp. black coffee, brewed
- 1 egg
- ¼ cup of sugar
- ¼ cup flour
- 1 tsp. cocoa powder
- Powdered sugar, for icing

Directions:
1. Preheat your air fryer to 330 F. Beat the sugar and egg together in a bowl. Beat in cocoa, instant, and black coffees; stir in flour. Transfer the batter to a greased cake pan. Bake for 15 minutes. Dust with powdered sugar and serve.

Chapter 15. Everyday Favorites for Your Family

586. Butternut Squash with Chopped Hazelnuts
Preparation time: 10 minutes
Cooking time: 20 minutes
Servings: 3
Ingredients:
- 2 tablespoons whole hazelnuts
- 3 cups butternut squash, peeled, deseeded, and cubed
- ¼ teaspoon kosher salt
- ¼ teaspoon freshly ground black pepper
- 2 teaspoons olive oil
- Cooking spray

Directions:
1. Preheat the air fryer to 300°F. Oiled the air fryer basket with cooking spray. Arrange the hazelnuts in the preheated air fryer. Air fry for 3 minutes or until soft.
2. Chopped the hazelnuts roughly and transfer to a small bowl. Set aside. Set the air fryer temperature to 360°F. Spritz with cooking spray.
3. Put the butternut squash in a large bowl, then sprinkle with salt and pepper and drizzle with olive oil. Toss to coat well.
4. Transfer the squash to the air fryer. Air fry for 20 minutes or until the squash is soft. Shake the basket halfway through the frying time.
5. When the frying is complete, transfer the squash onto a plate and sprinkle with chopped hazelnuts before serving.

587. Air Fried Shishito Peppers
Preparation time: 5 minutes
Cooking time: 5 minutes
Servings: 4
Ingredients:
- 24 pcs shishito peppers
- 1 tablespoon olive oil
- Coarse sea salt, to taste
- Lemon wedges, for serving
- Cooking spray

Directions:
1. Preheat the air fryer to 400°F. Oiled the air fryer basket with cooking spray. Toss the peppers with olive oil in a large bowl to coat well. Arrange the peppers in the preheated air fryer.
2. Air fryer for 5 minutes or until blistered and lightly charred. Shake the basket and sprinkle the peppers with salt halfway through the cooking time. Transfer the peppers onto a plate and squeeze the lemon wedges on top before serving.

588. Avocado Wedge Fries
Preparation time: 10 minutes
Cooking time: 8 minutes
Servings: 12
Ingredients:
- 1 cup all-purpose flour
- 3 tablespoons lime juice
- ¾ cup of orange juice
- 1¼ cups plain dried bread crumbs
- 1 cup yellow cornmeal
- 1½ tablespoons chili powder
- 2 large Hass avocados, peeled, pitted, and cut into wedges
- Coarse sea salt, to taste
- Cooking spray

Directions:
1. Preheat the air fryer to 400°F. Oiled the air fryer basket with cooking spray. Pour the flour into a bowl. Mix the lime juice with orange juice in a second bowl. Combine the bread crumbs, cornmeal, and chili powder in a third bowl.
2. Dip the avocado wedges in the bowl of flour to coat well, then dredge the wedges into the bowl of juice mixture, and then dunk the wedges in the bread crumbs mixture. Shake the excess off.
3. Transfer the well-coat avocado wedges in a single layer in the preheated air fryer. Spritz with cooking spray.
4. Air fry for 8 minutes or until the avocado wedges are tender and crispy. Shake the basket and sprinkle the avocado with salt halfway through the cooking time. Serve immediately.

589. Bacon Pinwheels
Preparation time: 10 minutes

Cooking time: 10 minutes
Servings: 8
Ingredients:
- 1 sheet puff pastry
- 2 tablespoons maple syrup
- ¼ cup brown sugar
- 8 slices bacon
- Ground black pepper, to taste
- Cooking spray

Directions:
1. Preheat the air fryer to 360°F. Oiled the air fryer basket with cooking spray. Roll the puff pastry into a 10-inch square with a rolling pin on a clean work surface, then cut the pastry into 8 strips.
2. Brush the strips with maple syrup and sprinkle with sugar, leaving a 1-inch far end uncovered. Arrange each slice of bacon on each strip, leaving a 1/8-inch length of bacon hangs over the end close to you. Sprinkle with black pepper.
3. From the end close to you, roll the strips into pinwheels, then dab the uncovered end with water and seal the rolls.
4. Arrange the pinwheels in the preheated air fryer and spritz with cooking spray. Air fry for 10 minutes or until golden brown. Flip the pinwheels halfway through. Serve immediately.

590. Candied Pecans

Preparation time: 5 minutes
Cooking time: 10 minutes
Servings: 4
Ingredients:
- 2 egg whites
- 1 tablespoon cumin
- 2 teaspoons smoked paprika
- ½ cup brown sugar
- 2 teaspoons kosher salt
- 1-pound (454 g) pecan halves
- Cooking spray

Directions:
1. Preheat the air fryer to 300°F. Spritz the air fryer basket with cooking spray.
2. Combine the egg whites, cumin, paprika, sugar, and salt in a large bowl. Stir to mix well. Add the pecans to the bowl and toss to coat well.
3. Transfer the pecans into the preheated air fryer. Air fry in batches for 10 minutes or until the pecans are lightly caramelized. Shake the basket at least two times during the cooking. Serve immediately.

591. Cauliflower Parmesan Fritters

Preparation time: 10 minutes
Cooking time: 20 minutes
Servings: 6
Ingredients:
- 2 cups cooked cauliflower
- 1 cup panko bread crumbs
- 1 large egg, beaten
- ½ cup grated Parmesan cheese
- 1 tablespoon chopped fresh chives
- Cooking spray

Directions:
1. Preheat the air fryer to 390°F. Oiled the air fryer basket with cooking spray.
2. Put the cauliflower, panko bread crumbs, egg, Parmesan, chives in a food processor, and then pulse to mash and combine it until chunky and thick lightly.
3. Shape the mixture into 6 flat patties, then arrange 3 of them in the preheated air fryer and spritz with cooking spray. Air fry for 8 minutes or until the patties are crispy and golden brown.
4. Flip the patties halfway through the cooking time. Repeat with the remaining patties. When the air frying is complete, serve the fritters immediately.

592. Cheesy Jalapeño Cornbread

Preparation time: 10 minutes
Cooking time: 20 minutes
Servings: 8
Ingredients:
- 2/3 cup cornmeal
- 1/3 cup all-purpose flour
- ¾ teaspoon baking powder
- 2 tablespoons buttery spread, melted
- ½ teaspoon kosher salt
- 1 tablespoon granulated sugar
- ¾ cup whole milk
- 1 large egg, beaten
- 1 jalapeño pepper, thinly sliced
- 1/3 cup shredded sharp Cheddar cheese
- Cooking spray

Directions:
1. Preheat the air fryer to 300°F. Oiled air fryer basket with cooking spray. Combine all the ingredients in a large bowl. Stir to mix well. Pour the mixture into a baking pan.
2. Arrange the pan in the preheated air fryer. Bake for 20 minutes or until a toothpick inserted in the center of the bread comes out clean.
3. When the cooking is complete, remove the baking pan from the air fryer and allow the bread to cool for a few minutes before slicing to serve.

593. Classic Latkes

Preparation time: 15 minutes
Cooking time: 10 minutes
Servings: 4
Ingredients:
- 1 egg
- 2 tablespoons all-purpose flour
- 2 medium potatoes, peeled and shredded, rinsed, and drained
- ¼ teaspoon granulated garlic
- ½ teaspoon salt
- Cooking spray

Directions:

1. Preheat the air fryer to 380°F. Oiled the air fryer basket with cooking spray. Whisk together the egg, flour, potatoes, garlic, and salt in a large bowl. Stir to mix well.
2. Divide the mixture into four parts, then flatten them into four circles. Arrange the circles into the preheated air fryer.
3. Spritz the circles with cooking spray, then air fry for 10 minutes or until golden brown and crispy. Flip the latkes halfway through. Serve immediately.

594. Classic Poutine

Preparation time: 15 minutes
Cooking time: 25 minutes
Servings: 2
Ingredients:
- 2 russet potatoes, scrubbed and cut into ½-inch sticks
- 2 teaspoons vegetable oil
- 2 tablespoons butter
- ¼ onion, minced
- ¼ teaspoon dried thyme
- 1 clove garlic, smashed
- 3 tablespoons all-purpose flour
- 1 teaspoon tomato paste
- 1½ cups beef stock
- 2 teaspoons Worcestershire sauce
- Salt
- Ground black pepper
- 2/3 cup chopped string cheese

Directions:
1. Boil a pot of water, then put in the potato sticks and blanch for 4 minutes. Preheat the air fryer to 400°F.
2. Drain the potato sticks and rinse under running cold water, then pat dry with paper towels. Transfer the sticks to a large bowl and drizzle with vegetable oil. Toss to coat well.
3. Place the potato sticks in the preheated air fryer. Air fry for 25 minutes or until the sticks are golden brown. Shake the basket at least three times during the frying.
4. Meanwhile, make the gravy: Heat the butter in a saucepan over medium heat until melted. Add the onion, thyme, and garlic and sauté for 5 minutes or until the onion is translucent.
5. Add the flour and sauté for an additional 2 minutes. Pour in the tomato paste and beef stock and cook for 1 more minute or until slightly thickened.
6. Drizzle the gravy with Worcestershire sauce and sprinkle with salt and ground black pepper. Reduce the heat to low to keep the gravy warm until ready to serve.
7. Transfer the fried potato sticks onto a plate, then sprinkle with salt and ground black pepper. Scatter with string cheese and pour the gravy over. Serve warm.

595. Crispy Cinnamon Chickpeas

Preparation time: 10 minutes
Cooking time: 10 minutes
Servings: 2
Ingredients:
- 1 tablespoon cinnamon
- 1 tablespoon sugar
- 1 cup chickpeas, soaked in water overnight, rinsed, and drained

Directions:
1. Preheat the air fryer to 390°F.
2. Combine the cinnamon and sugar in a bowl. Stir to mix well. Add the chickpeas to the bowl, then toss to coat well.
3. Pour the chickpeas into the preheated air fryer. Air fry for 10 minutes or until golden brown and crispy. Shake the basket periodically. Serve immediately.

596. Crispy Green Tomatoes Slices

Preparation time: 10 minutes
Cooking time: 8 minutes
Servings: 12
Ingredients:
- ½ cup all-purpose flour
- 1 egg
- ½ cup buttermilk
- 1 cup cornmeal
- 1 cup panko
- 2 green tomatoes, cut into ¼-inch-thick slices, patted dry
- ½ teaspoon salt
- ½ teaspoon ground black pepper
- Cooking spray

Directions:
1. Preheat the air fryer to 400°F. Line the air fryer basket using parchment paper.
2. Pour the flour into a bowl. Whisk the egg and buttermilk in a second bowl. Combine the cornmeal and panko in a third bowl.
3. Dredge the tomato slices in the bowl of flour first, then into the egg mixture, and then dunk the slices into the cornmeal mixture. Shake the excess off.
4. Transfer the well-coated tomato slices to the preheated air fryer and sprinkle with salt and ground black pepper.
5. Spritz the tomato slices with cooking spray. Air fry for 8 minutes or until crispy and lightly browned. Flip the slices halfway through the cooking time. Serve immediately.

597. Air Fried Edamame

Preparation time: 5 minutes
Cooking time: 7 minutes
Servings: 6
Ingredients:
- 1½ pounds (680 g) unshelled edamame
- 2 tablespoons olive oil
- 1 teaspoon of sea salt

Directions:

1. Preheat the air fryer to 400°F. Place the edamame in a large bowl, then drizzle with olive oil. Toss to coat well.
2. Transfer the edamame to the preheated air fryer. Cook for 7 minutes or until tender and warmed through. Shake the basket at least three times during the cooking.
3. Transfer the cooked edamame onto a plate and sprinkle with salt. Toss to combine well and set aside for 3 minutes to infuse before serving.

598. Frico

Preparation time: 5 minutes
Cooking time: 5 minutes
Servings: 2
Ingredients:
- 1 cup shredded aged Manchego cheese
- 1 teaspoon all-purpose flour
- ½ teaspoon cumin seeds
- ¼ teaspoon cracked black pepper

Directions:
1. Preheat the air fryer to 375°F. Line the air fryer basket using parchment paper. Combine the cheese and flour in a bowl. Stir to mix well. Spread the mixture in the basket into a 4-inch round.
2. Combine the cumin and black pepper in a small bowl. Stir to mix well. Sprinkle the cumin mixture over the cheese round.
3. Air fry 5 minutes or until the cheese is lightly browned and frothy. Use tongs to transfer the cheese wafer onto a plate and slice to serve.

599. Garlicky Baked Cherry Tomatoes

Preparation time: 5 minutes
Cooking time: 6 minutes
Servings: 2
Ingredients:
- 2 cups cherry tomatoes
- 1 clove garlic, thinly sliced
- 1 teaspoon olive oil
- 1/8 teaspoon kosher salt
- 1 tablespoon freshly chopped basil, for topping
- Cooking spray

Directions:
1. Preheat the air fryer to 360°F. Spritz the air fryer baking pan with cooking spray and set aside.
2. Toss the cherry tomatoes, sliced garlic, olive oil, and kosher salt in a large bowl. Spread the mixture in an even layer in the prepared pan.
3. Bake in the preheated air fryer for 4 to 6 minutes, or until the tomatoes become soft and wilted. Transfer to a bowl and rest for 5 minutes. Top with the chopped basil and serve warm.

600. Garlicky Knots with Parsley

Preparation time: 10 minutes
Cooking time: 10 minutes
Servings: 8
Ingredients:
- 1 teaspoon dried parsley
- ¼ cup melted butter
- 2 teaspoons garlic powder
- 1 (11-ounce / 312-g) tube refrigerated French bread dough, cut into 8 slices

Directions:
1. Preheat the air fryer to 350°F. Combine the parsley, butter, and garlic powder in a bowl. Stir to mix well.
2. Place the French bread dough slices on a clean work surface, then roll each slice into a 6-inch long rope. Tie the ropes into knots and arrange them on a plate. Brush the knots with butter mixture.
3. Transfer the knots into the air fryer. You need to work in batches to avoid overcrowding. Air fry for 5 minutes or until the knots are golden brown. Flip the knots halfway through the cooking time. Serve immediately.

Conclusion

Now that you are here, don't think that it's finally the end. It is just your first step in your journey with your air fryer, and this helpful cookbook is full of delicious and healthy foods.

You can use this cookbook as a regular cookbook every day or on any occasion and follow the steps described as a routine. You can also take some ideas and make up your recipes and add your own twists. Apart from these recipes, you can also visit and participate in forums that offer lots of ideas and recipes. You can find thousands of discussions on the Internet that are open for public participation, and you can also share the amazing recipe you found in this cookbook in them.

There are several advantages of using an air fryer instead of frying the food in oil; we talk about it initially. Hence, the most important is that it does not use excess oil, which means you can gain the same satisfying crunch and flavor but in a healthier way. It also saves you the time you use when cleaning up the frying pans. No more greasy stovetops to clean up. A cool air that dehydrates the food right into your mouth! It also saves you the extra calories you consume every time you deep fry something. And keeping track of the recipes and using them will also help you to save money and buy smart.

The recipes in this air fryer cookbook are easy to follow once you understand that an air fryer is slightly different from a microwave oven. It does not need an equal quantity of oil or fat to be used every time. Some amount depends on the usage of the recipe. Some recipes need oil in them, while some need almost none if you play around.

The air fryer uses a system of hot air circulation to cook food without deep fryer oil. It circulates hot air to create a temperature gradient that dehydrates the food fast while it gets cooked in a way where the water inside the food turns to steam. The food can get fried, so it remains crispy while not adding too much fat to the body.

If you want to replace your deep fryer with an air fryer, this cookbook will help you get started. Why go to know more? Get your first air fryer and start experimenting with creating the best dishes for everyone. There is no limit to how far you can chase your culinary imagination, starting from breakfast to dinner, meats to dessert, and many more. Enjoy these air fryer recipes and share them with others.

If you are a little creative with food, you probably know your taste buds aren't that different from anyone else. You should consider the rest of the family and adjust the recipes to everyone's liking. While you are at it, it would also be good to adjust the recipes to what you personally enjoy. Look at the ingredients you will need to spice up and adjust the recipe according to your preferences. When it comes to everyday meals, not all family members enjoy the same type or quantity of veggies or the same spice level in the food.

You might find it easier to skip on specific ingredients that you are not too keen on. If you wish to impress or surprise your loved ones with a special dish, it is good to include those ingredients that they love and exclude others.

Some of the ingredients in this cookbook are available in the market year-round. If you want to cook something for the entire family, pick recipes that don't call for exclusive ingredients. With some planning, you could create a few dishes for the whole month that would use ingredients available in the year-round variety.

When you are picking the ingredients for the recipes in this cookbook, you can also pick out vegetables in season. You can forget about the high-priced veggies you see in the market over the winter and stock up on only the vegetables in season.

Now that you know the basics, it is good to get started with the recipes you plan to cook using this cookbook. The recipes you find in this cookbook are tasty, healthy, hearty, and can be cooked using any air fryer type. So, thank you and happy air frying!

A Short message from the Author:

Hey, are you enjoyed the book? I'd love to hear your thoughts!
Many readers do not know how hard reviews are to come by, and how much they help an author.

I would be incredibly thankful if you could take just 60 seconds to write a brief review on Amazon, even if it's just a few sentences!

If you have purchased the paperback version, just going to your purchases section in Amazon and Click "Write a Review" or scan the following QR code to write it quickly:

Thank you for taking the time to share your thoughts!
Your review will genuinely make a difference for me and help gain exposure for my work.

STEPHAN TYLER

Printed in Great Britain
by Amazon